The Untold Saga *of*
La Salle: Expedition II

HARD RIVERS

CRAIG P. HOWARD

RIVER GROVE
BOOKS

Published by River Grove Books
Austin, TX
www.rivergrovebooks.com

Copyright ©2016 Craig Howard

All rights reserved.

No part of this book may be reproduced, stored in a retrieval system, or transmitted by any means, electronic, mechanical, photocopying, recording, or otherwise, without written permission from the copyright holder.

Distributed by River Grove Books

Design and composition by Greenleaf Book Group
Cover design by Greenleaf Book Group
Cover image by Marc Leiberman
© iStockphoto.com THEPALMER / © Roberto A Sanchez, Photos on pages 12, 34, 43, 46, 60, 67, 163, and 219 by Marc Lieberman
Photos on pages 49, 79, 90, 103, 135, 145, 186, 188, 197, 206, 215, 233, 246, 257, 277, and 304 by Barton Dean
Photos on pages 116 and 295 by Douglas Sohn
Sketch on page 111 by Terry Cox
Map adaptation on ix by Bradley Basker
Author photo by Michelle Manning

Cataloging-in-Publication data is available.

Print ISBN: 978-1-63299-090-7

eBook ISBN: 978-1-63299-091-4

First Edition

This book is dedicated to the memory of Ralph Frese—canoe man, naturalist, history teacher, a dreamer and a doer who embodied the spirit of the voyageur—and to the men and women who follow in his paddle strokes.

"We would not take a sea voyage for the sole pleasure of seeing without hope of ever telling."

—Blaise Pascal

CONTENTS

Knocking on Death's Door, Part 1   1

On the Road to Find Out

Reliving the Dream   9
"Why Not?" to Things That Never Were   21
Take Up Your Paddle and Follow Me   33
Heart, Hands, and Voice   49
Good Help Is Hard to Find   66

Wild World

Go Placidly Amid the Haste   79
Undercurrents   89
Wicked Point   103
The Long March   115
So Long to Civilization   134
The Wilderness in Fall   144
Knocking on Death's Door, Part 2   162

Into White

The Autumn Winds Blow Chilly and Cold   185

Old Man Winter   196

Blood on the Shoulder   214

Hard Rivers   233

Flow, River, Flow   245

The Father of Waters   257

Longer Boats

I'll Get Down to the Sea Somehow   275

An Estuary of Loose Ends   293

All Experience Is an Arch   303

Acknowledgments   325

About the Author   329

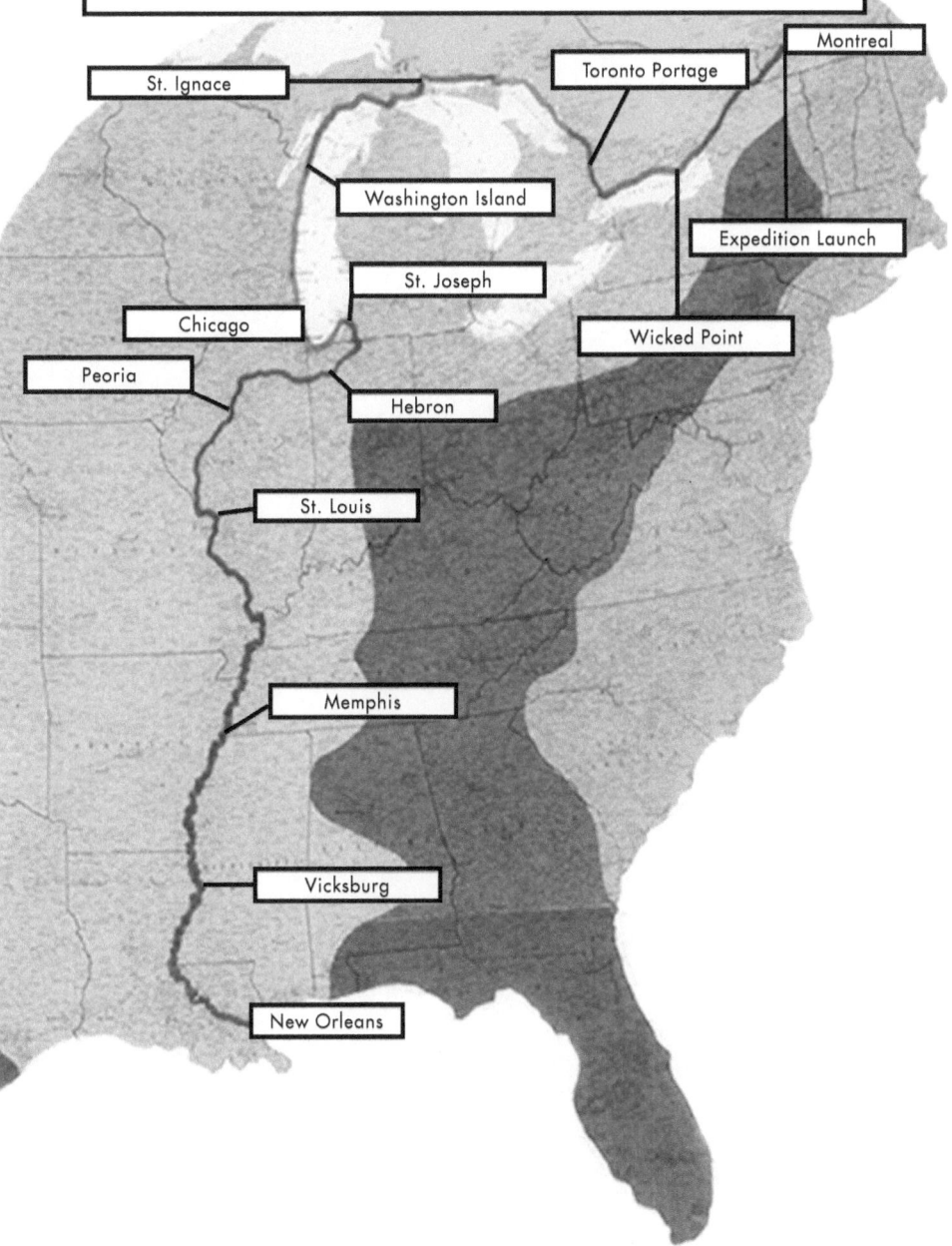

KNOCKING ON DEATH'S DOOR, PART 1

(Oct. 23–Nov. 4, 1976)
Lake Michigan shore and Washington Island

A foreboding settled over the members of La Salle: Expedition II as their canoes moved under the Mackinac Bridge and into Lake Michigan. The teenage boys and their young leaders moved from island to island over open waters, exposed to unpredictable winds and swells. Danger was a constant companion; November was the deadliest month for lake travelers and on Saturday, Oct. 23, 1976, the water was already near freezing.

"We know how bad Lake Michigan can be—especially in December," one traveler wrote in his journal. "We're all hoping for a mild November/December, but it's not looking good. I think I can safely say this will be the most dangerous part of the trip."

Meanwhile, as families back home awaited news of the journey's progress, they couldn't turn on the radio without hearing the Top Forty hit by Gordon Lightfoot, "The Wreck of the *Edmund Fitzgerald*," based on the deadliest shipwreck in Great Lakes history. Twenty-nine crew members had met their end when the iron ore freighter capsized in stormy Lake Superior just one year earlier and scarcely more than 200 miles away.

By midweek the young crew was in Manistique, about eighty-five miles down the coast of Michigan's Upper Peninsula. A strong wind whipped across the campsite, making it nearly impossible to walk, let alone set up a shelter. Snow continued to accumulate as the voyageurs packed themselves in for the night. Lightfoot's song was everywhere the paddlers touched shore. They may not have been aware of how recently the *Fitzgerald* had gone down; but they knew they were entering the same waters that had swallowed La Salle's ship *Le Griffon* in an autumn storm in 1679.

Still more frightening, the men would be passing by "Death's Door," a strait linking Lake Michigan with Green Bay, flanked on one side by Wisconsin's Door County and on the other by Washington Island. Winter was no respecter of persons, as these men—following in the canoe strokes of the great La Salle—were about to find out.

The snoring in his own tent shook one young man awake early on the first day of November. The predawn sky was alive, sparkling with stars. The day was sunny, and the wind came out of the southwest toward the canoes. The crew paddled eighteen miles and made camp at Jackson Harbor, a forested shoreline on Washington Island's north side. They were three days ahead of schedule—and feeling restless.

With time to kill, one of the men found a tavern in the woods—unlikely, but welcome—and the crew enjoyed the company of locals, who warned the voyageurs about the waters they were about to cross, "*Porte du Mort*" as La Salle's French company would have called it, so named because of the number of men who'd drowned trying to cross it. The wind and the shallow floor of the bay combined to generate very large waves quickly. According to the legend, a voyageur had to wait for the devil (wind) to turn his back (reverse direction and knock down the waves) before he could run through the door.

"We were more than a little afraid of making that crossing," one of the men recalled years later.

On the morning of Nov. 4, the men found a thin layer of ice along the shoreline. It wasn't much, but they had to break it before they could launch. The men pushed off just before 8:00, already more than an hour late.

Right away the wind picked up, sending a strong northwest wind over the island, creating choppy water that curled and foamed in the reef off shore.

About a mile and a half out of Jackson Harbor, the canoes rounded a point of land and headed south, and the whole expedition went sideways—literally. The wind shifted suddenly and strongly out of the northeast, quickly building to thirty miles per hour. The six canoes had been on the calm leeward side of the island. Now, however, they were immediately exposed to waves six feet high and coming at them broadside. The waves rolled under the canoes and broke over the gunnels. The water rushed off an arc of shallows so fast that it joined the wind in forcing the canoes toward the shore.

The men in the six canoes pulled hard against the waves, but the surf tossed them around like matchsticks in a bubbling pot. The waves became especially wild as the canoes came within half a mile of Hog Island—a sharp rise of ground with a granite escarpment running atop its center like the ridge of a razorback hog.

The fact that La Salle in his canoe braved a storm through these same waters was no comfort at all to these modern voyageurs. Cold spit came off the waves and stung their faces and fingers. An overturned canoe here was not just difficult but potentially deadly. Each boy could ask himself, "Is this what I signed on for?"

"We were paddling our asses off, but we were unable to break this pattern of swells," a voyageur later recounted. Waves rocked and tossed the small watercraft; the men struggled and bailed, but they couldn't keep up. The Great Lakes water poured over the gunnels, and one of the canoes became a bathtub.

Its four occupants thought they were sinking; they *were* sinking. Just back from the doctor to have his broken foot immobilized, one paddler was terrified that his new cast and heavy clothes would drag him through Devil's Door to the bottom of the lake, life jacket and all.

One by one the canoes raced to rescue their troubled crewmates and bring the half-submerged vessel to the rocky shore of Washington Island. Men hopped out, racing to assist those in worse shape.

They carried their companion with the leg cast to higher ground; while the waters were choppy, the land was dry—the winds hadn't brought rain, which would have made the whole endeavor even worse. As the men helped their stricken comrades ashore and out of their wet clothes, others brought food and blankets to warm them and fight hypothermia.

They picked up anything that could burn, and soon a fire was going. Cloaks made of Hudson Bay blankets were out, and soup was heating up. A couple of the men cracked jokes to help lighten the mood.

But as the men huddled for warmth, filled their bowls, and congratulated one another on making it through the "Porte du Mort," a grim realization settled among them.

"I don't know how we got so careless," one would recall later.

In their scramble to safety, they'd neglected to keep count. There should have been six canoes. Instead there were only five.

"We looked out from the shore and couldn't see any canoes on the lake," a voyageur said. Indeed, one was missing.

One crew quickly headed back into the roiling waters. Others found a local man willing to take them out in his cabin cruiser—their only option, given that every other boat on the island had already been put up for the winter.

But the fifteen-foot waves were too rough; and the men were nowhere to be found.

The pilot of a news helicopter flying over the area kept radio contact with the expedition leader on the cabin cruiser. "We're over Hog Island," the pilot reported.

Nervous seconds passed.

The loss of four young men was not what the voyageurs imagined two years ago when they signed up for this eight-month, 3,300-mile, once-in-a-lifetime adventure. They were retracing as authentic voyageurs La Salle's 1681–82 trip to find the mouth of the Mississippi River and claim America's heartland for France.

But this was still the twentieth century, not the life-and-death struggle it was for the seventeenth-century explorer. Notwithstanding the *Edmund Fitzgerald*, this was supposed to be the unfolding of history, not the unfolding of tragedy.

The pilot's radio crackled again, and his voice came back. "We see a submerged canoe about a half a mile out and drifting with the wind." He paused for a few seconds. Then he said the words they dreaded most: "There's no sign of survivors."

ON THE ROAD TO FIND OUT

RELIVING THE DREAM

The dream returned nightly to Reid Lewis.

The August sun burns the shoulders of rugged outdoorsmen. Wooden paddles slip in and out of the river. A pair of canoes surge over the water, and hearty male voices sing, "*C'est l'aviron qui nous mene*"—It is the paddle that carries us.

Like a video, the dream rolls through Reid's mind in high-definition vignettes. In one, seven men stand on the banks of Lake Huron, heads bowed. Jesuit Father Charles McEnery, a thirty-six-year-old canoeist with experience in the Boundary Waters west of Lake Superior, offers a prayer.

"Father in Heaven, we begin this expedition in Your hands, not knowing some of the trials, not knowing many of the joys. But we do begin with a hope and a great spirit, a spirit which the first *voyageurs* had."[1]

With the final amen, the men push their craft away from the Michigan shore toward Mackinac Bridge. The water is thirty-nine degrees Fahrenheit, where survival for a capsized sailor is measured in mere minutes.

It is a fine day in this dream. The man in the stern raises a sail along the tiny mast lashed to the front seat of the canoe. A man in the middle of the canoe holds the guide lines at the bottom corners of the canvas. The sudden speed makes the men giddy as children with a new toy. The game turns when the wind picks up. Without a

---

[1] Vignettes of the Jolliet-Marquette reenactment of 1973 are taken from H. Dean Campbell's 1974 self-published *A Second Impression* and Bob Osborn's film *The Last Voyageurs*.

keel to provide stability, a canoe can go only so fast before capsizing becomes a serious danger. The canoes skim waves cresting as high as eight feet. Suddenly the men struggle simply to survive.

The scene shifts.

Calm again, the men quench their thirst, lifting clear lake water with their paddles and letting it drip into their mouths. As the canoes approach a beach, children playing near their families' summer homes see the travelers, dressed in their seventeenth-century voyageur clothes. At least one canoeist sports an earring. "Mommy, mommy, the pirates are coming!" the children shout.

Fade to gray skies.

Calm water gives way to foul weather. A rogue wave breaks over the gunnel—upper edge—of the Marquette canoe. Father Chuck and Dean Campbell, a historical interpreter for the Illinois Department of Conservation, bail furiously. They keep from being swamped as wilderness guide Lee Broske and engineering technician Bill Dwyer stroke for shore.

The scene moves to downtown Green Bay.

Reid's brother, Ken,[2] dressed as a coureur de bois—literally "a runner of the woods"—speaks in broken English, as if he were French fur trader Pierre Moreau.

"I have been twenty-four years a canoe man and forty-one years in service," he begins. "No portage was ever too long for me, eh? And fifty songs could I sing. I have saved the lives of ten voyageurs. I have had twelve wives and six running dogs. I spent all my money in pleasure, but, were I young again, I should spend my life the same way over. There is no life so happy as the life of a voyageur!"

Now the camera zips through brief Wisconsin scenes:

Eureka, where townsfolk haul out a jukebox and line a makeshift dance floor on the street with beer cans; Portage, where a band plays the French national anthem, the *Marseillaise*, and a travois carrying the canoes and four hundred pounds of gear leaves deep

---

[2] Only last names will be used on subsequent references, except in the case of the Lewises (Reid, Ken, and Jan) in order to avoid confusion.

gouges in the soft asphalt; and Wauzeka, where a possible member of the militant American Indian Movement enters camp and archly asks if the men have found any holes in their canoes . . . yet.

The film drifts into slow motion.

Canoes on the Mississippi gobble up the distance on the last three days of the journey south—sixty miles one day, then seventy miles the next, and eighty-two the last day. The little crew now includes fourteen-year-old Boy Scout Jeffrey Leclerc, portraying "*le petit sauvage*," the Peoria Indian boy given to the original French voyageurs in Wisconsin to help guide them.

Darkness falls, and the Marquette crew, looking for the Jolliet canoe, paddles blindly.

They hear the rush of water against an object very close by. Moments later they pass an enormous shadow, an iron buoy the size of a Volkswagen bobbing in the water, anchored to the river bottom to mark the channel. With a current moving up to six miles per hour and a canoe moving downstream at four miles per hour, running into a buoy is like driving a car without seat belts through an unlit parking lot into a brick wall.

Blackout to the sound of buzzing cicadas. The lens opens to bright sunlight.

The men paddle, swatting at mosquitoes. The strain of paddling against the current shows on the men's sweaty faces. The water eddies against a wing dam jutting out from shore to streamline the Mississippi River channel. The men must either stroke against a current running too fast to overcome or step into the water to "line" their canoes, pulling them over or around the wing dam while straining in rapids up to their armpits. "Paddling upstream for twelve hours a day is like shoveling rock," one man complains.

The film zooms in on flies, then zooms out to show those flies on floating trash.

The men disembark on the polluted Des Plaines River at the Chicago portage. Biology teacher Jim Phillips speaks to a small crowd of onlookers. He describes the clear waters that carried Louis Jolliet and Father Jacques Marquette.

"Three hundred years later the voyageurs find an oozing, stinking river and weedy, trash-littered banks at this historic site. This looks like the legacy we're going to leave to the most important citizens here, the youngsters in this crowd. I don't feel particularly happy, nor do I feel particularly proud, to belong to a society that can do this to an environment in the name of civilization."

* * *

Reid relived the adventure in his sleep, but when he awoke he lived it, too. On leave from teaching French for Elgin Unified School District 46 (U-46), Reid gave presentations to schools, churches, and civic groups about the voyage, a Tri-centennial reenactment of the 1673 discovery of the Mississippi River by Jolliet and Marquette. Reid's trip had run from May 17 to Sept. 19, exactly the same calendar schedule that Jolliet had kept.

Reid Lewis

Today at a middle school, Reid told twelve- and thirteen-year-olds about the Jolliet-Marquette Tri-centennial paddle. He explained how important conservation is to their world. He sang French paddling songs and told the story of the voyageurs, reminding the kids that the French not only settled the Mississippi River Valley but also came to help a fledgling republic in 1777 gain its independence from England. He was Jolliet again.

"I was taught," Reid said in slow and broken English, "that our country was developed from the east to the west by the covered wagon. If they tell you that, you say, '*Excusez moi*, that is not so,' because our part of the country was developed from the north to the south, not by the covered wagon but by the canoe. And it was the French that did it!"

Well, it had been Ralph Frese's fault, really. The Tri-centennial voyage had been his idea, and he had recruited Reid and the others. Nearing fifty now, Frese had first fallen in love with canoeing at age fourteen, when he bought a secondhand Mead Glider for fifteen bucks. The thirty-five-pound canvas kayak had made Frese the "admiral of my own navy." He had the perfect workshop, too, in which to build a frame for the kayak, hitch it to his bicycle, and carry it to nearby lakes and rivers.

Carl Frese & Sons Blacksmith Shop stood between the nineteenth and twentieth centuries like an anvil in the stream of time. The building in Chicago's Portage Park neighborhood had previously housed a silent-movie theater and a small-scale airplane assembly plant. Outside the front door at 4019 N. Narragansett and Irving Park Road, Pontiacs and DeSotos and La Salles whirred by. The thrum of engines and occasional horns mixed with the soot and carbon monoxide in the street. Inside the shop, the slamming of hammer on metal rang out before the forge, an echo of the age of horse and buggy.

After he left military service, Frese found himself making canoe kits for Scout troops and introducing the kids to the outdoors. Soon enough, he realized that children were not inheriting pristine waters, and he decided to devote his time to protecting the environment. In

1957 he launched the Des Plaines River Canoe Marathon, a race every May of nearly twenty miles that became one of the largest of its kind in the United States. Routing the race between Cook and Lake counties, Frese hoped to initiate a dialogue about the habitat of their common waterway. Public interest in his race led to the Mid America Canoe Run on the Fox River and the protection of nearly eighty percent of the Des Plaines River in Lake County by the Lake County Forest Preserve District.

"The canoe is the only mode of transportation invented by man that leaves no sign of its passing," Frese frequently said. He liked the fact that the canoe itself was not a pollutant.

By the 1960s canoes and kayaks had overtaken blacksmithing on Narragansett, and Frese's Chicagoland Canoe Base became the most unusual watercraft store in America. Patrons could buy canoes and kayaks, Scout kits, or custom canoes made on-site. They could buy a bewildering array of gear and supplies, and a library of books and DVDs on watercraft, water sports, wildlife, and environmental issues.

Frese's passions for canoeing and conservation led to another interest, the role of the canoe across the ages; he appreciated its historic value. On the board of the Chicago Maritime Museum, Frese contributed more than 120 watercraft to the museum's collection. They came from four different continents and Polynesia and ranged from dugouts to birch bark canoes to folding kayaks. In the Windy City region, Frese was known as Mr. Canoe.

Reid's Boy Scout days had taken him in and out of Frese's canoe shop. Eventually, the teenager found himself paddling with Frese in weekend portrayals of Jolliet and Marquette, wearing ragtag costumes at Starved Rock State Park about one hundred miles southwest of Chicago.

Reid graduated in 1958 from Taft High School and entered the University of Illinois, where he studied French. Those studies continued at the University of California at Berkeley, at the Alliance Française, and at the Sorbonne in Paris. In time, Reid's teaching took him to Crown Point High School in Indiana and later to

Larkin High School in Elgin, a town west of Chicago on Illinois's Fox River. Reid, however, carried with him his onetime mentor's love of paddling, of history, and of adventure.

At Crown Point, Reid had taken his students on canoe explorations in early October to West Lafayette, where the Feast of the Hunters' Moon was an annual celebration of the region's French Heritage. He put up to eighteen students in a single thirty-four-foot canoe that Frese had fashioned. Reid would take them fifteen to twenty miles down the Wabash River to the campgrounds, where they sang the songs and ate the cuisine of the voyageurs, whose days in America largely died out with the French and Indian War.

Back in the classroom, the kids complained about studying the subjunctive tense of verbs, a tricky bit of French grammar.

"But you already know this," Reid said slyly.

"No, we don't," the students insisted. "When did we learn this?"

"You sang it last month at the Feast of the Hunters' Moon," Reid crowed, connecting their experience on the river with their understanding of French. In 1971, Dean Campbell initiated an annual French colonial rendezvous at Fort de Chartres in Illinois, south of St. Louis, and Reid began taking students to the national landmark there, too.

About that time it dawned on Frese that Illinois—in fact, the whole Midwest—was approaching the 300th anniversary of the 1673 European discovery of the Mississippi River by Louis Jolliet, another son of a blacksmith. Frese saw an opportunity to bring to the public the gospel of peaceful recreation through canoeing, of river conservation, and of the historic role of paddle craft in development of the Midwest. What would seize the imagination? What would grab the public's attention?

Frese conceived of a true reenactment of the voyage. Not a site-specific photo opportunity that dramatized in an hour's time the journey of several months. No, he wanted to re-create the look, the feel, the length of the trip itself, with canoes that looked like the real thing, clothing that looked and felt like the garb of another century, and men who could share this sense of rediscovery with Americans along the way, in thick French accents if not in the language itself of the voyageurs. Reid, whom Frese called "a born leader," was a natural to play the role of Jolliet.

"Now the problem was how to finance something like this," Frese observed, "because it would cover a period of four months, and it would entail a lot of gasoline, telephone calls, effort and so on, which had to be paid. It was at a gathering of historical reenacters at historic Fort de Chartres in southern Illinois that one person heard me."

Dr. George Arnold, a professor at Southern Illinois University at Edwardsville, was also a member of the Mississippi Parkway Commission, the Great River Road Commission. Since the 1940s the panel had worked to bring travel and tourism to the states bordering the Mississippi River. Like Frese, Arnold had contemplated possible celebrations for the river's Tri-centennial. He invited Frese to St. Louis to present his ideas to the commission.

"They loved my idea because it was the only one that would involve most of the states along the Mississippi," Frese said. Of course, the sponsors also wanted the reenactment to have a representative from every state along the route. It was not the first political stumbling block Frese would encounter or the most difficult. This one he deftly turned aside. "I pointed out to them [that] I needed local people that I could choose, with special talents and close enough that we could practice in costume and prepare for the journey," he said.

Thus Frese—canoe enthusiast, conservationist, and regional historian—gained the sponsoring group he needed for the idea he had. And he set to work creating the two twenty-foot canoes that would be needed for the long trip ahead. They were built of fiberglass to endure the scum and pollution of twentieth-century rivers, not the more sensitive birch bark of the seventeenth century. Bark canoes also had to be gummed frequently along their seams to avoid leaks, a problem that the molded hulls of fiberglass avoided. Frese used Sitka spruce to make the gunnels, ribs, thwarts, and fixed seats. He lashed the gunnels to the hull with strips of vinyl to simulate the root lashings used hundreds of years earlier. He designed both canoes in the early Algonquin style, with upswept ends. Each weighed about 150 pounds. Finally, a birch bark applique would give the crafts a realistic look.

The authentic look of the canoes, the period clothes the men wore, and the ancient French paddling songs the men sang attracted small crowds wherever they camped. The men fought the heat, the mosquitoes, sore muscles, and the current as they visited the lakeshores and riverbanks of nine states in a successful retracing of the voyage of discovery.

In some ways, however, the Tri-centennial trip was a lot like the path of a canoe—a transit that left no sign of its passing. Newspaper coverage stopped. Film crews moved on. No great cultural or environmental initiatives were attributed to the Tri-centennial paddle through America's heartland. But its ripples continued to move in a widening arc through the lives of the Tri-centennial crew.

Not long after the 1973 trip ended, a reception for the crew at the Peggy Sommers Studio brought together the now ex-voyageurs and Ken Lewis's acting friends. Both groups brought extended family and friends. One of Ken's friends was Howard Platt, an actor generally recognized at the time for a recurring television role as Hoppy the Cop on the NBC comedy show *Sanford and Son*, Norman Lear's follow-up to the groundbreaking *All in the Family*. Platt brought his sister, Judy, to the reception, and Ken introduced her to Broske, who later married her. Broske had been born in Chicago but raised by an uncle on the shores of Hudson Bay. Ken said Broske could survive in a wild forest for months with a pocketknife and a cord of rope. Stocky and strong, Broske worked part-time as a high-steel worker who had put the antenna on top of the Sears Tower (now the Willis Tower) in 1973, making it the tallest building in the world for the next quarter-century. He hated being enclosed in a tent or other structure, even as innocuous as a tarpaulin stretched over canoes. During the trip he would often sleep in the crook of a tree or on the beach instead and once meditated in a pouring rain.

The reception gave the voyageurs a chance to swap stories about the trip. Broske recalled the night near the end of the trip when he discovered their canoes had been stolen. One of the canoes turned up in shallows, filled with water. While Broske went to talk to the authorities, Phillips saw a light shining toward the lake. Quickly, he told Dwyer and the others to kill their own flashlights.

"Hey, out there, how about giving me a ride?" he called. Shortly, he saw the other canoe with two young men aboard. Claiming to know how to paddle, Phillips persuaded the pair to pull closer to shore, where he took the stern seat, which allowed him to control the direction of the canoe. The two young men, he noticed, were under the influence of drugs or alcohol. As the group paddled, Phillips took a wide arc in the water toward the voyageur camp then abruptly turned the craft into shore, where they were placed under arrest. The thieves should have been grateful, perhaps, that they did not fall under frontier justice that angry coureurs de bois would have exacted three hundred years earlier.

By now most folks knew that Phillips was The Fox, the anonymous environmental crusader who had created "ecotage"—sabotage of industries that polluted the water and air—before the Environmental Protection Agency began its official role. The Fox became legendary as nationally syndicated columnist Mike Royko wrote about Phillips's exploits and *Time* magazine did a story on him in October 1970. Phillips recounted many of his escapades in *Raising Kane: The Fox Chronicles*, written under the pseudonym Ray Fox. In 1969 Phillips carried on a campaign against Armour-Dial, a soap company that had been polluting Mill Creek, which fed the Fox River west of Chicago. He blocked a catch basin where effluents were being dumped. Then he left a message warning the company against polluting the stream and drew a picture of a fox's head bracketed with an F and an X. He distributed flyers and posted banners on highway overpasses. He recruited a loose network of teenagers from nearby high schools to slap embarrassing stickers with a Fox emblem on bars of Dial soap. His crusade grew to include US Steel as he employed many of the tactics later used by Greenpeace and other environmental activists.

In another part of the studio that night, Campbell recalled the time the crew heard a pistol shot and, upon investigating, found a husband and wife who had shot a water moccasin. Campbell had accepted the couple's invitation to come home with them. Together they trudged a mile through a cotton field, over a levee, through a creek, and onto a dirt road that led, astonishingly, to a plantation house that could have served as Tara from *Gone with the Wind*. The 120-year-old mansion and its Greek columns sat on a 2,800-acre plantation. Two days later, Campbell went for a walk after dinner and came across another plantation home, this one newly built.

"If a six-pack of beer were lost in the Sahara Desert, you'd trip over it," Phillips said.

Father Chuck remembered climbing up from the Chicago River to the city's Pioneer Court while Chicagoans leaned over the railings of the bridges and fireboats threw multicolored streams of water over the channel. Then he celebrated mass on an overturned canoe with Mayor Richard J. Daley and Cardinal John Cody in attendance.

After the expedition, Ken, like Broske, also married a girl named Judy, who no doubt thought his roving days were over. But adventure was in Ken's blood, as it was in Reid's, handed down to them from their father, Perry, a lawyer who worked out of an office at La Salle National Bank in Chicago. Growing up, Ken and Reid didn't have a TV or a car. The boys were seven or eight years old when their dad began taking the family on trips, each one a surprise. They never had a plan. Mr. Lewis called the outings "shunpiking," a deliberate effort to stay off the interstates and follow the "blue highways" of the map instead. During a drive, Mr. Lewis would turn to his wife and say, "Let's let the colts out into the pasture," and they would stop and let the boys explore the countryside.

Once they stopped for a horse auction. Another time they sampled oysters right off the boat. Perhaps the most memorable stop was at a regional airport near Washington, D.C., where Mr. Lewis let Ken and Reid try on seat belts on a small plane. As they did so, the pilot climbed into his seat and announced, "Those who are not taking off should get off the plane now." As if on a lark, Mr. Lewis said, "Don't get up. Let's just see where it's going." It turned out that he had bought them tickets for a flight to Cuba.

"Sometimes we think our lives are supposed to move naturally from A to B to C," Reid said. "But how often does that happen?" More often some event takes place that slides us in a new direction, from A to C or A to D. How we deal with those new directions may determine how well we live our lives, he observed. "Our parents were teaching us how to travel through life," Reid said. "You can see, with that upbringing, how you have to be flexible. It was fun, and getting there was half the fun."

In the afterglow of their successful voyage, the crew left the seventeenth century behind and quickly went back to their twentieth-century lives. Ken resumed his role as a creative director writing copy for trade shows and other commercial presentations. Dwyer and Broske returned to their own pursuits. At least for a while, McEnery resumed his duties as a priest, though he would eventually doff his collar for a wedding ring. Jeff Leclerc had years of high school ahead of him. Campbell went back to his job with the Illinois Department of Conservation, and Phillips returned to a job he had taken with Kane County.

In many ways, however, Reid could not get past the adventure. Truly, he never really wanted to shake it off. When audiences responded enthusiastically to his stories, as they invariably did, they reflected Reid's own sense of discovery. The test of endurance, the thrill of the crowds, and the excitement of reaching a wider public about its French heritage never left him.

Additionally, education always meant more to Reid than verb conjugations and useful tourist phrases. He knew that experience was a great teacher. For him, the recent trip through the Midwest had also reinforced how a display of culture could reach people outside the classroom. Even for spectators, experiencing history brought an appreciation of it and mobilized people to act to improve the places where they lived. The power of that realization continued to work like an undercurrent, tugging at Reid's psyche for months after the canoes were beached.

"WHY NOT?" TO THINGS THAT NEVER WERE

As 1973 wound down, Reid began to gather strands of thought. The media, which had followed the Civil War centennial in the previous decade, now lit the flame of interest in the American Revolution Bicentennial, pointing toward July 4, 1976, the 200th anniversary of the Declaration of Independence. Reid noticed, though, that the entire conversation seemed stuck on the East Coast. True, that was where conflict with the British government had resulted in independence. But the western end of the new American nation was French. America's chief ally in the Revolution was France. The vision of what America could become was that of French explorers. No one appeared to be telling that story, and the Francophile in Reid took exception.

At the same time, the Founding Fathers were being held up as perfect creators of a perfect republican democracy. As such, they were less objects of emulation than idolatry. But Reid believed that there was a way to make the work of pioneers more accessible, understood as real work by real people whose example could be followed every day, not simply ignored as being beyond the ability of Americans today. Reid extended that thought to encompass the young people he had taught. They did not see themselves as important in themselves, powerful enough to effect change. And there were plenty of people who reminded them of their limitations.

In December Reid's strands of thought coalesced one day when he was in the shower. An idea began to form for another adventure.

He let the idea percolate for a few months. At Easter the Lewis clan gathered at Ken and Reid's aunt and uncle's home in suburban Morton Grove. The house was full of people, so Ken and Reid took their hors d'oeuvres to an upstairs bedroom. As they nibbled, Reid turned to Ken and said, "You know what? I've got a great idea. The American Revolution Bicentennial is coming up. Wouldn't it be great to do another trip to mark the occasion?"

Reid called it La Salle: Expedition II. He envisioned a reenactment of the 1681–82 voyage by René-Robert Cavelier, Sieur de La Salle. The explorer had been given the task of finding the mouth of the Mississippi River and building a port there for sailing ships on the Gulf of Mexico, which the Spanish considered their private lake in the New World. Like the Tri-centennial trip, this would be a true replica, mirroring La Salle's itinerary exactly.

Like the Jolliet crew of eight, the La Salle crew would have exactly the same number of paddlers as the original trip—twenty-three—and each would carry the name of one of the original Frenchmen. The historic La Salle had paid a group of men to go with him. Unlike that voyage, La Salle II, as Reid saw it, would be made up principally of suburban teenagers traveling for eight months and living outdoors throughout the winter. It was a journey that had never been attempted before—at least not in the way Reid envisioned.

Reid knew the expedition would require time to plan, recruit, and finance. But he couldn't make it a true Tri-centennial. By 1981 the Bicentennial would be over—and the possible funding sources dried up. By timing their arrival at the Gulf of Mexico on April 9, 1977, however, the expedition could celebrate exactly 295 years later and at the same spot in the Mississippi Delta where La Salle claimed the Louisiana Territory for France.

This emblem of La Salle: Expedition II marked barrels and chests in expedition canoes as well as the nonprofit corporation's newsletters and stationery.

Reid wanted the trip to project authenticity in all respects. The reenactment would, like the Jolliet one, accept home cooking from people along the route, as the original voyageurs accepted hospitality from Native American villages they passed. But the boys would use authentic diet on the trail, authentic utensils, and cooking pots. The boys would also make their voyageur clothes, muskets, and canoes and learn the French paddling songs.

The commitment to authenticity would come at a cost, however. La Salle's calendar for 3,300 miles would be twice as long as Jolliet's and run through the entire winter, when water underneath the canoes would not be a given thing. And that was just for starters. Reid would need three times as many paddlers and canoes, clothes for both warm and cold weather, provisions for eight and a half months instead of four, and arrangements for hundreds more campgrounds and performances.

Like Frese, however, Reid was both a visionary and a man of action. To his companions, he was a "pusher," a term put forward with some admiration. Reid was someone who kept plugging away at his goal because, to him, it was always possible. "The greatest day is the day you decide to do it," Reid said. The rest is simply doing it. "Never once did I think, 'This isn't going to work.' There's always a solution, unless you give up on it." Reid may have been the only person who could have pulled off such an audacious quest.

While his sense of adventure provided Reid the impetus, he always claimed three key issues motivated him to seek another voyage of exploration. The first was to extend the message of America's French heritage during the Bicentennial year. The Tri-centennial expedition had done so well. Reid thought a second trip could reinforce the French role in US history while bringing the message to those who missed it the first time.

The second was to showcase the pioneer strength of twentieth-century American kids. The previous year, 1973, had witnessed the end of "the first war America had lost," as the United States ended its involvement in Vietnam. Sixty thousand young men and women had died and many thousands more had been wounded.

The conflict had driven a wedge between generations in America. Many parents who had fought in World War II and the Korean War to halt totalitarianism had clashed with their children, who saw no purpose in defending a totalitarian regime on the other side of the globe. During the conflict, some young men fled to Canada, retreated into college deferments, or burned flags and draft cards to protest the war. Those actions offended many adults, who also took offense at children who thumbed their noses at cultural norms by growing their hair long, experimenting with illegal drugs, and blaring rock 'n' roll.

However, Reid taught those kids, and he had grown weary of suggestions that teenagers were lazy, privileged deadbeats who eagerly took the easy way, unwilling to dig deep to achieve something difficult. He watched the growing cynicism among his students—mere tots during the years of President Kennedy's Camelot—who didn't see how they could ever make a difference in the world.

Finally, Reid saw the voyage as an opportunity to develop valuable educational resources in a wide array of disciplines for schools in America and abroad. It would certainly help as a tool to sell the expedition as a primarily educational venture. But Reid also understood the way that academic subjects, separate in the classroom, are linked in the real world. The prospect of putting such interdisciplinary tools in the hands of young people delighted him.

"In my own education, from high school and grade school and in the university, everything was so compartmentalized," Reid recalled, "and it was always a major victory to me to have one class actually related to another subject. Educators are very slow to be innovative. You have to kind of creep up on them and show them how it will work."

The prospectus for the project stated:

> One of the most important tangible results of the Expedition, of enduring value to educational institutions and other interested organizations, will be the development, publication, and international distribution of nineteen

interrelated Educational Resource Units, based on the collective experience of the adult and student crew members and the Expedition's board of professional advisors.

This board of advisors, many of them hands-on experts, anticipated the sweeping educational component for the La Salle trip. The advisors included history professors from several universities: Illinois, Southern Illinois, Marquette, and Ball State. Harry Volkman, meteorologist from Chicago's WGN-TV, and S. James Gooding, an antique arms researcher from Ottawa, were advisors. The board included environmentalists from the National College of Education and UNESCO, the United Nations Educational, Scientific, and Cultural Organization; outdoor recreation specialists from Nova Scotia, and geographers from Johns Hopkins University and the University of Chicago.

Like Frese before him, Reid had to select a crew for the expedition. Because two of his goals were to renew confidence in youth and to advance education, Reid knew that he wanted teenage boys for his crew. High school students would be eager to go, but he also knew that he had to have adults to steady the group and counsel them when it was needed. His brother, Ken, was an easy choice. Over the years, the pair would work together on five different expeditions.

"I had a wife at the time," Ken said. "I said, 'I'm in,' and then I had to tell Judy about it." She was not happy. Ken would be away from home for eight months, and she was less happy still that he made that decision without consulting her about it ahead of time.

Reid thought teachers would be ideal aides, and he wanted their areas of interest and expertise to represent a range of disciplines in order for the educational component of this expedition to work. He also realized that the men and boys, like those on the 1973 expedition, would have to come from the same general area in order to coordinate their preparation and train for the challenges both on and off the water.

Ron Hobart, twenty-five, fit the profile that Reid wanted for his adult voyageurs. He was the head of the science department at Central Junior High in Elgin. He also taught in Elgin High's alternative school, where he had to develop rapport with teenagers who had issues that kept them out of mainstream classes. Hobart also had field experience in biology and geology. Hobart's outdoor credentials for this assignment included work as a conservation officer for the state of Minnesota. He had also been a YMCA camp counselor and was an experienced canoeist. And he was willing to go.

John Fialko, twenty-seven, was also willing to go. He taught metals and machine shop at Larkin. He was quiet but well regarded by his students.

"Reid walked into the lounge one day while I was working on some papers for class," Fialko recalled, "and he opened up that big notebook of his and showed me the first typed description of everything, and he told me what he wanted. And he wanted somebody to work on tools and equipment primarily, and things were pretty nebulous at that point. After a week or so, I told him I'd be willing to work with it. I felt I needed a change from work, and that would be a good one for it. He hit me right where I was interested." But he warned Reid that he came with limitations. "I told Reid two things that I remember. One was that I don't like to work with groups of people and, secondly, that I couldn't swim."

Fialko preferred to work alone or with two or three people at a time, but he took part during the trip in crew performances before hundreds of people. He was a quiet man who focused more on the task at hand, but he would spend more than two and a half years with many young people who focused as much on relationships as jobs. "I would have made a better mountain man than a voyageur, I would think," he said. Fialko used his skill with his hands to help Frese create canoes and build muskets. Later he would construct sledges and repair damaged equipment, serving as armorer for the trip.

Reid had known Dick Stillwagon, thirty-six, from his days at Crown Point, where he had been the football coach and taught judo. He also taught general science, biology, and health. Stillwagon had received a National Science Foundation grant for biology in 1963. He had led wilderness canoe trips and field biology courses. As a senior member of the National Ski Patrol, he also possessed a valuable asset—advanced first-aid and rescue training. By default that made him the expedition "surgeon," but his skills would be invaluable on the trail.

While he was more Reid's contemporary than any other adult on the expedition, Stillwagon was unique among the La Salle II personnel. He had a family. He and his wife, Rowena, had met when they were fourteen years old. They had four children, and the oldest, Jeff, would be going off to college almost as soon as his father first dipped a paddle in the St. Lawrence. While Stillwagon was away on this adventure, Rowena would be a single parent, making sure that Jeff's siblings—high school senior Andy, sophomore Diana, and eight-year-old Anissa—got up, got breakfast, got dressed, and went to school every day. Rowena would be the one to buy the groceries, do the laundry, and deal with family finances during his time away from home.

Terry Cox, twenty-six, had been a senior at Crown Point High when Reid was there, but he had not been one of Reid's students. As a gymnast, however, Cox knew Stillwagon as a member of the Athletic Department at Crown Point and respected him. After college, Cox had moved to the Chicago area in the fall of 1974. He started teaching US history and coaching freshman-sophomore gymnastics at Downers Grove North High School in the western suburbs.

Classes had barely started that year when French teacher Holly Devaud asked Cox if he could provide some background information on a fellow she had invited to speak at North about the Jolliet-Marquette Tri-centennial expedition. The day Reid appeared at the assembly, he stopped by Cox's classroom for a Q&A session with students. As he was leaving, he mentioned that he needed a history teacher for another, much longer trip he was planning.

"He asked me if I would be interested, saying he'd been having a difficult time finding a history teacher that was willing to go. My students wanted to sign me up on the spot," said Cox.

Cox told his wife, Pam, about Reid's presentation and his plans but said nothing about the need for a history teacher. In the next few weeks, Pam heard Reid's presentation firsthand as he spoke to Elgin schools. Pam taught home economics at Central, where Hobart was on the faculty. Reid recruited the home economics teachers to help with the making of authentic seventeenth-century clothing for the trip, and soon both Coxes were part of La Salle: Expedition II.

"When the opportunity was presented to me, the thing that intrigued me most of all was the physical challenge," said Cox. "I was somewhat complacent with my life. I guess I wanted to see if I could once again be 'Terrible T in the Shape of a V.'"

One of the adults who signed on to the expedition did not come from Elgin schools or Reid's circle of acquaintances. This was Joel Monture Knecht, twenty-one, a Canadian descendant of Mohawk Indians. His mother had heard about the expedition and told her son. He then called Reid and volunteered, relocating to the Chicago area because he believed in the project. On the surface, he seemed to be a good fit with the group. He had taught American Indian history and culture, and his expertise ranged from Indian beadwork to moccasin making to black powder gunsmithing. He spoke French, and the Mohawk and Lakota languages. He also had experience camping, canoeing, and rock climbing. Knecht's age made him gravitate more toward the boys than the adults.

The French explorers always required a priest to accompany their travels. La Salle—like Jolliet—was no exception. The Tri-centennial trip had demanded a Jesuit, but the La Salle reenactment would need a Franciscan to be authentic to the original voyage. The choice was Father Loran Fuchs, fifty-one, headquartered at St. Anthony Friary in St. Louis, Missouri. Father Loran taught Latin, English, religion, and library science, none of which was a critical area explored by the educational projects of La Salle: Expedition II. On paper, however, he had extensive camping and canoeing experience and had served for six years as chaplain for the Voyageur Wilderness Programme in Quetico Provincial Park in Ontario, Canada.

The priest's involvement did not come from a personal desire to participate, however. It was not until a directors' meeting on March 9, 1976, that the impetus to put him on the crew became clear. Reid asked the adults to tell why they had become involved in La Salle: Expedition II. For some it was a sense of adventure. For others it presented a chance to educate others. Father Loran said he joined because his superiors told him to get involved. Over the coming year, many voyageurs would come to believe that he was a reluctant participant.

Father Loran's motivation was not the only difficulty. Reid candidly told the other adults that Father Loran had a drinking problem. Stillwagon, Hobart, and Cox voiced objections, but Reid and Ken believed that the expedition would be good for the priest, that it might even help him kick his dependence on alcohol.

The enterprise also needed a person to direct the expedition's liaison team, someone to contact all those points along the route that La Salle touched, to book venues for performances and schools for classroom appearances, to bring in audiences and work up enthusiasm for the crew's appearances. That person would also have to flag in the canoes, make sure there was firewood, and set up and take down audio equipment for the performances. Of course, she would not be doing laundry for seven smelly men and a fourteen-year-old. She would have to do it for twenty-three smelly men.

Three years earlier, Frese had chosen Phyllis Eubanks from the Visitors' Center in Springfield to head the support team for the travelers. Campbell knew her and brought her to Reid's home and introduced her to Frese. Eubanks was a member of the Young Women's League and involved in New Salem Village, a historic re-creation of young Abraham Lincoln's Illinois home. She began to make the necessary contacts a full year before the canoes started their journey south, working with Frese's friend Father Donnelly, who served the expedition as historical advisor, developed a daily itinerary, and guided the making or buying of equipment.

During the trip, Eubanks drove two or three days ahead of the canoes to contact key individuals and groups. She secured campsites, made sure firewood was available, and ensured venues were provided for the men to address audiences. Eubanks was known among the voyageurs as "Mother Marquette," and she did more than connect the canoeists with their audiences. She did laundry for the environmentally conscious men, who certainly wouldn't wash their clothes with soap in the rivers on which they paddled.

Journalist David Lane provided press coverage with help, after Green Bay, from Gary Gordon, then twenty, who was finishing an internship for the *Press-Gazette* there. Dave stayed just one day ahead of the canoes, securing food, preparing campgrounds, and waving the men in using a phosphorescent Frisbee they could see in the gloaming. Meanwhile, the Mississippi Parkway Commission helped provide contacts for Eubanks and worked hard to raise money and to promote it along the Great River Road. Eventually, six states along the route helped defray expenses—Michigan, Wisconsin, Iowa, Illinois, Missouri, and Arkansas.

All Reid thought he needed to find his new "Mother Marquette" was to walk into his own home and turn around. Reid's wife, Jan, a middle school English teacher in U-46, would serve as director of support services, helping to keep the new voyageurs afloat and on schedule.

"If Jan hadn't believed in it from the very beginning," Reid said, "the expedition never would have happened." Not only did she accept the responsibility of directing liaison efforts, she sold her car to help fund the trip and joined Reid in absorbing many thousands of dollars in debt that would weigh on their family income for years.

Janine Sholes had married Reid in December 1974 when he'd already made up his mind to go on this second canoe expedition. Accepting that Reid would be gone for several months was one thing. Taking a working position with the enterprise was something else. Yet they were newlyweds, and love carries a lot of weight in sharing the load. Reid has been effusive in his praise for Jan's efforts on behalf of the expedition, and with good reason. Reid knew what Eubanks had achieved, and he thought he understood what he was asking of his bride. As it turned out, he was asking much more.

"As far as Jan is concerned," Reid said in a post-expedition interview, "when we were going together and had already gotten into this, she knew me from the Jolliet-Marquette Expedition and she backed us from Day One and did every possible thing she could, especially after we got married, typing letters, answering phone calls, taking days off work . . . because she knew it was an overwhelming task."

Reid was a master of understatement. The Lewises originally thought they would have secretarial help, arranged through La Salle National Bank. But the bank was shorthanded and had to back out. The expedition had no money to afford a secretary, so it all had to be done by the Lewises or anyone they could get to type. And typing was the least of Jan's concerns.

Reid knew nothing would be achieved without money, and he knew how important the Mississippi Parkway Commission and the various state Tri-centennial commissions had been in that regard to the 1973 trip. For that reason, it was important to Reid to gain the sanction of the American Revolution Bicentennial Commission. To do so, he began to gather endorsements from high-profile individuals and strengthen the legitimacy of his La Salle project.

Fluent in French, Reid found it relatively easy to find Frenchmen willing to lend their names to a project that would highlight French language and heritage in America. Reid's involvement with water conservationists like Frese and Phillips also helped in attracting the endorsements of undersea explorers Jacques-Yves and Philippe Cousteau. Countryman Marcel Marceau also gave his name (and thereby the famous mime's voice) as a "distinguished friend of La Salle: Expedition II."

Headquartered in Chicago's iconic new Sears Tower, the giant retailer had on its board of advisors another great explorer, the conqueror of Mt. Everest, Sir Edmund Hillary. He too agreed to endorse the canoe trip Reid had planned. So did Ara Parseghian, head football coach at Notre Dame and, previously, Northwestern University. The expedition would be traveling through the campuses of both schools.

Chicago-born conservationist Sigurd F. Olson also joined the list of distinguished friends. In 1974, the seventy-five-year-old author won the John Burroughs Medal, the highest award for distinguished nature writing. The canoeist and wilderness guide had served as president of both the National Parks Association and the Wilderness Society, and he was a director of the National Parks Service.

TAKE UP YOUR PADDLE AND FOLLOW ME

The young crew Reid wanted would probably have less experience as canoeists than Jeff Leclerc and certainly less than the adults on the 1973 trip, so the La Salle crew would have to put in a lot of training—two years of it. And for the same reason that Frese demanded the Jolliet voyageurs come from one area where they could train, the La Salle crew had to come from a relatively restricted part of the Chicago area, preferably near Reid's home in Elgin.

This meant he would have to gain approval from the board of education. Reid discussed his intentions with Superintendent Paul Lawrence, a man for whom he has nothing but praise. Lawrence was extremely accessible, the kind of fellow Reid could call and quickly get to see.

That access made it possible for Reid to go straight to the top and get a decision on a question rather than passing it through channels.

With Lawrence streamlining the process for him, Reid next came before the school board and laid out his plans. He admitted that the biggest concern was lawsuits. When asked how he intended to address that concern, he told the school board that he would take out a million-dollar liability policy. Reid opened the floor to questions. The board peppered him. For every question they put to him, Reid had an answer.

"Well, it looks like you've thought of everything," Lawrence said, putting his positive spin on the presentation while punctuating its conclusion. The board approved the project. The time had come to talk to the class of 1976.

An assembly for junior class boys was held for Elgin high schools on Thursday, Sept. 12, 1974. Reid had discussed his experience with the Jolliet Tri-centennial trip in earlier presentations at the high schools. The charismatic adventurer now explained that he wanted to take sixteen boys on an even longer trip for the Bicentennial. Reid promised participants $1,000 toward college expenses, plus fifteen hours of college credit.

Prospective members of the La Salle II crew do calisthenics on a field in Elgin.

In recruiting boys for his epic expedition, Reid wasn't looking for functionaries as much as he was trolling for visionaries. He may never have considered the process this way, but he was seeking disciples. Sure, Reid wanted boys who had strength of arm and strength of character. But he also looked for boys who really believed in preaching history, heritage, and the holistic nature of humans and their environment. They must be willing to leave their families and follow his ways. And they must be willing to sacrifice themselves for the greater goal they all pursued.

Boys interested in the expedition were to fill out a four-page application, providing their academic background and answering questions about their activity in scouting, camping, swimming, and canoeing. The form asked an applicant if he could "carry a tune" or play an instrument. There were questions about hobbies and sports, clubs, travel, physical disabilities, allergies, and employment. The application asked: Would you object to wearing a costume throughout the expedition? Do you have difficulty speaking in front of a group of people? Will you be able—and are you willing—to spend considerable time and effort preparing for the expedition? There was also an open-ended question to let each boy amplify on how he might be an asset to the expedition.

The application forms were to be turned in by noon the following Monday, Sept. 16. "Late forms will not be accepted," the application said. Reid meant that. The ability to follow directions was an important consideration, and the deadline was not a loose one. Students would be selected based on background and specific interest or talents. The first cut would be posted Oct. 1.

"I knew of Reid long before I met him," said Rich Gross, who was in the gym for Reid's presentation. As a student at Kimball Middle School, Gross had heard from older siblings about this French teacher at Larkin High who seemed larger than life, cracking jokes and taking students on canoe trips to historic places. Gross looked forward to taking Reid's class, but by the time he became a Larkin freshman he was too late. "When I got to ninth grade, he wasn't there. He was on the Jolliet-Marquette expedition."

John DiFulvio had attended Lewis's French class as a sophomore. He had also spent several years camping with his family for two weeks on a sandbar in the Mississippi River. The La Salle reenactment seemed like a natural fit to him.

Bill Watts also fit the profile of a New Age voyageur. He had seen the flyer at Larkin and thought the expedition might be fun.

Watts was nearing completion of his Eagle Scout requirements and had done a lot of camping with his troop. He possessed skills as a canoeist that became obvious as the selection process got under way. He also enjoyed history, though he knew little or nothing about either La Salle or Reid.

In the bleachers, there seemed to be two different kinds of responses. Bob Kulick said everyone next to him in his row was eager to go. Clif Wilson, sitting with "half a dozen of my stoner friends," turned to them and said what a great idea he thought it was. "I guess I didn't grasp the fact that so much of it would be outdoors," he commented years later. "I'm not an outdoorsman." His friends told Wilson he was crazy and the venture was ridiculous, but his family backed him all the way.

"Every father likes to see his son have that 'military experience,' and I think he was kind of the same way," Wilson said of his dad. "My mom was also supportive, but she was looking more at the risk, the dangers involved: 'You're going to freeze to death this winter' and stuff. My sisters were all for it, especially my two older sisters, because they agreed with me that I wasn't ready to go to school."

Steve Marr, who had done some trailer camping with his family, told his father about Reid's presentation, "and he got excited about it," just as Wilson's father had. That excitement became infectious, and Marr decided to get involved.

Not every applicant heard Reid's presentation that day. Keith Gorse deliberately missed the assembly altogether. That was his free period, and he thought sitting in the library talking to girls was a lot more important than the assembly. But when he went to his next class, the trip was all any of the guys wanted to talk about. He went down to the office during his next free moment, got an application, and filled it out.

Mark Fredenburg wasn't at the assembly, either. He wasn't even in the target group. He was a senior, not a junior, and he planned to spend his next two years at Elgin Community College before transferring to a four-year school. His first class after the assembly was an AP English class, and a junior boy next to him wouldn't shut up about the crazy trip Reid had laid out for them. Fredenburg and his brother were Eagle Scouts with a wealth of experience in camping and canoeing, hunting and fishing. To be able to pursue such a life beyond high school was a dream. Setting aside thoughts of college for a bit, he dropped by the office after school to pick up an application. They were already gone. That didn't stop him from tracking one down, though. Fredenburg's parents, like Gorse's, were of two minds. His father was on board, but his mother was not at all enthused, fearful for the dangers he might face on such a trip.

About 165 boys thought enough of the adventure to turn in application forms. Fewer than ten percent would be selected. Once the pool of applicants was set, Reid scheduled a mandatory evening assembly with the boys and their parents. Like the application deadline, the word "mandatory" was a litmus test for applicants. If the boy wasn't willing to make time for this first requirement, he would probably not be willing to meet later requirements. Gorse, who had missed the initial assembly, almost missed this required meeting as well. He had been excited about the trip, but he also nursed hopes of becoming a foreign-exchange student.

"The night of the meeting came at Elgin High and I was in a bad mood, so I told my parents I wasn't going to go and to never mind," Gorse recalled. "I'd skip it and go to Germany instead. And they said, 'Why don't you try, just go ahead and go in case the thing with Germany falls through,' so I took off for the high school. . . . I don't think I could have [gone on the trip] without them because there were a lot of things I had to neglect at home."

Reid gave the same presentation he had made for their sons, but to parents he stressed the dangers. He used the language of insurance—words like "death" and "dismemberment." He wanted to make sure the parents understood that there would be severe risks involved. He candidly told parents that he was asking for three years of their sons' lives. Reid said there would be two years of training. There would be mandatory work on educational projects in music, geography, weather, clothing manufacture, canoe building, history,

French language, and other disciplines. That work would require at least one night a week plus three weekends a month by early 1976. Reid stressed the enormous physical challenges the boys would encounter, and tests of mind and will.

The parent assembly had a chilling effect on the enthusiasm shown the previous week. Roughly one hundred boys withdrew their applications or quickly dropped out of consideration.

Evelyn Gross, the mother of four sons and two daughters, listened to Reid's presentation and thought hard about the decision she and her husband would have to make. Rich, her fifth child, was among the applicants. The family had taken camping trips all over the country, but this was not a vacation Reid was talking about. This was an eight-month test of endurance through the winter. But a mother remembers things.

On his first day home from kindergarten, Mrs. Gross remembered, little Rich had come home, plunked his lunch kit down firmly, and announced, "I quit." She asked him in all seriousness what was wrong. What had led him to this momentous decision?

"You told me I would learn things in school, and all we did all day was play," he said angrily. The next day Gross and his mother went to school and explained to the teacher that her student was quitting. The teacher also treated Gross's decision with adult respect and asked why. He repeated his objection.

"I'm so sorry," she answered. "I promise, Rich, that if you come back, you will learn things every day and this will never happen again."

Gross was a determined young man, his mother knew, and holding him back was really not an option. In the end, she said, "It would have hurt him more to tell him no."

The task of whittling even sixty-five crew applicants down to sixteen still seemed daunting. While considering how to trim the number of boys, there were calisthenics and outdoor excursions. On Nov. 2, 1974, the boys lay randomly on the ground in a forest preserve where Ken had taken them to practice the kind of steady breathing they might have to do during a full day of paddling a canoe. Each boy balanced a stack of books on his stomach and breathed slowly and evenly. A couple walked by with their dogs, and it must have been a mystery to them why a long-haired, bearded man strolled among this odd assembly, every so often intoning the mantra, "Good. Good. That's right."

Unknown to the boys, the training itself was part of the selection process, and it got under way in earnest that winter. Reid arranged a campout for the applicants at Kettle Moraine State Forest in Wisconsin. It was cold, of course. There were no plumbing facilities or running water. To accommodate the boys' families' vacation schedules, the training took place over a series of weekends between early December and early January.

The boys went backpacking through the woods, with Reid setting a fast pace, forcing the kids to keep up. He wanted to put the boys under stress to see how they would respond. When it came time for the group to set up camp, Reid made the boys responsible for gathering wood and starting a fire. He deliberately asked for volunteers to see which boys were willing to step forward. "Some people have the knack for looking the other way," he quipped.

"There was one boy lagging behind the others on the trail. He came in last and was so frustrated that he took his backpack and dashed it on the ground and against a tree. We took note of that," Reid said.

For water, the group melted snow, which they later learned was a mistake. Experts told the members of the expedition that precipitation actually scrubbed pollutants from the air, collecting heavy metals and other impurities as it fell. "We did that based on ignorance," Reid said. He paused and grinned before adding, "We already knew not to eat yellow snow."

The boys had slept for what seemed like only a few minutes when Reid woke them up for a two-mile run. It was two o'clock. The fire had died. The boys scrambled to put on their clothes as their bright dreams dissolved in the darkness.

The adult crew members graded each camper on a four-point scale, from poor to fair to good to excellent. The scale was applied to eight categories: cooperativeness, compatibility, initiative, resourcefulness, consideration for others, endurance, ability to follow instructions, and good disposition. After the rigors of the winter campout, more applicants dropped out. Clearly, La Salle: Expedition II would be no picnic. For some, the prospect of spending two years of their lives working toward eight months more of winter camping did not sit well. It would also be two years that interfered with their social lives—dates with girls, school dances, football and basketball games, movies on the weekends, TV watching, and an endless stream of memories. And for what? There was no guarantee of a place in the canoes. And high school kids had never done this before; maybe they couldn't pull it off. It was a risk many refused to take.

"I wanted to go so bad in the beginning, I was always hoping others would quit," Gorse remembered. "And once we got down to things, other people did quit, people that had already made it once the final crew was picked. Some of those dropped out, and I thought that was foolish."

Those who dropped out, however, presented others with a fabulous gift. While Fredenburg took advanced placement courses and had earned Boy Scouting's highest award, he had the feeling that something was missing. He was nearly an adult, but he never really felt he measured up. Whether he lived with a self-imposed standard that kept him forever reaching some sense of accomplishment or whether others expected more of him than he could deliver, Fredenburg lacked the confidence that a boy of his achievement should have had. When he was designated an alternate despite his years of outdoor experience and told he would be staying in Elgin during the expedition, he was very disappointed that he "wasn't crew material." It only reinforced his feelings of inadequacy. Surprisingly, it was his mother who counseled him to stay with the program. No one can see the future, she said, and maybe a spot might open up. He took the advice, and as crew members dropped out, a place opened up for him.

The adult leaders also wanted to find out how committed the

boys were to the team itself. Pretending to be reporters, they interviewed the applicants. They asked open-ended questions to see how the boys handled themselves. If they were backed into a corner, would they respond to save themselves or to protect the group?

"Our real purpose [in undertaking the expedition] was education," Reid said. "When we came off the water at the end of the day, our job was just beginning. No matter how tired we were, there were always the performances and the interviews and the questions waiting for us. Our purpose even influenced our choice of crewmen. We didn't want the strong, silent types. We needed men who were outgoing, who could paddle all day through a snowstorm and then turn around and tell a class of fourth graders what it felt like to do that."

By May the original 165 applicants had dwindled to twenty-nine hardy souls. On May 24, the adults again rated the boys, this time on a +/0/- scale across ten criteria.

As the adults continued to assess the applicants, certain assumptions were made. The men wanted boys with a proven record of native intelligence and natural leadership. These qualities tended toward academic achievers, sports team captains, and National Honor Society types. The result, Reid and the other directors admitted, was too many chiefs and too few Indians. Each boy who had risen to the top was a youth of proven ability, and every one of them had an ego fueled by knowing that he was. The expedition needed people who were dedicated enough to do whatever was asked of them, people who could easily set ego aside and do what was necessary to further the needs of the expedition. But there were several boys in the applicant pool whose intelligence was not of the book-learning variety and whose character could not be measured by how many extracurricular activities they had joined. And despite a bias against them, these boys found a strong advocate among the adult leaders in Fialko.

"John Fialko is one of the nicest men who ever walked the earth" is the comment most often heard by every person who had anything to do with La Salle II. As a shop teacher, he appreciated hands-on learning and the kind of mind that saw practical solutions to problems in a physical world. He recognized the value of boys that the selection process had somehow overlooked or tried to weed out. Among those he championed for the expedition were Sam Hess, who had taken classes with him at Larkin High School, and Randy Foster, who attended Elgin High.

"The trip saved me. I hated school," said Hess, for whom academics never came easily. Hess had dyslexia, a learning difference commonly recognized and accommodated in today's schools but little understood in the mid-1970s. Dyslexia made it hard for Hess to read textbooks and, consequently, made studying difficult. His grades did not reflect his mental ability, but he was like a ship without a rudder. He stayed with the training, however, and responded in positive ways to the challenges it provided. Hess was one of the last boys to win a spot in the expedition crew, and he did not disappoint.

Foster was one of nine children, and he was under pressure to help support the family. Like Hess, he also had a learning difference, which set him apart from the college-track students. In his alternate universe, Foster "hung out with the bad boys" at Elgin High School. At the time, Elgin had an open campus that allowed students to come and go. Students did not have to be on campus if they did not have a class. Foster believes the open campus was bad policy because it allowed students, who often exhibit poor judgment, too much room for mischief. At the time, however, he was happy to have such freedom.

One day in late February 1976, Foster's class schedule allowed him to get a ride to school from a neighbor after the first bell of the day had rung. Shortly before this, and unknown to him, the rough group with whom he was associated had taken part in what he describes as a race riot with black youths. His group was packing up afterward in the school parking lot as Foster arrived. The police appeared suddenly, and he was immediately caught up in the police dragnet. Innocent in a court of law, the would-be voyageur became collateral damage anyway, tarred with the same brush as his associates. The school suspended him for ten days. Nevertheless, Foster's place in the canoes was secure, owing much to Fialko's advocacy.

By the beginning of the Bicentennial year, the crew was virtually set. Those mentioned as part of the crew included Father Loran Fuchs, Knecht, and Ken, the five teachers (Reid, Cox, Stillwagon, Hobart, and Fialko), and fifteen students: Gross, DiFulvio, Wilson, Gorse, Foster, Fredenburg, Kulick, Watts, Campbell, Rick Connolly, Peter Fatz, George Lesieutre, Gary Braun, Marc Lieberman, and Jorge Garcia. By the end of the spring Connolly, Fatz, and Knecht would leave the company. Hess, Marr, and Doug Sohn would take their places.

(L–R) Rich Gross, Keith Gorse, and Gary Braun test water in the Fox River in Elgin as part of their educational projects.

The crew came from two different high schools. While half the kids came from Elgin, many of the boys hailed from the suburbs of Bartlett, Streamwood, and Hanover Park. The boys represented a variety of socioeconomic backgrounds, family sizes, academic achievements, and personality types. Some leaned on religion or faith; others were agnostics or atheists. Some were willing to sacrifice themselves, while others were significantly self-absorbed. It was a rich environment for conflicts.

Toward the end of the selection process, there were four alternates in addition to the sixteen boys chosen. By the time the actual expedition neared, however, all four were gone, including two who had been considered particularly talented. To have alternates available, Reid added Sohn and Sid Bardwell, who agreed to join as members of the liaison team.

Another one of Fialko's protégés, Sohn possessed a willingness to sacrifice himself for the good of the group. His sister had always been known as "Beckwheat" and he as "Buckwheat." Sohn displayed an eagerness to work and a determination to succeed in the tasks he was assigned. The character he displayed on the trip became a beacon for more academically able students trying to develop maturity of their own. As he sat in class March 4, 1976—five months before La Salle II was to launch—he had not even made the grade as an alternate. Someone entered the classroom and handed him a pink slip of paper. On it were written the words: "You are a member of La Salle: Expedition II." It was Sohn's birthday.

"Doug wasn't a great student or a conventional leader," Cox said. "Yet he proved to be one of the hardest working, most dependable, least complaining members of the crew. He was a rock. Why we as adults couldn't see that from the get-go is a bit unsettling."

Bardwell was the son of the superintendent of School District 59 in nearby Elk Grove Village, but he was a student at Evanston High, near the family home. In the spring of '75 Bardwell and a friend had rafted down the Mississippi River from La Crosse, Wisconsin, to St. Louis. Reid came to one of the District 59 junior highs to discuss the Jolliet-Marquette trip, and Bardwell's father invited his son to come out for the day to hear the presentation. Bardwell and Reid had lunch that day, and the teenager told him about his "Huck Finn" experience. He naturally came to mind when Reid found himself without adequate backup. Bardwell was the only student voyageur to come from outside the U-46 school district.

However, Bardwell was a year younger than the Elgin crew. He had meant to graduate in three years, but he still needed a fourth year of English. After meeting with English teachers and the superintendent, a course of study was worked out for him that involved reading and journal writing. He would also face six weeks of classes right after the expedition, during which he would have to write a lengthy paper on his experiences.

On Oct. 22, the adults brought the kids to their first La Salle: Expedition II press conference. Gorse gave a short talk on the voyage they all planned to make. At first, he was nervous, but he became more comfortable speaking to his audience and did well. By the end of the expedition, every one of the young men would be veterans of public speaking, able to handle himself well talking with a single reporter or speaking before a crowd.

Through the fall and winter and into the spring, the boys worked to make their voyageur clothes, to learn their voyageur songs, and to make progress on their educational projects. In January 1976, U-46 turned over a warehouse to Reid's group for use as a workshop and meeting place. By the end of June, the modern voyageurs had come up with a nonsense name for their expedition retreat, referring to it fondly as "Camp Wa-De-Do-Da." The building was the site of some memorable episodes, including the night that Kulick, running late and plagued with poor brakes, slid across the icy parking lot and plowed his beat-up Ford Maverick into a snow bank.

For months some kids worked diligently on their projects and others with less enthusiasm. But the boys were still boys, strong-willed teens whose pursuit of fun sometimes clashed with the work Reid expected them to put in. Wilson, in particular, frequently asked for time off.

"I think that really pointed out to the expedition leaders that maybe I wasn't as dedicated as I should have been," Wilson said. "I'm also very vocal. I really think the project directors had a couple of points where they would have preferred if I just went home."

It was this kind of behavior that made even his closest friends doubt Wilson's ability to see the expedition through. "Nobody thought I'd make it," he said, "not so much that I couldn't make the eight-month part. They didn't think I'd stick out the two years beforehand. I had never displayed those tendencies before . . . but I wanted it badly."

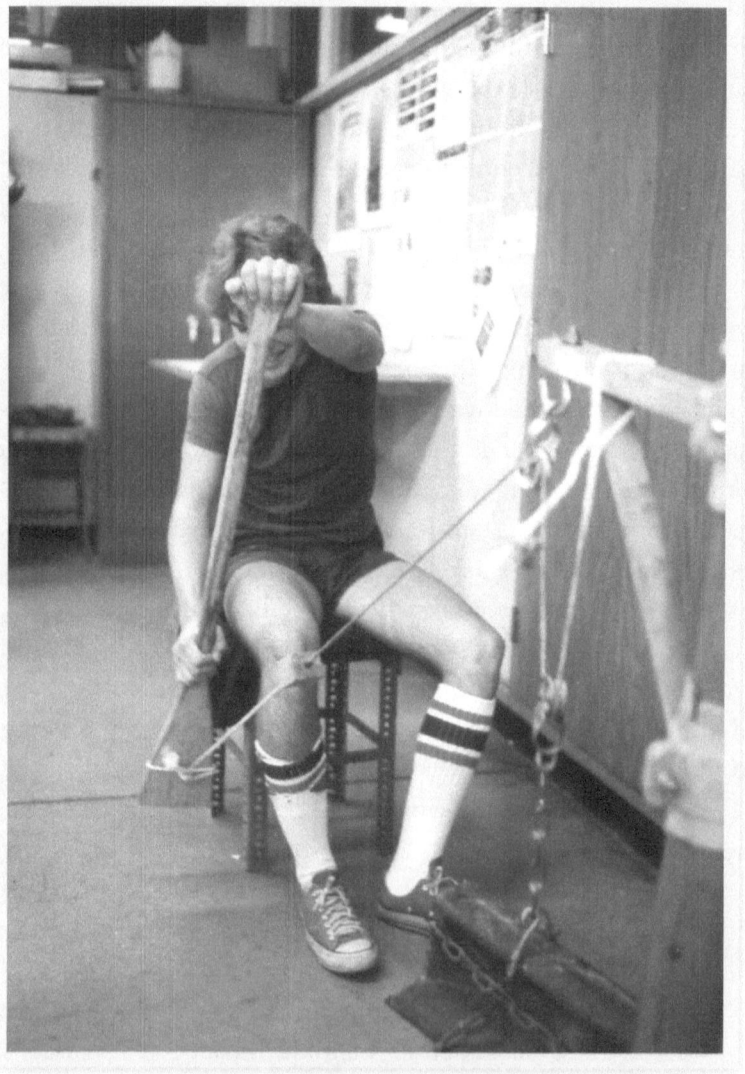

Clif Wilson practices his stroke using a paddle tied to a pulley.

Gorse, DiFulvio, Kulick, Lieberman, and Wilson formed a quintet of boys with a similar outlook on life, their bond made stronger by their interest in La Salle: Expedition II. All of them also liked to party. They styled themselves the Radical Five after an incident in May when they'd gathered to work on outdoor projects at a conference center thirty miles south of Rockford. Wilson had come in his parents' camper, which provided a perfect party vehicle.

"I was probably the partier of the expedition," Wilson recalled. "And we had been frustrated in our attempt to get the crew together to drink. So we got some beer and we stocked up the fridge with the beers and we participated in all the day's events, just like we were supposed to. We got a little juiced on the way up, but just a little and were able to clean up our act and participate in the afternoon's events and the evening events. Then we went back and continued to drink. We were severely chastised that night. I don't think we felt as guilty as we were supposed to feel. We just wanted to have a good time."

The directors pegged Wilson as the ring leader. Hobart was especially angry about the boys' behavior; Stillwagon expressed his anger as well. Hobart went to talk with the boys alone. He found several of the crew at the camper. Four of the "Radical Five" had been joined by a couple of others, and they were waiting for two more when Hobart showed up. The adult delivered a tongue-lashing. Some kept their heads down the whole time. Kulick actually thanked him when he left, but not everyone was ashamed of their behavior.

The drinking incident came up again during a break in the weekly directors' meeting on Sunday. Now Reid was upset. Hobart called Wilson and arranged a meeting at Reid's house that night. Hobart and Cox were there, too. Wilson told the adults how important the trip was to him, but they challenged him to explain what he had been willing to give up for it. That silenced him. They indicted him for acting as if rules applied to others, for violating their trust, for ignoring his responsibilities to the group, and for doing the least amount possible. The tongue-lashing hit home for a while, but the adults took their foot off the gas and the emphasis shifted 180 degrees. By the time they were finished, the subject was no longer what Wilson could do for the expedition but what the adults could do for him.

Later that week at Crown Point the crew held a feedback session that got intense.

Reid expressed his outrage over the drinking, but Wilson by now was ready. He said the adults had not made it clear that drinking was forbidden. Other students agreed with him. They challenged the way decisions were being made for the crew. It was a warning of things to come.

In order for the boys to work efficiently in camp on the trail, each was assigned to one of six canoes in July. The canoes were paired, and their crews were to share a shelter and form a work module.

The crew members also received their French names, the names of those who had accompanied La Salle himself down the Mississippi River to the Gulf of Mexico. There were a few petty noblemen. Reid, of course, was to be the Sieur de La Salle himself. The crew would carry their French names as if they were part of their clothes. The names were something they would put on in the morning and keep on till it was time to sleep. Then they would doff them like a hat. The names were part of the authenticity the expedition demanded. But authenticity would waffle. Trust would be bent into an ill-defined shape. The thrill of discovery on the water would surrender to the fatigue of boredom on land. And French names would be lost along the way like luxuries discarded by pioneers on the Oregon Trail.

HEART, HANDS, AND VOICE

(L–R) Marc Leiberman, Clif Wilson, Dick Stillwagon, Chuck Campbell, Bill Watts, and John Fialko sing during one of the hundreds of performances the La Salle II crew gave before, during, and after the expedition.

The journey through the heart of America presented physical challenges. The boys had to develop the strength, aerobic stamina, and paddle skill needed to stroke through all kinds of waters fifty-eight to sixty times per minute for up to eight hours a day for eight and a half months.

Early in their own training Stillwagon, Hobart, and Cox came up with a point system to reward themselves for aerobic activities. "Today I ran 2.5 miles and cross-country skied for an hour . . . That's good for 12 points," Cox recorded in his journal for Saturday, Jan. 10, 1976. He gave himself six points for an hour of racquetball on March 1, but "Hobart hit himself above the left eye. He needed four stitches (0 points)."

After the crew was selected, physical fitness was coordinated by directors Cox and Stillwagon and students Campbell and DiFulvio. They worked out activities that they hoped would build both fitness and paddling prowess. The first time the crew hit the water, they took aluminum canoes down to the Fox River on Feb. 1, 1976. The day was windy and bitterly cold, with temperatures between five and ten degrees below zero.

"We looked like ice sculptures when we were done, with ice on our gloves, knees, legs and faces," Cox recorded. "Ken's toes were freezing, even with his three pairs of cotton socks. Randy's thighs were on fire and Bob Kulick said he couldn't feel his toes. Now we certainly have an idea of what lies ahead."

A week later they worked through a course Hobart and Fialko had laid out on the relatively narrow Fox River. In two-man canoes they loaded and launched, turned left and right, paddled at speed, reversed course, ferried from one bank to another, landed, and unloaded. It was a sunny winter day in the upper thirties, and the crew enjoyed the practice, though it did expose some weaknesses among them.

The fitness group believed that, aerobically, voyageurs ought to be able to run four miles in 34 minutes, a pace of 8:30 per mile. Theoretically, each boy had been running on his own since the crew was chosen. Ken and Cox laid out a four-mile course south and west of Elgin Community College. It included a hill at the start and another half-mile climb about two and a half miles into the run.

The first group run took place on Valentine's Day. Three of the boys and Father Loran did not run that day, but everyone else participated. Of those nineteen, eleven met the thirty-four-minute standard, and a twelfth just missed it. Led by Lesieutre's 28 minutes flat, half a dozen met or exceeded a 7:30 pace. These included Stillwagon and Hobart among the adults and Braun, Lieberman, and Kulick among the teens. The seven who did not meet the standard had times ranging from 35:20 to 52:00. Ken did not do well, but

Knecht brought up the rear. He may have done so simply to support one of the boys, who also struggled in at the end. The first run helped determine the fitness gap that training had to make up.

That night Stillwagon and Cox "chewed a little ass" at the crew meeting. Hobart watched the boys' reactions as Stillwagon ripped them for their laziness. They had not taken their fitness seriously, he said, and it showed. Hobart later told him that the kids had been silent during their dressing down but knew that the adults were right.

The next day, Feb. 15, the crew took a proficiency test on the same canoeing course they had practiced on the previous Sunday. Temperatures were in the sixties. As Hobart gave instructions, a grand sight greeted the boys. Fialko and his crew—Foster, Gorse, and Gross—came around the river bend with the expedition's first finished canoe.

For this Sunday's event, the participants were graded on a scale. Three was *tres bien*—very well. Two was *bon*—good. One point was *pas bon*—not good. Zero meant *merde*—shit. Several months later, difficulties on the journey would be described in letters and journals as *merde* or *bad merde*. The participants were also timed, although Cox and Hobart agreed that, "at this point in our training, accuracy in handling is far more important than speed." Cox and DiFulvio turned in the fastest time. Fialko and Braun scored highest in proficiency, edging out Reid and Kulick with thirty-one of a possible thirty-six points. Both canoes scored *bon* or *tres bien* in every maneuver. Fredenburg and Garcia were unable to participate. The last "pairing" was recorded as Father Loran and The Lord—"no score, but hanging right in there."

The four-mile run reappeared March 13. This time sixteen crewmen met or nearly met the standard. Several showed substantial improvement. The slowest time this day was a full ten minutes faster than before.

On the Fox River the next day, canoe groups practiced for an hour at a time with the expedition canoe. They discovered that Frese's creation was bigger and less maneuverable than the aluminum craft the group had been using.

The plan on the trip was to paddle fifty minutes of each hour and rest ten minutes. To approach that standard, the crew took to the Fox again for three hours on Saturday, April 3, to paddle forty-five minutes and rest fifteen. The paddles, which they were making specifically for the expedition, were shorter than store-bought ones and enabled a rapid racing stroke. Some of the guys raised their pace to sixty strokes a minute and sustained it for a while. But their arms were dead just halfway through the session.

After spring vacation, training resumed April 25, a cold, snowy, windy day. The wind made paddling upstream very difficult. The short paddles meant that some canoeists took strokes in the chop and either didn't hit the water or failed to dig the paddle blade deeply enough to power forward. The crew was already beginning to see that their linen shirts, stitched together so carefully to preserve authenticity, were nearly worthless in the canoes. The river water and perspiration soaked them through, and it took forever to get them dry again.

Five days later, the weather had improved. Canoeing on the Fox that Friday afternoon, no one concerned himself with an obstacle course of maneuvers. The crew simply stroked in straight lines from one point to another. The result brought a surge of confidence to the crew. "The stroke suddenly came to me," said Cox, who had switched to a longer, fifty-four-inch paddle. By the time the session was over, the boys were yelling with joy.

In May the crew traveled to Berrien Springs, Michigan, for the chance to give school presentations and paddle their canoes on the St. Joseph River, where they would be paddling in December. On the 22nd the crew took part in the Des Plaines Canoe Marathon, where they practiced setting up a true voyageur shelter, stretching a tarpaulin over canoes and erect paddles. Finally, on Saturday, June 3, the crew took the canoes out on Lake Michigan for the first time. "It felt so good to be out on the lake," said Marr. "The sun was warm and the water was so cold. I got sunburned badly."

The swells of the lake offered a completely different sense of canoeing than the men and boys had experienced on any of the rivers they had paddled. Waves jolted their craft and soaked them. They dealt with crosswinds and a chop of up to four feet.

"You really felt you were at the mercy of the lake," Cox observed, adding prophetically, "it also served to remind us that we'd be on Lake Michigan the entire month of November, which historically is the most dangerous month for the lake." The yelling and screaming of April 30 paled in comparison to the raucous noise they made on the lake. "Keith [Gorse] said he wouldn't back out now if someone gave him a million dollars," Cox wrote in his journal. The air temperature that day around Belmont Harbor was around ninety degrees. The thrill would be gone by the time the voyageurs returned in December.

The adults knew that the crew members would spend every day of their continental odyssey in close quarters with one another. Such contact places enormous social and psychological demands on even the best of friends, and many of the participants were not—and would not ever really become—friends. Reid turned to experts to help him build these disparate personalities into a team, or at least to develop within them the tools they would need to deal with their feelings of anger, frustration, loneliness, or distrust.

Through the summer of 1975, Reid had corresponded with Will Kennedy, a psychologist he knew in Bloomington, Indiana. Reid had hoped to have a team-building session in the fall. Kennedy's letter of Aug. 16 explained how difficult it might be to get together by then. He had found two other professionals who could help assist in the process, Dr. Dale Guilsdorf and Dr. James Weaver. But their schedules made it hard to get together with students that fall, and it was important to have everyone there, he said.

"Building a team can be likened to building a wall of brick," Kennedy wrote. "Leaving a brick out here and there obviously causes the wall to look different from the one where all the bricks are in place. Groups have peculiar dynamics at work that place a very high priority on all members being present."

"Being present" meant far more than simply showing up for a training session, however.

One might have expected the boys to turn to Reid and Ken for guidance throughout the training and the expedition. Reid was the engine that drove the project and the rudder by which it steered. He and Ken had gone through the Jolliet reenactment and understood how the parts fit together, but that experience worked against them as much as for them. Too often they would rub their companions the wrong way, starting an explanation, "When we did the Jolliet trip . . ." The 1973 trip was not at all like the 1976–77 odyssey, and constant reference to it served to distance the veterans from some of the others.

Next to Father Loran, Stillwagon was the oldest adult in the expedition and a man who thought of his younger crewmates as students first rather than equals in experience and understanding. Though he cared deeply for the boys, he had a son that was older than they were, and their lack of deference presented a psychological hurdle for Stillwagon, who was strongly traditional and therefore distanced somewhat from the young voyageurs. While the boys deeply respected Fialko for his talents and selflessness, he was not a vocal person.

That left Hobart and Cox, who were younger, opinionated, and much more vocal than the other directors. While everyone understood that the expedition was Reid's vision, some came to see Hobart and Cox as its more natural leaders. Some of that was due to their relative youth. Hobart played guitar, sang, and understood contemporary music. These interests and abilities drew young people to him, and as the expedition's navigator, he literally gave the boys direction. Cox was scarcely out of college himself. He was an athlete who could stand on his hands and run the legs off of most of the boys. Emotional and unguarded in his opinions, Cox's natural inclination was to "tell it like it is." Some of the kids found his brutal honesty compelling and a rare quality among adults, who tended to be more circumspect. However, it was also a potentially divisive force among the adult directors when priorities diverged on the expedition.

As much as these, however, Hobart and Cox had the advantage

of "being present." Stretched to the limit to find money for the trip, Reid was often away from workshops and meetings the boys were required to attend leading up to the trip. Even during the expedition, Reid would spend hours away from camp, calling or writing to potential sponsors. Ken and Stillwagon lived several miles away from Elgin, and Fialko spent much of his time at the Chicagoland Canoe Base with a handful of the boys helping Frese build the canoes.

Hobart and Cox, unburdened by the responsibility of financing the trip, were always the ones most present, relating to the boys and their cares and questions. The teenagers of the crew gravitated to these men in their twenties, men who shared their youthful passions and embraced their own liberal philosophies. Hobart and Cox had their faults. They were not Supermen. But the cadets of La Salle II could see that they both cared deeply about each of them and their sense of truth, justice, and the American Way. When these two men found themselves at odds with Reid during the trip, it was their point of view that some of the boys adopted.

The team-building weekend took place Feb. 21–22 at Camp Edwards in Wisconsin. Kennedy and Dr. Guilsdorf, a professor at Governors' State University in Chicago's southern suburbs, began with relaxation exercises. The crew went through a number of visualizations and played some what-if games: You have a ticket to enter a treasure chamber where you can choose only one: What treasure do you choose? You're stranded on a desert island with a belt: What do you do with it?

A silent playback of a problem-resolution session revealed something important. Everybody seemed to want to talk at once, but few wanted to listen.

"People won't listen to you unless they feel they've been heard," Reid noted. He also said it was important to listen in order to understand others, not to help develop an argument. The discussions threw a light on the divisions among the crew members, and Kennedy had some warnings for Reid. He told Reid that the outspoken Cox would be trouble, a loose cannon that Reid couldn't control. But he also said the group as a whole lacked cohesion.

"You don't have an expedition," he said. "You have twenty-three expeditions, and you're not going to make it." At least La Salle II wasn't going to make it unless the crew learned to get along and work together, whether they liked each other or not.

Sir Edmund Hillary, who clearly had experience with difficult treks, had offered this word of warning to the voyageurs: "People are going to tell you it's the wind, the weather, the storms, the physical part of the expedition you're not going to handle. But you'll become acclimatized in the first month or so. Your problem is going to be interpersonal relationships."

After the group session, Guilsdorf had a private talk with Wilson, Foster, and Hobart. Some of the students, including Wilson, thought they could force Foster out. Adults hoped to avoid such talk, since Foster had earned his spot. However, this situation also remained unresolved and would stay that way, until the voyage had traveled several days down the St. Lawrence River. Even then the chasm between Wilson and Foster would never really close despite sharing the same canoe.

Many have said that the team-building sessions were too little too late to prevent the deep divisions that several times seemed to spell the end of the road for La Salle II. Others credit the sessions with holding the operation together. There is room enough for both conclusions.

"That team building did help hold us together. I think, without it, we wouldn't have been nearly as conscious, because by and large most people tried to do what we had been taught," Reid said.

"I have mixed emotions about the psychological training," Fialko said in an interview shortly after the trip. "Either we didn't have enough of it or we weren't together long enough beforehand or we spent too much time together or . . . I don't know. At times, it seemed that if somebody had a gripe with somebody else, they would bring it out, but then after a while things became more and more sublimated just to have less friction, I believe."

While there were times during the long trip that the participants forgot their training, Fredenburg said long afterward, "There were confrontations in the dark in the middle of nowhere that could have gone very differently" without the training the boys received in communication skills. The expedition was also incredibly empowering for students who had had only modest control over their circumstances before. At any point in the journey, any crew member could simply say, "I want to have a meeting," and the expeditionary force would have one.

Though Stillwagon served as the expedition's official medic, situations might come up in which others had to pitch in or even take over his duties. Reid wanted to be sure that everyone had first-aid training, so he contacted the Red Cross to give his crew a comprehensive course. Reid had contacted the Red Cross in early 1976 to obtain a trainer from Evanston to teach his crew the fundamentals of first aid. Despite several postponements, a three-hour Red Cross training session finally took place on Feb. 27, and instructor Dave Maxfield turned out to be a great help.

The men also received winter survival training. A team of experts came down from Maine to run the class March 5–7 at the naval training station in suburban Glenview. Instructor Tom Kirkpatrick gave the boys a reality check, telling them that it was only by luck that the original La Salle and his men finished their trip at all. They could all have been killed, he said.

Maxfield's second Red Cross session on first aid came the evening of Friday, March 12, a day of particularly bad weather. A couple of twisters touched down in the Chicago area that day; that evening Maxfield brought a film on tornado preparedness and told the group that he would gladly do a workshop on medical tape and how and why it is used.

The crew of La Salle: Expedition II planned to make hundreds of presentations, including skits and dramatic speeches given in character (and spoken in English) and ancient paddling songs (sung in French). For teenagers unused to public speaking (or singing, for that matter), this would also require substantial preparation in memorization and music practice.

Many of the songs the crew would sing came to the New World

from France in the late sixteenth century, conceived by the troubadours, or jongleurs, of the age. They encompassed cradle songs, children's chants, and love songs. There were songs for work, play, and religious occasions. In the forests of Canada these songs not only entertained the fur traders but helped keep a rhythm with their paddles as they swept through the lakes and rivers. The modern travelers, of course, sang tunes that are still popular today, like "*Alouette*," but most of their songs were of ancient origin. Perhaps the quintessential song of La Salle II was "*En Roulant*," or "Rolling My Ball," a call and response piece. The chorus goes, simply, "rolling my ball along, along, rolling my ball along":

> *En roulant, ma boule roulant,*
> *En roulant, ma boule.*
> *En roulant, ma boule roulant,*
> *En roulant, ma boule.*

The voyageurs also used rounds as chants to paddle by. One used by La Salle II paddlers is called "*Vent Frais*," or "Cool Wind." It perfectly describes sights and feelings experienced by the crew, especially in the waters of Georgian Bay:

> *Vent frais, vent du matin,*
> *Vent qui souffle au sommet des grands pins,*
> *Joie du vent qui souffle. Allons dans le grand vent . . .*

The words mean, "Cool wind, morning wind, wind which whispers in the tops of the great pines, feel the joy of the wind as it blows. Let us go forth into the wild wind."

Hobart, who had a strong singing voice, led choral practices, and helped Ken work the voyageur songs into a full program for audiences, just as the Jolliet group had done three years earlier. The program included a skit about how to build a voyageur from the ground up. DiFulvio took center stage in his underwear, and layers were added until he was fully dressed for a winter portage.

Ken and Hobart unveiled the program to the crew for the first time on March 10, five months out from the start of the trip, but only a couple of weeks before their first public performance at the Chicago Flower and Garden Show. The show provided a rich "target" environment for the crew to sing their songs and interact with the public. The boys gave twenty-one performances, which improved as the show went on. The practice helped reduce the natural stage fright that some of them felt and instilled confidence that they could do this.

Reid published a brochure in 1975 to invite interest and monetary support for the La Salle II enterprise. Titled "La Salle: Expedition II: Reliving the past to explore the future," the document announced, "By conducting nineteen different research projects, the Expedition members will provide materials and a model for an exciting interdisciplinary approach to learning which emphasizes active participation." Reid wanted to publish the materials and spark imagination, inspiring young people to follow their dreams into the modern wilderness of ideas.

Every adult served as a director for at least two projects, generally in his area of knowledge or expertise. Each teen crew member served on at least three different projects. A coordinator was to create a unified format for all the resource units and assure that the material met current academic standards. Student-teacher teams at U-46 would take the expedition's raw data and use it in a pilot program on expedition-related themes. Reid foresaw the voyageurs working with student groups after the trip was over, assembling printed and audio-visual materials.

There was more to each project than first met the eye. For example, mapping the route entailed much more than tracing the route through lakes and rivers across a Rand McNally road atlas. Lesieutre and Watts took a cartography class at the University of Chicago in which they became familiar with seventeenth-century maps. During the trip, Lesieutre worked with methods and instruments employed by seventeenth-century explorers, and Watts recorded distances, topographical features, mineral deposits, demographic information, and the types of plants and animals found along the route. This required historical research and observation comparing seventeenth- and twentieth-century environments, conservation practices, population movement, land development, and depletion of natural resources.

Huddled around maps of their route are (clockwise from lower left) Bill Watts, Jorge Garcia, Bob Kulick, Ron Hobart, George Lesieutre, Gary Braun, and Keith Gorse. The boys also studied meteorology, French colonial history, hydrology, and gunsmithing, among other studies.

In addition to the project work, the men and boys were required to fashion their own paddles and their own authentic voyageur clothes. This included using finger weaving to make sashes and sewing to stitch long-sleeved linen shirts and draw moose hide together to make moccasins. The men and boys would also cut out patterns to make parts for canvas pants and warm vests and to cut and sew wool blankets into capotes, a kind of heavy poncho that would provide some relief from the cold weather.

THE LIAISON TEAM

La Salle II had the appearance of a Jolliet/Marquette rerun, but it was far more complicated than the 1973 canoe trip. The new version needed to provide food, mail, and laundry services for three times as many people and for twice as long. The 1976–77 voyage encountered snow-slicked and icy road conditions that the first voyage did not. The logistics alone of making the arrangements for eight months of campsites and performances were staggering. Instead of the Jolliet trip's 165 performances, the La Salle journey required more than 500, and there were many more visits to arrange, too, for schools, hospitals, nursing homes, and churches. The visits and performances of the first trip basically stopped after the canoes turned upstream at the Arkansas River. There would be no such respite for the paddlers of La Salle II.

Jan was responsible for contacting several hundred communities, from tiny towns to major cities. These communities could and did change their minds about when and where the canoes would be met, what kind of greeting would be extended, what kind of meal (if any) would be provided, and what kind of venue would be available for the crew presentations. Often Jan would have to discuss the crew's arrival with several different agencies in each community, from chambers of commerce to elementary schools. Ages before the Internet and cell phones, mail and telephone landlines were the only way to communicate.

Her team would have to meet the canoes and flag them in. But the canoes were often held up by weather conditions, water conditions, or both, forcing the support team to double back to find them. Sometimes good weather or good harbors presented the crew with opportunities farther downstream, and the liaison team would find the scheduled campsite bypassed and empty. But if the guys had anticipated a meal and the food wasn't available, there might be hell to pay from a group of hungry adolescent boys. Hitting every mark was an impossible task. Not only were her efforts anonymous and unappreciated, she'd be blamed and vilified. And she would join Reid in debt for tens of thousands of dollars to make the expedition work for the benefit of her critics.

And she was alone. There was no Great River Road Commission to help her make connections. No Father Donnelly helped her build the itinerary or make connections spanning two countries and half a continent. Until the canoes were ready to embark, no one assisted her with publicity. Reid might help a little, but his focus was on fund-raising and crew preparation. Any chance she had to be "Mother Marquette" was buried under the thankless drudgery of doing La Salle II's grunt work.

In November 1975 Jan expressed her frustrations to her best friend, Marlena Scavuzzo, a teacher in the Orion, Illinois, school system south of Moline. She and Jan had met in college in 1968 while living across the hall from each other. Both were headed toward teaching careers and found many interests in common. After Jan graduated a year ahead of her friend and quickly found a job, the pair vacationed together and enjoyed each other's company. Scavuzzo was a bridesmaid at Jan and Reid's wedding and later became godmother to their daughter, Marni. That winter of 1975–76, Scavuzzo watched her friend drowning in the phone calls and paperwork of La Salle II, and her heart went out to her.

In March, the Lewises finally reached out to Jan's friend. Knecht, whose expertise was helping the crew to make authentic voyageur clothes, had suddenly left the enterprise. As the other director on the clothing project, Fialko was fully engaged in helping Frese build the canoes. Scavuzzo, twenty-five, was a seamstress. Jan turned to the one person she knew could step in and pick up the slack, and Scavuzzo agreed to serve as assistant liaison director. But she did not do so without qualms. She would have to give up an apartment that had been comfortable for her, to leave a job she liked, and to surrender much of her independence for most of a year to serve the needs of men and boys she did not know. Adolescents would be the last to say, "Thank you." But she also saw the adventure.

"I thought being the Bicentennial year, it would be something special," she said, "something different from what I saw other people doing, like painting fire hydrants and putting up the flag. This seemed to me to be a more meaningful thing." Her father never thought the expedition would succeed, but Scavuzzo's mother encouraged her participation.

Despite the existence of costume pattern books that might have approximated voyageur garb, Reid's insistence on authenticity demanded that the expedition spurn modern tools. The patterns and materials would be part of the educational materials Reid hoped to publish and make available to schools. He asked Scavuzzo to design basic shirt and pant patterns from scratch, then adjust them for size for each voyageur. Both summer and winter outfits had to be created, and the boys would have to be taught how to sew the pieces together.

Despite Scavuzzo's arrival on the scene, the dimensions of the liaison functions continued to overwhelm the Lewises, and they made another application form available to those who wanted to be part of the land support crew for the La Salle venture. These positions were even more selective than the crew spots. Of thirty-five student applicants, only two were chosen: Cathy Palmer and Sharon Baumgartner.

Many months earlier, crew members had begun to come to class with piece work as part of the La Salle project. Moccasin parts, beaded pouches, and linen sleeves kept showing up on their desks. Palmer shared classes with boys like Braun and Lesieutre. She saw them bring in their piece work, and talked with them about their experience with the expedition. She also gave them hell over the fact that no girls were part of the crew. Clearly, she told them, this fact would make this an inferior kind of journey.

In the spring of 1976 the girls began to hear that La Salle: Expedition II needed volunteers to serve on a support team, paralleling the crew's route and helping with a variety of duties that included mail delivery, stage crew, driving and logistics, laundering, and shopping for provisions. This time girls were welcome to apply. Suddenly there was another way into the adventure, and Palmer recognized this as a great opportunity. She was the second child and only daughter in a family of seven children. While her parents must have had some concern about their daughter leaving home for the unknown for the better part of a year, they wholeheartedly supported her decision to apply.

Palmer had held high school jobs in the movie theater and the bakery where her grandmother worked. Neither job had required much in the way of screening, so she found the interview part of the recruitment process intimidating. The girls each faced a panel of five or six adults. Palmer remembers the panel consisting of the Lewis brothers, Hobart, Cox, and Jan. The process put the girls through the same rigorous questioning that the boys had faced the previous year. How would she deal with homesickness on the trail? Was she able to change a tire?

Sharon Baumgartner had already graduated from high school and was a student at Elgin Community College when she heard about the need for liaison members. She came by the news naturally, however. In high school, her freshman speech teacher had suggested that Baumgartner apply for a position at the U-46 radio station, WEPS, and she was accepted into the program. Larry Drafall taught the radio program and ran the station. He had a dry, deadpan kind of sarcastic humor that many kids found compelling. "Mr. D" treated the kids as if they were thirty-five instead of seventeen. When Drafall needed an assistant to help him, Baumgartner's mother, Carol, interviewed for a position and was hired. Eventually, Baumgartner became a babysitter for Mr. D's children. One day in early 1976, Mrs. Baumgartner came home with one of the fliers meant for liaison applicants.

"Isn't that the thing Chuck Campbell is doing?" she asked her daughter. Baumgartner had worked at the station with Campbell, who was a year behind her in school and one of the La Salle II crew. He and Marr had also taken Drafall's radio class with Baumgartner. She joined the ranks of applicants and also found herself part of the team.

Reid knew he needed publicity and a good photographer. He was able to cover both of those needs in Michigan native Barton Dean, who'd moved to Los Angeles after college to seek his fortune in the entertainment industry "and couldn't handle it," he said. He returned to the Midwest and was finishing his master's degree program at Northwestern University's Medill School of Journalism in the spring of 1976 when he saw a job notice on the bulletin board at school. Dean had taught photography at night to continuing education classes in Flint, Michigan, and his training at Medill prepared him to write articles to promote the expedition as it traveled.

"I had canoed and camped a lot of the area [the expedition was to explore], and I'm kind of an outdoors person, so I thought I'd check it out," Dean said. He met with the crew while they were doing canoe trials on the Fox River. He did some audition pictures and was hired to start Aug. 17, six days after the trip got under way. He spent the summer painting houses to pay for a used Nikon and lenses.

GOOD HELP IS HARD TO FIND

La Salle: Expedition II paid several people to help make the expedition run smoothly. Despite their genuine efforts to help the project, however, many of these individuals encountered special problems. In some cases they became liabilities themselves while trying to raise money, develop authentic clothing, create educational materials, and produce a feature film.

Each of six canoes being built at the Chicagoland Canoe Base cost $5,000. The adults who had taken unpaid leaves of absence were to be compensated. Various experts in their field were to be paid. Each student was promised a $1,000 scholarship. There would be expenses for food, firewood, shelter, and a host of other things. Two vans, one of them purchased, carried provisions and audio equipment. Both ate up gas, oil, and repair bills. Then there were materials for clothing, muskets, and educational projects that had to be paid for.

"It will cost us, over a three-year period, about $595,000," Reid said during the trip.

While that sounded like a mind-boggling amount of money at the time, one fund-raiser questioned how the enterprise "could be done on such a shoestring," Reid said.

The answer was that it almost couldn't. Reid's parents contributed money and spent untold hours helping in the office donated by La Salle National Bank. Scavuzzo's father, a food broker, helped bridge the gap with samples from vendors, and people along the route stretched the food supply by feeding the boys with meals of various kinds. However, the journey of 1976–77 was, like La Salle's saga of 1681–82, a day-to-day financial burden, with directors scrambling to drum up cash and scrounge donations to keep the trip going.

(L–R) Crew members Steve Marr, Bill Watts, and Rich Gross listen intently as a bearded John Fialko discusses musket construction during pre-trip planning.

"You either believe in it or you don't," Reid said. "You can't wait until you can afford it or it is convenient."

Expedition funding that Reid imagined would roll in as a result of high-profile endorsements never matched the glitter of the names on the marquee. Despite Sir Edmund Hillary's endorsement, Sears, Roebuck & Co. contributed no funds for the trip. Virtually every one of the supporting organizations was a nonprofit itself, not in a position to fund the trip.

Money issues had dogged the 1973 expedition, too, but at least Frese had enjoyed the support of the Mississippi Parkway Commission, which anticipated a boost in tourism from a project encompassing all of its member states. The same was not true of the 1976 journey. Only three years after the first canoe trip, the directors of the Great River Road could say of the second one, "Been there. Done that." Besides, the new trip didn't celebrate the American Revolution as much as pre-Revolution history, and it didn't originate in the United States at all but spent its first several hundred miles in Canada.

"One great frustration for La Salle and for us has been getting the financial backing for the expedition," Reid told an interviewer halfway through the voyage. "Most of the money will come from individuals all along the route. We don't need big government to do everything." In fact, it was big business and big government that had paid for the 1973 trip.

The overall economy was one problem. The country fell into a recession as both the inflation rate and the unemployment rate in the United States reached 9.2 percent. In Elgin itself the United Way campaign failed to reach its goal for the first time since 1932 and both the YMCA and the Bicentennial Committee fell far short of their own goals.

The American Revolution Bicentennial Administration (ARBA) was another problem. Instead of contributing to projects like La Salle: Expedition II, ARBA pumped most of its resources to state commissions and giant corporations, prompting a populist reaction to the "Buy-centennial." ARBA's board chairman, US Sen. Edward Brooke (R-Mass.), said, "It is the people from the state and private sectors that will have to bear the brunt of the work."

The Illinois commission contributed $20,000 to La Salle II, one of the largest local donations it made. Of its $1.35 million budget, however, the IBC spent $550,000 on the sound-and-light show at the Old State Capitol—a bit more than the $38,000 spent the previous year—and another $390,000 on operating expenses.

Reid and his team consulted the Donors Forum, which profiled foundations and charitable trusts. The Adventurers Club of Chicago provided connections to donors, but really large contributions were rare. When it came time to pass the hat along the route, audiences and school groups might produce $50 here, a couple of hundred dollars there. The amounts trickled in as the cash poured out.

The Illinois Humanities Council provided a $20,000 grant to La Salle: Expedition II, but half the money went to pay for a series of speakers at forums the voyageurs were required to attend. Most forums were poorly attended by the public. Crew members were privately critical of most of the speakers, whom they believed to be boring at best and ill-informed at worst.

A grateful Reid said the executive director of the National Bank of Paris in Chicago "was incredible. He believed in our project from Day One. He lent my wife and me $10,000 on our signatures, no collateral." While the loan did help the project's cash flow, it did nothing to help the bottom line. The money still had to be repaid.

On Dec. 11, 1974, La Salle: Expedition II was officially formed as a nonprofit corporation, and Reid could begin in earnest to solicit tax-deductible funds. Nearly one year later, so little money had come in that Reid sought a professional fund-raiser. A nationally known company was hired, but its connections never worked for La Salle II. By that time the expedition was out $13,000 in fees. Sumner Rahr, who had just started his own firm in 1974 to help nonprofit institutions, picked up the slack, charging $3,500 a month. But he had Chicago contacts, not national ones.

"They've worked hard," Reid said of Rahr and Company after the trip ended, "but they haven't gotten much money for us. The only thing I can conclude is that we're just hard to raise money for."

When Reid met in early 1976 with the parents about fund-raising, one father expressed concern that the expedition was "subsidizing" the adults and said the teenagers should be paid more than $1,000. He also asked whether his son would get a thousand dollars if he didn't go to college. Two days later he told Reid that he didn't want his son to go on the expedition. The boy dropped out four days later, and the directors replaced him with Hess.

On Feb. 18, less than six months before the expedition began, Jan told project managers that her husband was now devoting himself full time to fund-raising and might miss many of the Wednesday and Friday meetings. She reported that only a third of what they needed had been donated or pledged. The national fund-raiser had cost them money, and Rahr had barely started on the job. Clearly, Reid had been the best fund-raiser, but his involvement came at a price, too.

"[My] spending all that time [on fund-raising] really hurt us, in that I couldn't oversee more of the other activities that were going on," Reid admitted shortly after the journey ended, "and I think that hurt us in the long run from the leadership standpoint. We had almost a headless monster on our hands. Everyone started doing things pretty much on their own, and that became pretty much the tenor of the expedition. I had to be doing the only thing we were having trouble with, and that was raising money."

"A lot of the crew resented him missing stuff. This was unavoidable," John Fialko commented. "He had so many things to do. We always were understaffed."

"There were a lot of things that didn't get done because of the amount of stuff to do all at once. We could have used five years" instead of two, Reid said. Or they could have used three Reids: one to raise money, one to oversee the trip, and one to make sure the educational projects were completed, published, and used.

Expedition directors hoped to reap a financial harvest from the Chicago Flower and Garden Show scheduled for March 20–28 at McCormick Place on the Lake Michigan shore. The show was the largest flower show in North America and expected to draw tremendous crowds to the convention floor. The La Salle II display was built around the French symbol, the fleur-de-lis. The booth carried the slogan "Planting the Lily of France in the New World."

The voyageurs performed and passed out tens of thousands of brochures over the nine-day show. As a moneymaker, though, the flower show withered and died. The show brought in about $700, little more than the cost of gasoline for the expedition faithful to drive back and forth between Elgin and Chicago. Much more lucrative was a visit three days later to the Elgin Junior League, which pledged $5,000 to help fund the expedition after hearing the crew perform.

When U-46 had its spring break in 1976, Rahr sent the directors out on fund-raising trips to major cities. There they discovered why few big donors were contributing. Just like the father of the boy who dropped out, companies balked at the fact that a substantial part of the expedition budget was in salaries. Fialko, Stillwagon, Cox, and Hobart—all of whom would be on unpaid leave from their jobs—were each to get $25,000, about what they would have received in salary for the year they were giving up.

Hobart was divorced. Fialko was newly engaged. A lack of income for them was perhaps unjust but not critical. For Reid and Jan Lewis, who contributed their savings and took out personal loans for La Salle II, the expedition was "our baby," and they reasoned that no one will give you money if you're not willing to risk your own. Ken and Cox had wives at home, however. Judy and Pam would have to carry on as single wage earners maintaining households that two incomes had kept going. The Coxes had already contributed $1,500 to the expedition funds. Stillwagon's wife, Rowena, had four children to support. A loss of income altogether would have been devastating, but the family made do.

"We did get a little cash from the expedition," Rowena said, and "I have always kept our expenses to a minimum anyway." Jeff, their oldest, had received some small scholarships to Purdue and had always been self-sufficient. He worked to help put himself through school. Meanwhile, their younger son, Andy, helped preserve another source of income. In addition to his teacher's salary and coaching stipend, Stillwagon had earned some money by managing rental properties for a local bank. While he was away, Andy took over many of those property management duties. Rowena herself did some sewing to bring in some money, too.

During spring break, at least, Stillwagon found someone to be regional chairman for La Salle: Expedition II in Michigan. The man was Dave Upton, a former state senator whose grandfather had started Whirlpool Corporation. Upton would be a staunch supporter of the voyageurs to the end of the trip. Stillwagon also found that the Berrien County (Michigan) Bicentennial Committee, working with Upton, had created a special commission for La Salle II and did not flinch when Stillwagon said the expedition was looking for $70,000 from Michigan and Indiana and mentioned the salaries.

Among other expenses, the expedition expected to pay Knecht to help design and supervise construction of authentic voyageur clothing. In fact, Knecht may have assumed when he arrived that he would be receiving a regular stipend from the nonprofit corporation. That wasn't the case.

At twenty-one, he was scarcely older than the boys preparing for the voyage. But his seat in the canoe was based on expertise, the kind that the adult teachers were providing in science, mechanics, history, and the arts. The question might have been asked, "Will he be more an adult who can supervise or a student who requires supervision?"

Knecht and Cox were codirectors of projects relating to historic research and governments in French colonial America. Cox developed a sharp distaste for Knecht, who he believed was an egotist who didn't care about any project work but his own and would not pull his weight, either in a canoe or out of it. However, Knecht formed a friendship with Hobart, with whom Cox was close. Knecht and Hobart even went through a "blood brother" ceremony, cutting their fingers and exchanging gifts.

As 1975 turned into 1976, the adults began to see the drawbacks in the young Canadian. Knecht spent more time researching and developing his own clothing instead of helping to bring the same kind of progress to the group. He was frequently late or absent from workshops, and his physical conditioning was poor.

In January Knecht went to Canada to buy moose hides, leaving Lesieutre and Campbell in charge of a day-long workshop on sewing voyageur shirts. A week later he showed up in a ridiculous costume and smoking a cigarette. After speaking with Reid for forty minutes after a canoeing session Feb. 8, Knecht was a no-show at the afternoon workshop. Even the boys objected. Reid agreed that he would have to go if he skipped team-building the weekend of Feb. 21. In fact, he had quit that morning, but Reid didn't want to let his clothing expert leave without trying to persuade him to return, an effort which succeeded, at least for a while.

However, after five more weeks of personality conflicts, communication difficulties, and financial issues, Knecht parted ways with the expedition. He showed up at Camp Wa-De-Do-Da one evening in late March and told the crew he was leaving. Nine months later, Knecht attended the crew's appearance in Elgin on their way to the Gulf of Mexico. He seemed to have made peace with his departure from the enterprise and wished the men well, according to Fialko, who added, "He said he was really proud of what they had done so far."

Reid wanted to develop K-12 materials from the expedition, and he wanted them to be reproducible, interdisciplinary, and consistent with current curriculum guidelines. He needed someone to coordinate projects, work with educators to put student-created materials into a standard design, and develop lesson plans before working with publishers to get them to the general public. The scope of the work was enormous.

The person chosen to lead this task was Sonia Vogl, a graduate of the University of Michigan. She was writing her dissertation on curriculum having to do with the Great Lakes environmental quality when she was brought to Reid's attention. Vogl said she never had a contract with Reid or La Salle: Expedition II, and no one ever spelled out her specific duties. About all she knew, she said, was that she was to enlist teachers to help in creating K-12 curriculum centered entirely on La Salle.

Nevertheless, she organized a class for U-46 teachers through the National College of Education, based in Evanston. Unfortunately, those who signed up were almost exclusively elementary teachers, Vogl said. Each teacher paid a fee to the school and received continuing education credit. Some were invested in Reid's vision, but others were simply there for the credit. And once they received that, their interest in the curriculum project evaporated.

While bringing the teachers up to speed, Vogl was also invited to Camp Wa-De-Do-Da to engage the boys in the curriculum development. After passing out information about the projects on Jan. 7, 1976, she found herself peppered with questions. Who were the end users? What would the final form be? Did the scope of research have to be narrowed? How would crew members exchange information? Could the work be completed after the trip? It was a start.

Through brainstorming sessions with the boys, she had by March 10 compiled a list of more than 120 parallels and connections linking the world of the voyageurs with the twentieth century. However, it was the expedition itself, not the projects, that absorbed the boys' attention in the old media warehouse, and Vogl began to see herself as "pretty extraneous" to their operation.

At the beginning, Vogl believed that Reid's ambitious vision for the curriculum might be possible. But as the attitudes in her class and at Wa-De-Do-Da revealed themselves, it became clearer to her that the possibility of achieving that vision was remote. As the weeks turned into months, her husband also began to express concern about the amount of time she was putting into the projects and the fact that she had not been paid for any of it.

A coherent, educational format was slow to develop. Many pages of research were created, including Scavuzzo's clothing patterns, history of French colonial government in America, use of seventeenth-century navigational tools, mapmaking, and languages of New France. But many of the documents would have to wait till after the trip—journals, actual maps and geographical observations, weather patterns, and a host of other data.

Cooperation between Vogl and the teachers eroded for one reason or another, and when Vogl finally drew her first paycheck from the nonprofit corporation, she said, the canoes were in Canadian waters and the money from La Salle II was not enough to justify her continued service. It was November when she and the expedition parted company.

The attempt to produce a documentary of La Salle II was as stillborn as the efforts of Knecht and Vogl. Bob Olson had made *The Last Voyageurs*, an evocative video of the 1973 expedition, and Reid wanted to make a similar documentary of the La Salle II trip.

After Reid had assembled his adult staff, the group met in 1975 with different filmmakers to hear proposals. The directors were asked for their input. Hobart and Cox pushed to give the contract to the Canadian Film Board, which Cox claimed had the "money, staff, expertise, and experience" to fulfill the contract and produce the film, whose cost was estimated at $400,000.

Then on Feb. 15, 1976, Osborn showed up at canoe practice on the Fox to film the debut of Frese's first voyageur canoe replica for La Salle II. That night he showed his finished Jolliet '73 documentary to the crew. No more was said about the film contract. However, on April 9, the crew was asked to sign releases for Osborn to use their pictures in any way he chose.

"Ken and Reid just decided on him to make a film of the trip," Cox wrote on that occasion. "Why'd they make us go through the charade of having a voice?" As things turned out, Osborn lost a lot of money in his divorce, took $2,000 from Reid just to begin shooting film in Montreal, and stopped filming La Salle II within days of its launch.

Oddly enough, La Salle II received a continuing boost from a most unexpected source. Years before the *Back to the Future* film trilogy, the expedition billed as "Reliving the Past to Explore the Future" acquired its own Doc Brown. Like the scientist in the movie series, the real Doc Brown was an oddball visionary.

Dr. Emily M. Brown, a grandmother "pushing sixty," shared an optometry practice in Elgin with her husband, Willis. She was also an enthusiastic philatelist who conceived the idea of making and selling unique postal keepsakes with proceeds supporting the expedition. By traveling ahead of the canoes, she also spread enthusiasm for the crew wherever she went.

WILD WORLD

GO PLACIDLY AMID THE HASTE

(Aug. 11–17) Summer on the St. Lawrence

The opening strokes of La Salle: Expedition II took place on Aug. 11 into calm water. After days of dinners and performances in Montreal, there was a solemn ceremony on the banks of the St. Lawrence River. "La Salle" signed a will, Father Loran said a prayer, and the boys sang the *Te Deum*. Then they shoved off on the greatest adventure of their lives.

Canoes lie ready as a crowd gathers on a riverbank in Montreal to see the modern voyageurs push off on their great adventure.

The journey of 3,300 miles began with a baby step. As soon as the canoes were out of the downtown area and around the first bend, the crew pulled them out of the water for a brief portage around a railroad bridge.

The voyageurs struggled over slippery rocks, up the bank, around a railroad trestle, and down to the water again. The portage took place into the wind in humid, ninety-degree heat. And men and boys discovered that everything had to be lashed by a tumpline, a leather strap across their heads or chests. Quickly they found that the tumplines were improperly rigged. Either they slipped or the packs slipped or both did. They also realized that people had to be assigned specific cargo duties. A musket had been left behind by one contingent but picked up by another. The crew's first true experience with portaging was difficult, but it was their destiny to become experts. The canoes went back into the water and the crew paddled five kilometers more to a park in suburban Lachine, where they took on food and equipment. The crew left the park at four that afternoon for Châteauguay, upstream on the south side of the St. Lawrence, and a scheduled 5:00 p.m. dinner. Simply crossing the river took half an hour. Rocks along the far bank slowed them further. Battling the current, they were still three miles away after ninety minutes. Stillwagon, Braun, and Lieberman in a three-man canoe couldn't keep up with the others, and Stillwagon said he was shot at the end. Several others were hurting, too.

The crew had finger sandwiches and beverages at city hall before they were taken to a football field to give a show while mosquitoes ate them alive. Finger sandwiches proved wholly inadequate to feed a group of young men who had fought the current hard all day. As soon as the show was over, the travelers did exercises to ward off stiff limbs in the morning.

Lying in his sleeping bag that first night, Kulick looked through a space between the canoe and the tarpaulin and gazed at the moon. For him, the trip had finally begun. For the next eight months he would not be Robert Kulick. He would be Colin Crevel, voyageur. But not everyone had the same point of view.

"The first day, maybe even the first week, didn't seem like the beginning of the trip," Gorse mused, "because we'd pull into a town and we'd know that twenty miles back, and just a few minutes' drive, we could go back to where we started from. It didn't become real until I looked at a map later, toward the end of the St. Lawrence, and saw how far we had gone . . . That's when I started to feel like the trip had begun, because there was no turning back."

"I wasn't even convinced we were gone," Wilson admitted, "until I woke up one morning, cold." That morning the crew had been gone from Montreal for three months.

As Braun prepared beans for breakfast on Day 2—Hobart's birthday—Stillwagon patched the boys up. One after another came to the former football coach as if he were a small-town doctor and asked him to ease their blisters from a hard day of paddling and portaging. Wilson alone had eight blisters; Cox had five.

"We took a month to acclimate," said Wilson, echoing Sir Edmund's prediction. The boys had to get used to blisters at first, but they also had to develop routines, find their rhythms, and discover their strengths, "to divide the possible from the impossible." By the time they were through, they could go from landfall to a completed shelter in twenty minutes.

Six Canadians in a twenty-two-foot canoe acted as escorts for La Salle II while they were in the province of Quebec. They acted as quasi-official goodwill ambassadors for the province. The six belonged to a club called Les Portageurs that shot rapids in sixteen-foot canoes, but they had never used the longer one or paddled upstream before.

In Beauharnois, Les Portageurs and the La Salle II voyageurs finally got to know one another. After dinner the two groups hung around together another hour and a half. Ken and Reid sang a song. Then the Americans called for Les Portageurs, who sang two. Both groups demanded that the city and K of C officials sing, and they obliged with two more. On request, Cox told a tale he called "my bear story." Then it was off for a presentation to the public at a park along the river.

The voyageurs attracted a less welcome group when they arrived at the park. Three young men who had been smoking marijuana and drinking beer saw the canoes approaching. Cox characterized them as "freaks." The trio jumped into their own little canoe to escort the voyageurs in. In the daylight, they seemed harmless enough, but as they lingered long after sundown they took on a more sinister cast. Some of the locals told Reid that the "freaks" were famous for breaking beer bottles and throwing paint at anything in the park. Reid said they looked just like the people who stole a canoe on the Tri-centennial trip, and the Lewises were visibly uncomfortable. Reid had the crew put a rope around the campsite.

Two crewmen were up in shifts every hour, acting as lookouts all night long. Braun and Campbell were up from three to four a.m., and said some of the freaks had come back around 3:30. All in all, it had been a wonderful day, but dawn would bring Friday the thirteenth and a seventeen-mile paddle.

The voyageurs headed for the Beauharnois Locks, the first of three sets of locks the canoes would use to rise above rapids and falls. In the 1950s and '60s, the United States and Canada had built the St. Lawrence Seaway, streamlining the river and building a series of locks that allowed modern ships and barges to navigate the river from the Great Lakes to the Atlantic Ocean. As the trip moved south, the canoes would go through Canada's Beauharnois Locks in Châteauguay, the American Snell Locks south of Cornwall Island, and the Eisenhower Locks at Massena, New York.

The president of the St. Lawrence Seaway Commission had given permission for the travelers to use the waterway. Somehow the word got lost. The master of the locks insisted that the canoes be towed through and that they wait their turn for an available tugboat, just as a canoe group traveling from Montreal to Duluth had done.

Reid called the head of the seaway commission himself to try to expedite the situation, and as soon as he heard the man's voice, Reid knew he could talk to him. Clearly, French was the president's preferred language, and Reid spoke to him in perfect French. The canoes were subsequently allowed to enter the locks unaccompanied, the first time non-motorized craft had ever been granted the privilege of going through unaided.

A hard rain began to fall as soon as the canoes entered the first of two locks. Immediately, the group noticed that their ponchos offered no protection. But two guys driving behind them in a car shouted encouragement, and one of them showed up an hour after lunch with cold orange juice. The crew paddled the whole distance in the rain that day. At least the current didn't fight them. Only later did the travelers learn that the lockmaster had lightened their paddling burden by closing a dam. A Seaway Commission representative followed the canoes in a Travelall with his son all the way to Valleyfield. As the canoes rounded the last point he yelled out that the voyageurs had a lot of guts.

The St. Lawrence River impressed the crew. Much wider than the Mississippi over much of its length, the far shore often disappeared in haze. The canoes could be hundreds of yards off shore and still be a mile away from a tanker in the middle of the stream. That far out on the river, too, things on shore remained in sight longer, making progress feel especially slow.

On the 14th Braun cooked sagamite and burned his hands on the portable oven. The expedition left Valleyfield late. Foster was sick with an upset stomach and headache—the first casualty, and only three days out. He lay down in Fredenburg's canoe, and Bardwell took his place.

The canoes swept on toward a bay reserved for them on the north side of the river in South Lancaster, Ontario's Glengarry Park. The voyageurs entered the bay near sunset. The western light glared in their eyes, but they could hear the opening whine of bagpipes along the curl of the bay half a mile away. The tired paddlers responded to the music. At Ken's urging, they picked up their stroke in cadence with Braun's. Unseen, the piper worked the magic of his drone and chanters out of the shaded shore. The soft splash of wooden paddles into the lake mixed with the piper's eerie highland skirl in a concerto remembered for its beauty decades later. As the sun set behind the trees, the voyageurs made out a lone park ranger standing erect and playing in the gloaming, finishing only when the canoes scraped their bottoms in Ontario and darkness enveloped the piper.

A pleasant, English-speaking audience attended the voyageurs' presentation that night, illuminated by car headlights. They came around the campsite later that evening to ask questions. But general distaste for Braun's pea soup for dinner and a hard rain and strong wind during the night put dampers on the travelers' joy.

The wind never let up, but the crew took advantage of the wind, sailing for the first time at least a few of the seventeen miles that day. In each four-man canoe, three people were suddenly passengers, and they couldn't imagine that sailing was too difficult. All the sailor had to do, after all, was hold the line and lean backward into the wind, they thought. But for the voyageur in the second seat, sailing was anything but easy. To begin with, he had no fixed bench, as did the men in the bow and stern. He sat on a faux bale whose flat bottom wobbled on the curved edge of the hull. Little more than a stick served as the "mast" holding a makeshift canvas sail. What stabilized the jerry-rigged apparatus was the lone sailor, who might have to hold on for dear life as the ropes from the sails tightened over his hands and cut off his circulation, if not actually drawing blood from his cold, wet flesh. In the best case, breezes came from directly behind the canoe. Pity the sailor who had to make constant adjustments in his seating or the ropes to deal with wind coming from the side or gusting. For the sailors, paddling was often easier.

The crew's target that Sunday was Ontario's industrial Cornwall, whose paper mills created a stench that revolted men who were familiar with the steel mills of Gary and East Chicago, Indiana. The guys had been told to expect a crowd of about fifteen hundred people. Instead, perhaps fifteen people dotted the shore as the canoes pulled in. It didn't seem to matter later as the town set up a corn fest later for the visitors, who had come during Canada Week. A folk-rock group from Ottawa called Thirty-two Berets performed as La Salle II's opening act. The mayor gave each of the boys a miniature lacrosse stick, because Cornwall was apparently the only place in the world where wooden lacrosse sticks were still made.

A mile into their route toward the US locks the next day, the canoes dropped four feet into rapids that ran under a bridge. Most of the canoes lined around the trouble, though Braun cut his feet in doing so. Several crew members had not yet put on life jackets, and the strong current nearly proved disastrous. The crew of one canoe was lining around a cement point. Gross and Kulick were in the water. Gross pulled the bow line, or painter, and Kulick held onto the gunnel. When Gross gave the rope a rough tug, the boat shot away. Kulick suddenly felt his rocky footing drop off beneath him. He quickly sank into the swirling waters, out of his depth and unable to pull himself back up over the gunnel and into the canoe. Reid, who was on shore and heading for the canoe, reached the point, bent over his boat mate, and hauled Kulick up by his arms. The expedition's first potential disaster had been averted.

The boys moved through the American locks much more quickly than they did the Canadian locks. At the Eisenhower Locks the liaison team met them with lunch and the first meat they had had in three days. As the water rose in the lock, the crew looked up and to the right to see a hundred people above them waving and applauding. The calm water of the lock was not matched by the water outside. The chop on the river bounced them around as they exited, and it stayed with the canoes for a few miles before they camped in Massena.

Stillwagon had done a lot of groundwork before the expedition by involving 4-H groups throughout the length of the trip. The men and boys were grateful that the clubs provided meals for them, as they did in Massena, but some began to wonder how they would fare when the expedition left civilization and dealt with the isolation of Georgian Bay. Adults also wondered what would happen in Illinois, where Stillwagon was required to work with the state 4-H officials instead of the local clubs. There was no way to predict what word, if any, might have trickled down to the individual 4-H clubs. Would split pea soup and bannock bread be their daily companion?

As the crew left Massena's town beach the morning of Aug. 17, the sun rose at their backs and threw its light off the water ahead of them, a glistening of diamonds. No buildings lay ahead. There was only the water, the trees, and the sky.

Fourteen miles down the river, Cathy Palmer faced a dilemma. Among her duties was the job of flagging down the canoes and guiding them into their scheduled campsites. On this occasion, she noticed that the campsite was inside a curl of land and out of sight from the river. The guys might never see her wave the flag, and they might paddle on for miles before the liaison team could catch up with them. Without giving it a thought, Palmer leaped into the river and swam well out into the St. Lawrence to flag the voyageurs in. That evening a hundred people came from a town of only eight hundred to hear a presentation performed on a flatbed truck. The turnout turned conversation to a discussion of big towns and small towns, exactly the kind of discussion the J&M crew had had three years earlier.

"It's funny how small-town folks offer better things than big ones," Campbell commented in a letter home.

"Large towns give you wine and finger sandwiches, and small towns give you mounds of food," Cox recorded. "These people understand a hard day's work and good food."

For Reid, a hard day's work didn't end at sundown. He was still trying to raise money for the enterprise. He often left camp to go to the motel where the liaison team had set up shop. There he had access to a telephone, and he would continue to write fund-raising proposals and draft letters to potential sponsors well after the crew had gone to sleep. While doing so, he sometimes took dinner on the fly, eating a hamburger or a few slices of pizza while writing or working the phone. Exhausted from paddling all day, and multitasking while sitting on a soft bed in a warm room, Reid may have found it easy to fall asleep at the motel or cast an eye toward the television the liaison team watched in the same room. However, the crew lay on the ground, sometimes in the rain, fended off mosquitoes, and slept in bags. Reporters following the voyageurs began to notice Reid's absences from camp and questioned why.

"I deflected as best I could for as long as I could, but they kept asking," Bart Dean, press liaison, recalled. "I knew it was just a matter of time before one of them published the story and discredited the expedition's claim of authenticity."

One night he asked Reid how he should answer such inquiries. Dean's innocent query disturbed Reid because he thought Dean, in asking the question, had taken the part of detractors. In spite of his own flash of anger, he also understood that it was important to project the right image as the canoes traveled upstream. Reid stopped eating fast food and sleeping in motel rooms after that.

The boys had received a hero's send-off in Elgin on Aug. 3. They had been fawned over for another week in Quebec and Montreal. As they paddled through Canada and the United States, crowds applauded the boys. The media gathered around them as officials and other adults patted the boys on the back. Children asked for their autographs. Hordes of young females mobbed the boys, cooing at them and meeting them for long walks, meals, drives, and make-out sessions, though everyone was well aware of lines that could not be crossed. To these girls each voyageur lad may have seemed like a rock god, with long hair, skin tanned by the sun, and an upper body grown muscular by long hours of physical labor. This kind of reception gradually became a dividing line of sorts between the crew and their support team.

The incredible adulation gave the boys a sense of self-importance that many of them recognized, but whose consequences most did not understand. More than a few assumed an attitude of the privileged, that others existed to do their bidding. Bardwell, who traveled with both the support team and the crew, believed that the boys' attitudes grew out of gender roles prevailing in America at the time. The boys' mothers had generally been the ones to care for them as they grew up. Now, he believed, the guys expected similar care from Jan and Scavuzzo, and objected when it didn't meet their expectations.

"They had a job to do and they did a fantastic job," said Marr, who months later would spend six or seven weeks as part of the liaison team. The trials of the women were often lost on the crew, however.

Scavuzzo found that the same boys who so patiently had taught her to drive a stick shift in Montreal began ordering her about or found fault with her for not performing tasks that were never hers to begin with. She chalked that up to youth and immaturity, but she was less forgiving when she found Jan and herself criticized by the adult men, particularly Cox and Hobart, who passed along their feelings to the boys. Nobody cheered for the liaison team, Scavuzzo observed, but she expected at least some modest respect for the many things she and Jan continued to do for the boys. That was not forthcoming. Instead of respect, the women found contempt. The gap in expectations between groups became a gulf as attitudes calcified.

In the first ten days, however, equipment was the big issue. The men and boys had discovered by now that the canvas pants they wore never seemed to dry out and could not be tightened around the waist. They began to write home for woolen ones, which not only dried out quickly but also provided more warmth as the summer receded into autumn and winter. The temperature fell into the forties the night of Aug. 17. The sleeping bags, donated by the Canadian government, suddenly felt comfortable. The three-foot by seven-foot sacks weighed twenty pounds apiece. They had an inner layer of wool, an outer layer of light canvas, and were good to about twenty degrees Fahrenheit. In August, that sounded like more than enough protection. By November, there would be doubts.

UNDERCURRENTS

(Aug. 18–26) The Gate to Lake Ontario

In two weeks' time, some were already feeling the sense of separation from loved ones, some of whom had spent the days with them in Montreal just a week earlier. Homesickness would grow for several of the men and boys. Less worthy feelings also grew. Personality conflicts had already begun to appear. Ken had rankled many of his mates by yelling at them and quarreling over small things. Some felt that he had drifted out of touch and seemed to be in a world of his own. He tended to talk down to the boys, all of whom felt that they were virtual equals on the trip and many of whom more than matched him physically. Annoyed by the petty conflicts, the crew had begun to take a dislike to him. Finally, Ken apologized for his irritability. He explained that he had been a smoker from the age of eleven and, knowing that he would have little access to cigarettes in many areas along the route, he had quit a two-and-a-half-pack-a-day habit cold turkey. The withdrawal had affected him dramatically. Even months later, he would put himself through heavy physical exertions—like running and push-ups—to keep from thinking about smoking.

Another conflict was less easily resolved, and it came to a head on Aug. 18 after a difficult passage between a bridge and the dam near Cornwall Island. Five canoes made it through the swift spot, but Watts's canoe failed four times to make the transit before giving up, getting out of the boat and pulling it, or lining, around the problem. Bardwell was paddling for Foster, but the problem had nothing to do with Bardwell.

The crew included (seated, L–R) Jorge Garcia, Ron Hobart, Terry Cox, George Lesieutre, John DiFulvio, Chuck Campbell, Randy Foster, Gary Braun, Doug Sohn, and Clif Wilson; (kneeling, L–R) Rich Gross, Dick Stillwagon, Sam Hess, Mark Fredenburg, Keith Gorse, John Fialko, and Reid Lewis; (standing, L–R) Ken Lewis, Steve Marr, Marc Lieberman, Loran Fuchs, Sid Bardwell, Bill Watts, and Bob Kulick.

"[Wilson] was doing rock 'n' roll in his head, and [Foster] was doing country," Watts said. Wilson's rhythm, in particular, was out of sync with the crew's. "We knew we were doing something wrong. We had done well on the Fox, but now we lagged behind the others."

Foster and Wilson had never gotten along with one another. Wilson was the only son of a well-to-do family in which he was given a lot of freedom. Foster was part of a very large working-class family that expected him to pull his weight economically. Oil and water, they were put in the same canoe anyway, and it was the only boat that did not include an adult. Now Wilson took his case to Reid and threatened to quit if Foster wasn't removed from his canoe.

That night in Cardinal, Ontario, Wilson met with Hobart and Fialko to make his case. The two men called Garcia and Watts into the discussion and asked them about their boat mates. Watts, the stern paddler and helmsman, had seemed reluctant to speak up about the conflict. Garcia was perhaps the quietest of the voyageurs throughout the trip. Given the opening, however, they both told Wilson in detail why he, not Foster, was the problem. As a mirror to his own behavior, Garcia's and Watts's reactions hit Wilson like an emotional right cross. He had to absorb what they said, and he spoke for an hour with Reid later that evening.

"Even a friend won't back you up if you're not pulling your weight," Cox commented in his journal, "and the last two days [Wilson] has not helped load or unload their canoe. He just stuffs his bag and lets the rest of the crew do the work. As I write this he's sitting behind his canoe pouting." But Wilson, in fact, was processing input from Cox, Reid, Watts, and Garcia.

In Ogdensburg, New York, on Aug. 19, the city opened up the Frederic Remington Museum for the crew, allowing them to view some of the finest art ever rendered of the Old West. A local boy had offered the travelers a package of eight hot dogs as the canoes arrived. Marc, who played Henri de Tonti, La Salle's trusted lieutenant, declined the offer, saying he wouldn't feel right about it unless there was enough for everyone. Soon afterward, Hess, Wilson, and DiFulvio were seen gobbling the hot dogs, and Stillwagon had to tell Wilson to put down a beer that had somehow materialized in his hand.

"You can tell we aren't into being voyageurs or team players yet. Guys can't always just be looking out for themselves like that. We have to start working more as a group. But how long will that take to set in?" Cox wondered.

On the other end of the spectrum, Cox noticed that Sohn did more than pull his own weight in his canoe. "[Sohn] is an animal," he observed. "He powers that canoe by himself. He really leans into each and every stroke. Today John F. was trying to get Fr. Loran and [Marr] to work on their strokes. When the others contribute anything that canoe flies."

Two days later, after covering roughly thirteen miles to Brockville, Ontario, it was clear that the confrontation with Wilson had had a positive effect. All the canoes made good time.

"[Wilson] and [Foster] have really been digging the last two days, and they're not the last ones in any more. [Watts] and [Garcia] talked to me at some length last night, and they're really excited about their newfound success," Cox wrote. "[Watts] said the best thing that happened was when they had their meeting and [Hobart] told [Wilson] there would be no changes in the crews. Their [module] was the first one to have a camp set up last night. I sure hope their problems are behind them, and us. If [Wilson] is man enough to accept the fact that he can't have his way all the time, this trip will be the greatest thing that ever happened to him."

Fialko also noticed the difference. "[Watts's] canoe now leads the pack at times. They seem to have gotten together finally," he wrote in his journal.

Unprompted, Wilson said candidly years later that he was a contrary and difficult teenager at the beginning of the expedition. He said Cox took him aside and counseled him, explaining that he couldn't continue that way and that others depended on him. Wilson said he began to watch Sohn to see how he handled himself. Like Wilson, "Buckwheat" was a bow paddler. He was responsible for getting the others into and out of the canoe and setting the stroke for his mates. Wilson said he made Sohn his role model, and he came to understand how much the men in his canoe depended on him. He began to accept responsibility, not merely in his job as a bow man, but in a general sense as part of his module, part of the expedition, part of something larger than himself. That didn't mean that everything was rosy between Wilson and Foster. But it did mean that they would be able to work together to make things work for the good of the whole group.

As the tour downriver continued, rain gave way to sunnier skies. Temperatures moderated, finally dropping into the seventies. The shoreline rose to high bluffs lined with fewer hardwood trees and more birches and pines. The homes became estates, and some houses seemed more like castles. The crew was feted by the Brockville Historical Society and the Champlain Society, made up of fifty wealthy families trying to preserve French language and heritage in that corner of Ontario. The day did not go without a hitch. Campbell described a mild mishap along the shore as a motorboat came past the canoes.

"[Stillwagon] was standing in his canoe when a wake from a boat came and he lost balance," Campbell wrote in his journal. "He fell across about five to six feet to our canoe, bringing our gunnel under and filling the canoe with five to six inches of water. We can survive rapids but may destroy ourselves on the beach."

Families constantly lived in the knowledge that their husbands, fathers, or sons were exposed to the elements, traveling with privation over dangerous waters where the potential for tragedy always flowed alongside them. But the men of La Salle II also traveled on a current of love and goodwill. Parents, wives, sweethearts, and friends sustained them with their prayers, their letters, and their visits. Rumors of disaster on the trail sometimes infected the Elgin community: the crew was six days behind schedule or so-and-so had broken a thumb. Families did not give in easily to rumors, but they did not shy away from seeking answers.

The voyageurs crisscrossed the St. Lawrence River as they made their way toward Lake Ontario. Some days they covered as little as six miles, on others up to seventeen miles. One day they performed and camped in Canada. They next day they made their presentation and slept in the United States. The original voyageurs, like the Native Americans, had wandered on both shores. On Aug. 22 the expedition headed south in a New York State of mind.

There the lovely Alexandria Bay area is the beginning of the Thousand Island chain. In 1908 George Boldt, the owner of New York City's Waldorf Astoria Hotel, began to build a castle for his wife. After the man had spent $2 million on the exterior of Boldt Castle, the story goes, he threw a big party, calling in his chef, who had previously created Waldorf salad for the hotel menu. Boldt asked him to develop a new salad dressing for the occasion.

They named it Thousand Island dressing. But soon afterward, the tycoon's wife died, and Boldt discontinued construction. The interior was never completed.

As La Salle II paddled into the area from Ontario that Sunday, the boys found the river as busy as Chicago's Dan Ryan Expressway on a Monday morning. Tour boats, speedboats, rowboats, and sailboats crowded the river. The canoe men had come solely to entertain Alexander McNally III, a friend of La Salle: Expedition II. Reid had delayed their departure till the heat had set in that afternoon, trying to time their arrival at 5:00 p.m. As it turned out, McNally had to leave by that hour and they wound up entertaining his three sons instead. The expedition did spend time with the scion of the Rand McNally atlas fortune the next morning on his houseboat. McNally had raised the partially sunken *La Duchesse*, a beautiful 1904 vessel, at a cost of one dollar, while using the help of the local fire department. The original brass fireplace was a work of art, and the woodwork gleamed.

The crew learned that McNally had written the expedition a check for $2,000. The amount was only $500 more than the Coxes had contributed themselves, and Cox railed bitterly about Reid, who he said forced the crew to bow and scrape to a millionaire who had contributed so little. But Reid knew the truth and shared it with Kulick, who kept the official expedition journal. McNally had been responsible for other donations totaling $17,000, including $10,000 from ARBA, which La Salle II never would have had otherwise. President Gerald Ford had picked eleven people to hand out federal Bicentennial funds. The group was supposed to be nonpolitical, though it was anything but. As one of those eleven chosen, McNally had to claw through the political thicket with the other ten people to pry away money for Reid and his La Salle crew.

While the expedition diverted for the sake of McNally's $2,000— and whatever else he might have contributed or might contribute in the future—the expedition's lack of money sat at the root of a growing problem. That Sunday Dean intimated that he was "tired of paying for everything out of his own pocket," Cox wrote. Money continued to be an issue between Reid and Dean during the trip and between Reid and other adults for years. During the expedition, cash was in very short supply. Afterward, moths flew out of the empty pockets and even the distant future was painted in red ink. The fact remains that Reid, by enterprise and dogged determination, made good on every debt.

The crew had both warm weather and cold weather outfits. When the cold set in quickly, the winter clothes posed some special problems. The outer garments were mostly wool, which could not be washed easily, and much of the laundry consisted of underwear. The men generally put on their newly cleaned undergarments under continuously dirty outer garments. They slipped their feet in clean socks into cold, wet moccasins. Sleeping bags became smelly over time, but their bulk and the crew's constant need for them made cleaning them difficult.

"I think our sleeping bags were cleaned twice in eight months," Cox said, perhaps exaggerating. "To say they were rank would be a gross understatement." But any opportunity at cleanliness was always welcome.

"We were never such heroes to the crew as when we scheduled showers," Scavuzzo observed.

Despite disagreements, the members of the expedition began to come together in other, important ways. Routines began to make the crew more efficient. At first, only the wood hawks, fire starters, and cooks had their act together. Gradually, others began to pick up the pace. Shelters rose more quickly. Departures, which had taken place later than scheduled in the mornings, now got off on time.

After latecomers complained about unequal distribution of food, Stillwagon told the cooks that no one would eat until everyone was present. Because paddling all day used an enormous number of calories, food was on everyone's mind morning, noon, and night. Voyageur journals and letters filled up with descriptions of special meals, pleas for care packages and delicacies from home, and weariness at the dreadful monotony of split pea soup and oatmeal. Stillwagon's decree forced everyone to dance to the same tune and streamlined activity as much as anything could have.

The demands of paddling the canoes also transformed the

travelers into stronger voyageurs. Arms, shoulders, and backs grew muscle. Paddling to the left and right on alternate days, the voyageurs worked their oblique muscles and defined their abdominals into "six-packs" as the months rolled by. The canoe training that had been done over the previous two years was nothing in comparison to the sustained physical activity that now occupied the crew every day.

Reid had learned a "power stroke" during the Jolliet & Marquette outing. The stroke called for the paddler to lean back and pull with his arms. Reid insisted that the crew use it. The problem, said one veteran boater, was that the stroke "makes it easy to look like you're working hard when you're not." Through the experience of paddling every day, the fellows quickly learned who could pull his weight and who simply went through the motions. But everyone improved his technique, and weaknesses were balanced with strengths in each canoe.

"In the early going, we were overwhelmed by the physical challenge, the group dynamics," said Wilson. "As the river became wider and slower, we became wiser and more selective. By the time we entered Lake Ontario, we were way, way better than we were."

The campfire was an almost mystical place where the crew could kick back and be more themselves, a bit less guarded than they were in the daylight or at performances. Though the campsites also drew onlookers and the curious, the voyageurs were somewhat less in the public spotlight and had shelters into which they could seek refuge. Shadows covered them. Hobart would play guitar. Braun played some banjo. Sometimes there would be singing. Always there were conversations, some deeply philosophical. Always there would be the warmth and the dancing flames of the campfire itself.

In Ganonoque, Hobart and Dean were singing around the fire when they were joined by Jim Norris, the head of the city Recreation Department. He was also a photographer. About forty-five minutes after he arrived, when the voyageurs had bedded down for the night, a war cry split the darkness and dozens of painted savages screaming, "Gans on the warpath!" broke into camp and surrounded the startled crewmen, emerging sleepy and half-clothed from their shelters. Norris got a photo of Gorse as he peeked out of his tent. A girls softball team and members of the city's summer recreation staff dressed as Indians had organized and carried out their attack as a kind of tribute. Reid, who was in on the act, halted the cries by producing a calumet—a peace pipe. The girl who had masterminded the plot sat solemnly with Reid to smoke with him.

While the voyageurs contended in camp with chiggers and mosquitoes and hot, stinky sleeping bags, paddling took place on calm waters under sunny skies. It was still summer, but the climate was changing. Marr took a temperature reading on the morning of Aug. 24. It was fifty-seven degrees at 7:30. The expedition entered the city of Kingston, the gateway to Lake Ontario.

By now the travelers had learned that, in addition to food and attention, local residents along the way eagerly gave advice about travel in their area. Among the realities of this advice, the crew learned that estimates given by locals of distance over water were always understated, usually by a wide margin, and that everyone believed his area was the most dangerous stretch of water.

Another kind of misinformation made for a mad scramble into Kingston. Officials were told that the crew would arrive at 5:00 p.m. The crew thought they'd have to work hard to arrive by then, but they made great time and stopped for a leisurely lunch not far from the city. They played on a rope swing over the river, though the water was so shallow it was astonishing that no one hurt himself. The canoes got under way again about 3:00 p.m. and paused about a half mile from the landing site in order to arrive at five o'clock. Watts grumbled that La Salle himself never had to work his ass off in the morning so that he could sit outside a town and wait.

There were ruffled feathers in Kingston for other reasons, too. Wilson confided to Cox that Sohn was becoming angry with Father Loran, who had not been assigned a job in the module. The boys had thought that, with his camping experience, the priest would naturally lend a hand, but after getting everyone else up and out of their tents, he usually simply sat down, smoked, and wrote in his journal. When he told his group to roll out one morning, Sohn had answered, "Why? So we can go have a smoke with you?"

Perhaps more diplomatic than most, Ken said that Father Loran "didn't quite have the ease with the kids that we did. He was more reserved during the expedition." Father Loran was nearly fifteen years older than anyone else on the trip and almost twenty years older than most of the adults, and his physical ability didn't allow him to perform as strenuously as the others. He frequently complained about how much his back hurt, and he was out of the canoe for a period of four months. Bardwell became a de facto voyageur, at first to fill in for those who fell ill but eventually as a replacement for Father Loran.

"Father Loran was gone a lot," though "every now and then he'd jump back in the canoe for an hour or two," Cox said. Despite saying mass from time to time, Father Loran was not a pleasant companion, according to several crew members; some felt he was downright ornery. Toward the end of the expedition, the Memphis Commercial Appeal asked the priest for the highlight of the trip for him, and he gruffly responded, "When it ends."

Wilson said simply, "We had a common goal, and Father Loran did not share that goal."

However, the crew was still operating as a unit, and their land support group had healed earlier rifts.

"The whole liaison team is getting along fantastically now," Baumgartner wrote home on Aug. 27. "Cath [Palmer] looks after me like a mother and Jan and Marlena [Scavuzzo] are a blast to be around. I think in Quebec we were just getting used to each other and the situation, something that was a little rough."

Despite the scramble to get there, Kingston treated the voyageurs to dinner at the site of the Olympic sailing competition, which had been held in July. Neal Patterson, president of the Kingston Historical Society, told the boys how proud they should be of what they had already accomplished, recognizing that everyone who sees or hears them learns something about the joint heritage of their two nations.

It was here in Kingston by the Cataraqui River that La Salle maintained Fort Frontenac. He left this frontier outpost many times in the 1670s and '80s to explore the Great Lakes region, to build ports and posts in Michigan and Illinois, and to travel down the Mississippi to the Gulf of Mexico, where he would claim the land from the Appalachians to the Rocky Mountains for the king of France and name it all Louisiana. His travels touched Ontario, Quebec, and the Maritimes of Canada, and at least fifteen of the United States, from New York to Texas.

Peterson gave Reid, Cox, and Kulick a tour of a replica of Fort Frontenac, named for the governor of New France who worked with the explorer on several projects. Little is left of the original fort, except the remains of two stone walls, each ruin about two feet high and eight feet long.

That night, Dean came by to exchange arrival information for the next stop on the itinerary. He had just left the campsite, driving Bardwell's expedition van, when the crew heard the screech of brakes and the impact of metal on metal up the road. A Pontiac Firebird had slammed into the rear of the van. The collision broke the van's fuel tank, damaged the springs and shocks, and pushed the back fender in against a rear tire. The Firebird's front end was demolished. Dean said the kid in the Pontiac had admitted to speeding, but when the local police arrived, the officer said he would give Dean a ticket for making an improper turn. Stillwagon, Reid, and Cox joined Dean in a long argument with the officer, who finally backed down. To add further to the expedition's financial woes, the kid in the Pontiac had no insurance.

Though only about seventy people came to see the voyageurs in Bath on the 25th, they included an old couple from England. The man said it was the most exciting thing he had ever seen. He was struck not only by the research the boys had done but also by the dedication required for such a voyage. He began to write a long letter to relatives in England about what he had seen. He was not alone in his admiration. The next morning Campbell found an envelope addressed to "The Voyageur Men." In it was this letter:

"Hi! I'm one of the people of Bath. I'm sure we enjoyed your visit to our village. Watching you was very interesting and I liked it a lot. Since I'm only 13 I found it exciting. In school, at History class we took up the voyageurs, but to see it happen was really something different. Thanks again for making our village one of your stops. Good luck on the rest of your journey."

Bath represented the end of the first leg of the expedition: the end of their 150-mile voyage up the St. Lawrence. They were about to take on Lake Ontario, something more like an inland sea. But it had been the St. Lawrence River that had been on many boys' minds during their two years of training.

"It's really a great feeling knowing that one of the most dreaded parts is behind us," Braun exulted in his journal. "It's also really interesting how I've changed already. My whole outlook is different. I don't worry about almost anything. I feel like I don't have a care in the world."

The St. Lawrence was, in fact, a stroll in the park compared to what waited for them.

* * *

The practical Fialko took time to assess the performance of the team's gear three weeks into their odyssey. "The moccasins are OK," he noted, "but promise to be hell on the [Toronto] portage. We may have to wear liners, or half-soles, on anything rough. The heavy canvas pants that we were issued before we left Elgin are OK until they become wet, which is daily. And then they rub and chafe legs raw when we are walking in them. . . . The tomahawks are not holding up at all. . . . The welds are splitting . . . I think we'll be using modern axes before long . . . The guns have been performing well as long as they are kept absolutely dry. Even the fouling from a previous shot has to be sponged out and the bore dried. . . . Must also keep 'em well-oiled against the rust."

On Aug. 26 directors also assessed what was already a troubling financial situation. While the expedition camped in a farmer's field on Morrison Point across from Wapoose Island, there was a talk about what the lack of income might mean. There was probably enough money to sustain the enterprise during the trip, but expectations beyond April 9 were hanging by a thread.

"There was talk last night at the adult meeting of sending the liaison team home because of lack of funds, but the whole crew disagreed so much I think it was left alone," Baumgartner wrote in her Aug. 27 letter to her parents. "I was pretty upset, though, because it would be like yanking away part of my life."

Before the expedition left Montreal, the crew had agreed on guiding principles of safety and put certain rules in place for tactical operation on the water. One of those was to keep three canoes together at a time. That rule had already been violated. Canoes were to stay within reach of shore and each other. This usually meant that the canoes had to follow the contours of bays and inlets. They would test open water only if that course was the only one available or the best one under the right circumstances. Ken and Reid, in particular, had stressed the need to stay together, knowing how quickly the lake could change character. The people in Bath had also warned that the crossing from the St. Lawrence into the lake could be very dangerous.

As the canoes entered the lake on Aug. 26, they passed a series of islands to their left, which formed a kind of sheltered waterway. They went through the gap between Amherst, the largest of these islands, and Adolphus Reach, a peninsula to the west. They hugged the peninsula, according to their rules of transit, staying close to shore. The next day they were scheduled to swing around a bay to the lighthouse at the end of Long Point, the last cover before the open lake.

In the morning, the travelers awoke to calm air and quiet water. The temptation to strike out over open water hovered like an unspoken desire, a whisper from the devil on their shoulders. Hobart, who was the expedition's navigator, tried to counsel caution. Almost as soon as the canoes cleared Wapoose Island, however, Ken and Reid abandoned the route around the bay and shot directly south toward Long Point. Almost every other canoe took off in pursuit. Only Hobart and Cox and those in their canoe, the Frontenac, followed the original plan, avoiding the route the Lewis brothers had led the others to take. While the five canoes made good time across the bay, they had to wait half an hour for the lone canoe to catch up, and Hobart was very upset.

"Do you know why they have a quarterback on a football team?" Hobart demanded.

"Harsh words were exchanged," Ken recalled. During a fifteen-minute crew meeting on shore, Reid and Ken admitted that they had been wrong. Reid said it would never happen again.

"I was the bad guy," Ken said many years later. "We thought we had defined our strategy as clearly as we could. But I remember [that] morning, coming into Lake Ontario. The water was like glass, not a cloud in the sky, not a breath of wind." Under those conditions, he said, he thought that following the contour of the land would be "following a principle beyond its usefulness. We could save ourselves half an hour." He ultimately agreed that it was wrong to stray from the guiding principle, and subsequent events showed why.

WICKED POINT

(Aug. 27–30) A Rite of Passage

Little more than a fortnight into their voyage, the crew's campsite on Long Point next to an abandoned lighthouse was among the worst of the entire trip: a swarm of mosquitoes over a sea of mud in a pouring rain. Traveling with the voyageurs, Dean remembered the site vividly as a marsh, little more than muck with reeds poking out of it. The tents, sleeping bags, and equipment all sank down into three inches of fetid swamp water.

(L–R) Terry Cox, Keith Gorse, Chuck Campbell, and Ron Hobart fight the wind and waves as their canoe approaches Wicked Point on Lake Ontario.

"The water was warm, so you felt like you were sitting in pee," Dean said. "After the sun went down, the mosquitoes came out. We had to put masks on to keep from breathing them in. I spent six hours propped up against the back of a canoe, swatting bugs off and wearing a mask."

At some point, the crew ate well, though. A local man had given the guys some frozen perch and bass. Hobart and Stillwagon and Dean spent an hour fishing and brought in six more. Lieberman and Gorse caught a pair of bass from a dock. With a little maple syrup added to the cornmeal mush, dinner was a feast. A 4-H group drove three hours to spend some time with them that night, a sacrifice very much appreciated by the crew.

After dinner, four members of the Radical Five took a walk-and-talk, largely so that Wilson and DiFulvio could smoke cigarettes—something forbidden under expedition protocols, at least in public, to preserve an air of authenticity. The boys agreed that nothing would come of the educational projects that had absorbed so much attention during the previous year. Despite Reid's passion for them, the younger travelers simply lacked interest. Wilson had viewed project work as the last thing on his list of to-dos, something he could always do later, and he was surely not alone in that sentiment. Many of the boys said they would not put in the two months of project work expected of them after the trip was over. The failure of other projects only bolstered their desultory attitude. Olson's movie, for example, would never be made, and fund raising had been a disaster.

Kulick used the walk to vent some frustration. He griped that Reid and Gross, his canoe mates, both kept correcting his paddling stroke, insisting that he keep his top arm straight and bend at the waist. Kulick complained that he was more comfortable sitting up straight and using his arms more than his back. That way, he said, he put in twice the power—and produced more forward movement than either of the others, who he said "lily dipped" their paddles. DiFulvio, who sat in the stern of their canoe, backed his friend Kulick, who had other complaints as well. But it was Kulick's day for bitching, and he knew it. He speculated that others might be complaining in their own journals about him, and hoped not. But everybody had complaints at one time or another, and especially on a long voyage in close quarters under stressful conditions. A day later, observing how the guys were laughing and joking with one another in spite of being wet, cold, and sore, Kulick would call the crew "one heck of a group" and the bitching was forgotten.

Finally, the number of people talking about quitting the expedition also came up. Watts was upset by something and ready to go home. Dean still hadn't been paid, and he was threatening to leave, too. Some questioned whether Father Loran would last beyond November before quitting. Not three weeks into the expedition, there seemed to be a sense that La Salle: Expedition II was falling apart. At least the Radical Five had each other as a sounding board.

Wind overnight whipped up waves on the lake, and the crew woke to the sound of surf the morning of Saturday, Aug. 28. They ate apple cobbler for breakfast, since Garcia got up early to peel some apples that a farmer had invited the crew to pick. But the travelers remained in camp, mending equipment and writing letters. Ironically, despite having paddled for hundreds of miles and lifting heavy loads onshore, it was while packing up his sleeping bag that Father Loran threw his back out. This injury would continue to hang over the Elgin contingent for the rest of the trip.

The windy day was the first of several such days of respite along the route. It was still late summer, and the air temperature was comfortable. But the water temperature was perhaps ten to fifteen degrees colder than the air, and the strong wind blowing from the south brought a three- to four-foot chop on the lake. The wind, the water temperature, and the chop were all factors in canoeing on the lakes, and they affected the voyageurs differently, depending on their places in the canoes.

Each canoe had certain positions, and each position had its responsibilities. The man in the stern was *le gouvernail*. He served as helmsman, guiding the canoe, his big paddle acting as a rudder. In choppy water, his choices could mean the difference between a successful landing and a dangerous capsizing. Going with the waves could hurl a canoe uncontrollably toward a rocky shore. Paddling directly into the waves could drench a team while moving them away from their objective or exhausting them without making any forward progress. On the other hand, traveling parallel to the waves invited capsizing, a potential disaster in the cold water several hundred yards from shore. The trick was to ride, or quarter, the waves, breasting them at something less than ninety degrees safely.

The central paddlers were *le milieu*, the strength of the forward progress and the ones who bailed when the water came over the gunnels. In a three-man canoe, the lone milieu paddler might have to alternate paddling and bailing, when circumstances demanded both forward progress and staying afloat, or to choose one over the other to avoid disaster for the boat. On those occasions when the wind called for sailing, the milieu in the second seat was also responsible for holding the ropes that controlled the sails. Balanced on a movable seat in a craft without a keel, a milieu could be pulled dramatically in one direction or another, especially when the wind shifted. In such a case, capsizing was a real possibility. But sailing occurred only rarely.

The man in the bow, however, was *l'avant*, the one who bore the brunt of the waves in good times and bad, the one who stepped into the boat or out of it first to steady the craft in the swells or near rocks while the others entered or exited. *En français*, the singular was *l'avant* and the plural *les avants*, but the Elgin boys (pardon their French) Anglicized the term and universally referred to one as a *l'avant* or to the group as *l'avants*. Often the l'avant had to stand on shifting rocks or icy slopes or balance precariously on boulders above a roiling sea. At other times, he had to leap up to his neck in blindingly cold water. Cold weather would overtake hot before the crew left the Great Lakes, and the water, already chilled enough to bring on hypothermia, would be especially hard on the l'avants.

"L'avants got all the water coming in over you," Wilson said. "Your job was to jump out into water anywhere from two to seven feet deep and guide the canoe in. Your responsibility is to the craft, not your own body."

Each canoe had also been given a name, taken from rivers and places that were meaningful to La Salle, plus the emblem of France herself. The canoes were dubbed the Louisiana, St. Joseph, Frontenac, Montreal, L'Illinois, and Fleur de Lys.

Despite the wind, the voyageurs tried the next day to make a run for Point Petre, fifteen miles away. The lighthouse operator at Point Petre had predicted they wouldn't make it, that they would be lucky to make six miles. And they didn't make it, giving up and putting in at Charwell Point, but only three miles short of their goal.

"The first hour was OK—very choppy and wet, but we were moving," Cox logged in his journal. "The second hour my hands began to get cold and numb, even though I didn't have a shirt on and the temps were in the mid to upper 60s. But when we took our break after the third hour I thought I was coming down with hypothermia. I got so cold my hands felt like blocks of ice. I started shivering and my teeth started chattering. Gary [Braun] was almost as bad. He said his feet were freezing. Doug's [Sohn's] arms were nearly blue. But Clif [Wilson] was the worst of the bunch. He just shook, and he had the most pained expression on his face."

Sohn, Wilson, and Braun sat in the bows of their respective canoes, so each not only took on the headwind but also the spray of lake water hitting them in the face as they quartered into the waves. Cox, Lesieutre, and Gross also served as bowmen for their boats. The voyageurs stopped for lunch, hoping a little time out of the water on rocks warmed by the sun would reinvigorate them.

"We found ourselves getting wet and cold, really cold," Braun wrote in his journal. "I don't think I could feel the bottom third of my legs or my feet. We started fires and built a couple of lean-tos to keep the wind off us. Everyone was on the verge of hypothermia."

Hypothermia might have been an exaggeration. But after another hour on the water fighting five-foot swells and vicious headwinds, they had had enough. They beached their canoes on a rocky shore next to Duck Bay. Huge waves broke beyond Charwell Point, so the voyageurs decided to make camp and try to contact the liaison team, who had said they would cook dinner for the crew at the lighthouse, or breakfast if they couldn't make contact earlier. The Point Petre lighthouse operator, a man with eleven children, had let Scavuzzo use the kitchen there to prepare a spaghetti dinner. The liaison team was still waiting for the crew to arrive at the lighthouse, so Reid hiked to the nearest road and hitched a ride in that direction. But with no guarantee that the two groups could be brought together, Braun, Fredenburg, and the other cooks tried to prepare dinner from dried peas and beans.

The soup was ready when Reid finally returned, but he announced that the crew would eat at the lighthouse. To get there, however, involved a complicated shuttle by canoe to a swamp where the canoe men would have to wade through knee-high water before waiting at the side of a dirt road for the members of the liaison team to pick them up in vehicles and shuttle them in. Reluctantly, the cooks took the now-overcooked soup of peas and beans off the fire and set it aside for breakfast. Two canoes ferried the crew to the swamp as the sky drained its light and Reid tried to figure out where the landing site was located. Hungry and angry, the boys cursed it as "the dumbest thing we've done so far."

They waded through the cold water and scrambled up the muddy bank to the dirt road. There they found a dock that led directly from the lakeside to the road and would have spared them the stroll through the swamp. The first group waited for the rest of the crew. The sun dropped out of sight. The cold set in. The stars spilled into a cloudless, moonless sky. When the second group got there, they all stood in the road and waited. Finally, the crew could stand it no longer and started walking up the road to meet the liaison team. A mile later, Baumgartner came in a Volvo and Dean in a pickup truck.

After they arrived at the lighthouse, the keeper told his guests that the winds Sunday had been measured at 27 knots. With one knot equal to 1.4 miles per hour, that put the winds at 37 miles per hour. The travelers had scarcely left the relative safety of the St.

Lawrence River and already they were finding cold water and high winds unlike anything they had seen before.

"After today all of the bowmen are asking the same question: What in the hell are we going to do in late October, November, December on Lake Michigan? Everyone has to be concerned, but the bowmen most of all," Cox wrote that night. "We get soaked on a calm day. Frankly, it scared the hell out of me."

Up Monday at five for two doughnuts and burned beans, the voyageurs hit the water soon afterward. The sun shone, and the waves were no more than two or three feet. Conditions did not last. After lunch the canoe men fought six- to eight-foot swells, making it to Point Petre after an hour of arduous paddling. One canoe would rise above the one behind it to the height of a basketball hoop before disappearing into a trough.

"As we rounded Point Petre, we headed straight across a bay to Wicked Point, which was a bad move. It took us three hours to get there. We couldn't take any breaks because of the wind and waves," said Cox. About two-thirds of the way across the bay, Stillwagon suddenly took his canoe in toward shore. He and his boat mates, Braun and Lieberman, were half a mile away from the other canoes. "The next thing we knew he was gone. We turned towards shore and looked for him for a good fifteen minutes or so, when he came out of a little cove. They were on a piss break!"

The voyageurs took the delay as an opportunity to stop for lunch. The respite for bologna sandwiches, bananas, and cucumbers would be the last bit of calm they would have before spending the afternoon madly fighting Mother Nature's effort to smash them to bits. The plan called for the canoes to hug Wicked Point and ease into a little bay, then follow the shoreline to the next point of land. Beyond that second point lay the intended camp at Sand Banks Provincial Park. Between Charwell and Sand Banks, however, the mortal sailors found themselves in the hands of the gods, trapped between Scylla and Charybdis, the pounding waters of an angry lake and the hard anvil of a rocky shore.

"You were in ten-foot waves and often couldn't see anybody in the other canoes," recalled Marr. "I saw this rock. It was as big as a house, and we almost crashed on it."

The canoes swung around Wicked Point and the voyageurs tried to paddle into the bay. Just as they had the day before, thirty-mile-per-hour winds whipped the lake to a fury. Waves hurled the six small craft toward an arc of land lined entirely with boulders. There was no effective place to put in without courting wreckage. Instead the crew chose to make a run for it across the bay.

Gouvernails quartered their boats into the wind. The canoes bucked and dived and their crews dug hard for the far point. One man in each canoe did nothing but bail all day using thick, waterproofed canvas bags. Stillwagon's three-man canoe couldn't spare a man to bail unless water sloshed deeply into the boat. Stillwagon used his longer paddle to steer the entire time as Lieberman and Braun stroked for their lives. Fear painted the faces of several boys as the waves tossed their canoes around like flotsam.

The two-mile transit might have been covered in half an hour in calm seas. In this case, it took three hours for most of the canoes to make their destination. One canoe took four hours to make it, and the travails of its small crew during those four hours were little understood even by their fellow voyageurs.

L'Illinois, piloted by DiFulvio with Gross as l'avant and Kulick and Reid in the milieu, found itself far out into the lake, at least a mile and a half from the rest of the group. While the other canoes had ridden the waves to some extent, L'Illinois had crested the waves more directly, taking the little crew farther away from land. The sharp wind whipped past Gross's head and carried away even shouted conversation behind him in the canoe, and he had his hands full with efforts to keep the little craft from capsizing. But it was clear that there was something wrong behind him. The canoe was not making the kind of forward progress that it should have.

As gouvernail, DiFulvio may have preferred a more aggressive quartering path that would have kept the canoe more in touch with the others. As expedition leader, however, Reid was concerned about the safety of the boys and may have believed that a more direct path into the waves reduced the risk of capsizing. Whatever controversy there might have been, their fight to survive needed all hands.

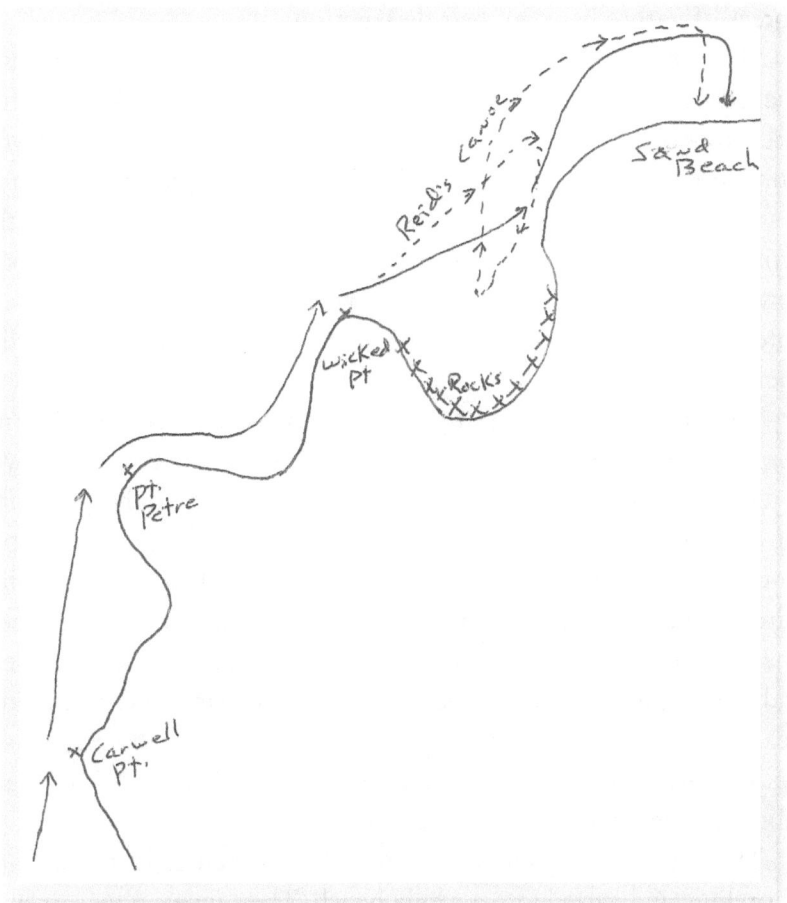

A hand-drawn diagram in Terry Cox's journal shows the twisting journey of L'Illinois crisscrossing the route taken by the rest of the canoes around Wicked Point.

By the time they turned to ride back into the shore, they had undershot their target by at least half a mile and crossed the track everyone else had followed. The pulsing waves threw L'Illinois back into the bay, swiftly toward rocks again. "La Salle" directed his team, shouting into the wind while drawing his paddle through the roiling seas. DiFulvio hauled on his rudder paddle, maneuvering hard against the pitching waves. Gross and Kulick called upon every reserve of strength they had to paddle and bail to counter the forces of nature bent on their destruction.

"It was a bad day from the get-go," said Gross. "The wind kicked up, and suddenly it's ten-foot waves, for chrissakes. We figured to quarter, quarter, quarter, then get into shore. When you come down the waves, the bow submarines. We would come up to a wave. We would quarter into the wave and drop down into the trough. The wave crashes over my lap, and I get a bath. I took a few waves like that and asked for my life jacket." The jackets were intended more for warmth than for safety. But, Gross said, the life jacket wasn't there.

The bow shot out over the crest of each wave. In that instant, Gross drew his paddle through nothing but air while hanging over a ten-foot drop to the surface. As the canoe slid down the other side of the wave into the trough, John's rudder paddle came up empty and lost any ability to guide the boat. Because their canoe pointed directly into the waves, even more water cascaded over the gunnels than it did in the other five canoes. The water was fifty degrees Fahrenheit, and Gross worried about hypothermia. He ripped the seams of his poncho and threw it over the front of the canoe as a spray skirt. Behind him in the canoe were Kulick and Reid, paddling like hell and bailing like crazy.

The other canoes made the far point, turned right toward the shoreline, and surfed into a sandy beach. The canoes, now traveling with the wind and waves, almost flew toward the shore. The thrill rose in their hearts as high as the terror in their throats. The waves broke upon the shallows in a ferocious amusement park ride.

"We felt like we were surfing—but it also felt like we really weren't in control," Cox wrote. "After the wave passed, you'd swear you were paddling in wet concrete. Then you'd hear a roar from the rear and it was off to the races again."

From the beach, however, many voyageurs wondered where DiFulvio's canoe had gone and even if it was gone for good. It was lost in the high waves out on Lake Ontario. Several people were worried, because it would be nearly impossible to try to relaunch the canoes for any kind of rescue attempt, now that they had reached shore. Finally, L'Illinois came ripping toward the beach, just as the others had done, racing fast and out of control. When the guys neared the beach, they jumped out to prevent a hard landing. DiFulvio leaped out, bent down, and kissed the sand.

"When I got out of the canoe, my feet hit the ground and I had no legs," Gross recalled. "Kulick saved my ass. He reached down and pulled me up and dragged me into shore." The l'avants had taken a beating. They all reported similar experiences, their cold, cramped legs buckling under them. Gross and Kulick, who sat right behind him, were exhausted by the fight for their lives. Reid, too, had feared for his life and theirs. But he also faced questions from the other adults about why his canoe had gone awry.

In that heightened state of anxiety, with adrenalin pushing the fear factor for everyone, voyageurs began assessing blame. Some were accused of poor conditioning. Some were accused of failing to follow directions. One person was accused of trying to do someone else's job. The finger pointing was pointless.

The boys had certainly tried to do their best under adverse, hazardous circumstances. If there were any implications to the contrary, they lacked merit, and a generation later Gross still bristled at the suggestion that he panicked in the waves. But fear leads people to say or do things they regret later. Reid's biggest regret, he says, almost in tears at the memory, came when DiFulvio, having guided their canoe to safety through those terrible hours, looked at Reid as if to say, "How did I do?" Reid said he should have acknowledged his achievement. Instead, Reid said, he turned away. But that was all in the postmortem. That afternoon, everyone was simply glad to be alive.

"Once everyone was on the beach it looked like New Year's

Eve," Cox said. "People were yelling and screaming and beating each other over the back and head. You'd have thought we'd made it to New Orleans."

Dean was on hand to take photos, but he also had some bad news. The park superintendent, watching the scene farther down the beach, refused to let the storm-tossed crew camp at Sand Banks. The park was closed, he said, and they faced fines of $50 each to remain. Because it was closed, he added, they could not set fires to warm up and dry off. The liaison team later said that they could not reach the man's superior by phone.

The superintendent arranged for the crew to use a private campground, but it was seven-tenths of a mile away—the length of eleven Canadian football fields, twelve if you play the US game. The portage was on a narrow path over a long hill and several fallen trees. Only what was needed for the camp was taken to the site. Everything else was left at the base of the hill, where Cox and Gross returned to keep an eye on things. That night the sky was fantastic with stars and the Milky Way shone with a special glow.

THE LONG MARCH

(Aug. 31–Sept. 21) The Toronto Portage

The drama of Sand Banks had made an impression on a voyageur who wasn't even there. Father Loran's back had kept him out of the canoe that day. He felt that he was a burden to the expedition and that perhaps it was time for him to go home. The rest of the crew of the St. Joseph—Fialko, Marr, and Sohn—wouldn't hear of it. They would carry him, if necessary. The loss of a priest would also compromise the authentic nature of a La Salle reenactment, and this was scarcely the time to find a replacement. With the other directors, Reid prevailed upon the priest to reconsider. Loran should go to a hospital in Toronto to check out his back problem, the adults told him.

The canoes would not reach Toronto for another ten days, and there would be another eleven days of portaging through the city before the canoes went back into the water. That gave the older man three weeks to rest before he had to make any real decisions about his participation. Reid hoped that the hiatus would be enough to bring Loran back into camp. At worst, he thought, the Franciscan could travel with the liaison team and rejoin the crew when he was able.

The terrifying hours around Wicked Point had been a rite of passage for all the expedition members, who now realized that their canoe training had not fully prepared them for the kinds of conditions they might face on the trip. They began to see another face of the trip, too, in the relative isolation along this coastline. Away from the fawning and gawking of cities and towns, the travelers drew their attention back to themselves. They drank water from the lake and prepared their own food. They developed efficiencies that gave them more time to consider their actions and each other. The sky cleared of city light and smoke. The stars popped.

After clearing downtown Toronto, voyageurs haul loads of a hundred pounds or more up and down the hills of Weston Road in the farm country north of the city as they head toward open water again.

On Aug. 31 good weather encouraged the voyageurs to paddle past their designated lunch site, frustrating the liaison team, which was supposed to meet them there. A retired schoolteacher living nearby drove Hobart and Reid for two and a half hours in a vain attempt to find them. Unfortunately, the van contained the crew's evening meal. Without provisions from the support team, the crew's cooks still made a stew, combining bacon and potatoes from the boats with produce the schoolteacher had given the men from his garden.

Camp was made on Baldhead Beach, six miles beyond Brighton. The site was part of a former shooting range for the Canadian military. Eight unexploded five-hundred-pound bombs still lay scattered around the property.

"Knowing you're sleeping on bombs makes it hard to get rest," Gross commented. "When we set up camp, we pounded our tent stakes very, very carefully."

The crew paddled through a misty bay the next day. The canoes moved like phantoms over the water, as if they were a dim memory of another time. At Presqu'ile in Brighton, the men were met by a small crowd. The liaison team was also there Sept. 1, but the brakes had locked on their green van, and it had to be taken in for repairs.

Over the next several days, the young men stretched themselves, traveling twenty-three miles to Cobourg on Sept. 2 and twenty more on Sept. 3 to New Castle, an unscheduled stop after Port Grady, which turned out to be a three-foot strip of sand and some houses you could count on one hand with fingers left over.

Lesieutre's parents came up to visit on a day of rest at Lakeview Park in New Castle. The vans were so full of equipment that Reid asked the voyageurs to take their personal effects from the vans and send them home with the Lesieutres. The vans had also filled up with gifts the crew had received from towns en route. Stillwagon was moving those to the Lesieutres' car when Ken walked up and announced a new policy: No one could get in the van without supervision from a liaison team member.

"Do you want a note from my mother?" Cox quipped, thinking that Ken was joking.

But it was no joke, and Stillwagon quickly gathered the other five men together to hash it out. Stillwagon may have felt that he was being whipsawed between Reid's directive to clear out the vans and Ken's "policy" requiring somebody else's permission to do the obvious. He said he was tired of being manipulated. Reid said that he could be La Salle and call the shots, and Stillwagon yelled that he was tired of the game-playing nonsense. After a quarter-hour of hollered profanity, the adults subsided into more mature discussion and realized that lack of communication was at the root of their problems.

In a post-trip interview, Reid admitted that he was short-tempered and emotional—byproducts of trying to operate an expedition by day and write fund-raising proposals by night. He said he should have explained the van situation more completely at the time.

"I think, in retrospect, that when you work with people, if you want to be effective . . . you put it in a way that people feel that they're being consulted," Reid said. The others said they recognized the pressures he was under and were eager to help when they could.

"I guess [Cox] and [Stillwagon] were really pissed at the decisions which were being made without any of their input," Braun wrote in his journal. "I guess they came out of the meeting feeling better."

Predictably, Fialko's journal was less judgmental, but it did specify the resolution: "Directors meeting tonight cleared up a couple of things. Mostly communication. More needed. Resolved that we spend more time explaining things to the crew."

Many months later, Reid praised Stillwagon, whose response to the difficulty he perceived led to the Saturday showdown. "One person I feel was a fantastic asset to the whole expedition was Dick. I could count on him implicitly. He was a very, very supportive person. I felt I could count on him, that he was a good leader. I've learned a lot from him, too, about suggesting things. He's less harsh than I am. He comes across as, 'This is the way I think it should be done, from my expertise.' See, that's one thing that I should have done in the beginning, and I think I lost some credibility from not doing that."

The morning after the showdown, Jan delivered checks to each director. Stillwagon had asked her about them earlier and said she became upset. The $4,200 payments ("Really $3,200 after taxes," Cox quipped) were partial compensation for the teachers who had lost paychecks to do the expedition. She said she'd had them for a week but that Reid had wanted to talk to the men before giving them out. Desperate for funding, Reid had asked the adult directors—the same day they had received their long-awaited checks—to contribute more than they already had. Stillwagon shared this urgent request—and his response to it—with his wife.

"I did hear today from Fr. Loran that all of the cash is gone & they don't know where more cash might be coming in," Stillwagon wrote on Sept. 7. "Oh, well, things will work out. That's Reid's problem anyway. He flew off the handle the other day & yelled at us about why didn't we put more money in the expedition & we weren't along just to have a good time. I told him that that was not how he had represented the expedition to me & I had no intention of putting another cent into it. He cooled off & I guess he's under pressure, but he just [has] to handle that himself. He's been better since his blowup, tho."

Reid approached the other adults with another situation that was becoming a problem. Although they had been gone less than a month, several of the boys were homesick. Directors believed that too many calls home were part of the problem. But not every problem could be read on the surface. Watts was very troubled and he had a reservation for a plane ride home, though he had told none of the adults.

"There was some homesickness, I'm sure, but there was a lot of frustration in the group," Watts recalled. "You could see a slight change in the command structure."

One night when he had a chance, he called home and shared his concerns with his father. Watts said he was done, and his father arranged plane fare for him to come home, but he also urged his son to sleep on it. A few days later they talked again. Mr. Watts reminded his son that he had made a commitment to the other guys and to the expedition, and he convinced him that he would always regret quitting. The plane ticket was never punched.

However, one of the directors overheard their conversation and shared the situation with the other adults. Reid thought it important enough to have another crew meeting to address the need for better communication, though no one ever confronted Watts about his concerns or his decision.

The mayor of Scarborough, a borough of Toronto, greeted the expedition dressed as Louis XIV on horseback. The crew could see Toronto's iconic CN Tower rising above a brown line of urban pollution that masked the lower levels of high-rise buildings. The Elgin boys paddled through sludge, scarcely believing that a few days earlier they were drinking water out of the same lake. Daytime temperatures still neared seventy degrees, and noses ended the day sunburned. But the overnight mercury readings were already in the low thirties.

Bardwell, who had been paddling for Father Loran, asked to paddle into Toronto, but the directors squelched that. Father Loran's canoe mates said they wanted him to be in a canoe for the paddle into the city, even if he couldn't stroke. It was still too early in the expedition for the boys to recognize either Bardwell's strengths or Father Loran's weaknesses. To his credit, Bardwell helped carry the load on the hard Toronto portage while Father Loran rested his back. Bardwell was downhearted, however, when he had to give up his seat again to Father Loran when the canoes slid back into the water for the paddle through Lake Simcoe and the Severn River toward Georgian Bay.

The expedition paddled thirteen miles or so from Scarborough to the city center on Sept. 8, pausing for two hours outside the landing point to have lunch. By chance, the beach they chose was the city's gay beach, an eye-opener for a bunch of relatively sheltered suburban kids. The adults attempted to have a team-building session there while waiting for the 2:00 p.m. arrival time downtown. The problems with homesickness and communications within the expedition were much on the minds of the adults, but lunch interrupted the flow.

Some of the boys simply walked off to discuss their problems in a clique. Among the Radical Five, it was the way they had always addressed their thoughts and feelings at home. It was more natural for them to rely on each other here than to share with a larger group, some of whom they did not trust. Already, the relationships the young men had brought with them had begun to affect the unity of the expedition.

The crew finally arrived at Ontario Place, an amusement park at the west end of the city waterfront, where they docked next to the World War II destroyer *Haida*. A "crowd" of about eight people met the crew, but Reid assured the crew that they were important people: representatives of the Ontario provincial government and the Toronto Historical Society. He had told the boys that they would get a shot of rum with the *Haida's* crew and that they would be served dinner. Neither of those things came to pass, and the travelers fixed their own chow. For the next two nights the men camped in historic Fort York surrounded by downtown Toronto. These would be their first nights indoors since leaving Montreal, and they would be their last for the next four months. The indoor accommodations left a lot to be desired, however, and some even chose to sleep outside. Once upon a time, each bed in the wooden blockhouse had held two soldiers in a frame six feet long by about four-and-a-half feet wide. The larger twentieth-century voyageurs could hardly consider these comfortable, but most of the crew would sleep soundly.

That night the crew shared beer and s'mores around the campfire with men who worked as guards and tour guides for the fort. They also sang ribald songs that seemed to offend Scavuzzo, who got up and left. The boys sang songs of their own, clean ones. Kulick marveled at how easily he participated in the singing, something he would never have done a year earlier, and attributed his new boldness to La Salle: Expedition II and its training.

The locals swore the fort was crowded with apparitions, and they told their guests ghost stories by the fire. Gradually, the boys slipped off to their tiny beds. In the middle of the night, Marr heard a banging on the bottom of his bunk. Convinced the guy below him was trying to play a trick on him, Marr whispered roughly for the voyageur to stop. Again, something banged against his bunk, and this time he barked his demand that it stop. Drowsily, the fellow in the bunk below answered, "Huh? Nobody's knocking on your bunk. Shut up and go back to sleep." Marr then picked up his gear and joined the voyageurs outside, the better to see any companion—or ghost—playing tricks on him.

He found an open space among the others, slipped into his sleeping bag, and relaxed. Shortly, however, he heard footsteps on a nearby gravel walkway. Quietly, he asked another voyageur if he heard the same noise. Immediately, the footsteps ceased. No one was there. It took a while to fall asleep that night.

The next morning, Thursday, Sept. 9, Kulick went through the courtyard to the restrooms on the other side of the fort. As he passed a set of stocks, he suddenly remembered that it was Wilson's eighteenth birthday. The Sieur d'Autray was about to have a rude awakening. Kulick laid his plans with Lieberman as soon as he returned to the blockhouse. They gathered a small mob of like-minded fellows around Wilson's bunk. Stillwagon slowly unsnapped the sleeping bag, rousing Wilson suddenly to the sight of about ten able-bodied conspirators. They marched him in his underwear out into the courtyard, singing "Happy Birthday" as they went. They put him in the stocks and enlisted the sergeant of the fort guard to lock him in. They wished their companion a happy birthday and said they might return later to let him watch them eat their breakfast. Too soon for them, the sergeant released Wilson a few minutes later.

At noon a bus took the voyageurs to the city hall in Nathan Phillips Square, where derelicts hung out. One of them told Wilson that he was the mayor of Ireland. Another wanted to borrow John Fialko's musket to shoot his grandmother. Afterward, while waiting for the bus, Kulick and Lieberman took a stroll around the block and attracted stares from residents, some of whom stopped the pair to ask them about their odd dress. During their time off, some of the crew tied two moccasins together for a football to use in an impromptu game. John had played for his high school team and missed the sport especially.

Except for an evening performance at the fort, the rest of the day was spent preparing for the portage. It had been a day and a half since the men had seen their watercraft. The canoes had no rudders of their own and little more than a suggestion of a keel, but they had given the entire crew purpose and direction for a month, and the men missed them.

That afternoon, however, a bigger problem loomed. Stunningly, no campsites had been secured for the portage anywhere in the city, and none of the parks they would visit had restrooms or running water, a fact Hobart and Cox had reported to Reid when they came back from the city. Reid apparently thought that Hobart and Cox had made reservations for space when they had scouted the portage route earlier that year. Jan and Scavuzzo, taking their cue from Reid's understanding, had done nothing to arrange campsites. The misunderstanding led to a stormy argument that the majority witnessed and everyone knew about. There was a lot of yelling. Finally, Jan and Scavuzzo got in their car and drove away. An exhausting eleven-day trek across the narrow neck of Ontario lay ahead.

Palmer and Baumgartner turned to the men and asked them how far they could move their loads before they needed a rest, how many trips they would need to move all their baggage, and how far they hoped to go in one day. Hobart and Cox had traveled the portage together earlier and knew what their targets were. They gave the girls' questions some thought and estimated that each man could carry a heavy load half a mile before he needed to rest. Then he would have to go back to the original location and pick up another load and carry it the half mile. The men would have to do that as many as three times before they moved all the canoes and equipment the half mile. Then they estimated that they might be able to do that perhaps as many as six times in a day, or three miles altogether.

Baumgartner and Palmer took the estimates as a mandate. They climbed into a van and started driving. Half a mile along the predetermined route they stopped, got out of the van, and started knocking on doors.

"Hi, my name's Cathy Palmer (or Sharon Baumgartner), and I'm with La Salle: Expedition II," the speech went. "Have you heard of us? We're reenacting Cavelier Sieur de La Salle's journey from Montreal to the Gulf of Mexico. We're also doing it authentically, so we're portaging through Toronto from Lake Ontario to Lake Simcoe, then on to the Severn River and into Georgian Bay. We need a place for the men to drop their canoes and their equipment and rest before retracing their steps and picking up another load. Can we use your yard as a stop along the way? May we use your bathrooms?" The girls showed newspaper clippings to validate their claims, begging for help in a leap-frogging trek through Canada's biggest city.

While the girls were doing this, Jan had begun to seek answers at the city level. Someone gave her the name of a person who might be able to help with campgrounds and security. She asked Hobart if he would go with her to meet the officer because some of the questions put to her over the phone were beyond her knowledge. Unfortunately, she didn't call to set up the meeting until 4:00 p.m. on Thursday, by which time the officer had left the station.

"Well, I wish somebody had told us this before," Reid said that night in regard to the lack of preparations. To Hobart and Cox, the comment seemed aimed at them. When they had returned to Elgin from scouting the portage route, they said, they had clearly told Reid that they had not secured campsites but only suggested places where they thought the group could stay. The job of reserving space belonged to the liaison directors, they thought. On Friday, Sept. 11, the morning the portage was to begin, Jan and Scavuzzo were still working out an itinerary for the lads. Officials in Toronto had approved none of it. The indecision about where to stay that night delayed the start of the march until 3:00 that afternoon.

The route that Cox and Hobart had mapped out included likely locations to bivouac each night. Most were large parks three miles away from the previous spot. Baumgartner and Palmer mapped out the rest stops in between. The crewmen called each half-mile segment a "*pose*," or placement, of their belongings. Every day, Palmer walked the first pose with the voyageurs to show the way to the first stop and Baumgartner would begin preparing lunch items. The rest was merely the grueling task of carrying heavy loads over and over and over until camp could be set up, tents pitched, and fires started. The girls, so close to the action of the portage, bonded with the crew during their mutual crawl through metro Toronto.

Finally, the crew began its portage, marching two and a half miles to Etienne Brule Park. A voyageur carried his share of a heavy canoe or more than one hundred pounds of gear for the pose, dropped his cargo and rested before walking back to the start and doing it all over again. Every pose required five separate trips, including three bearing a full load. Instead of walking 35 map miles in their 11-day portage, many of the guys each trudged up to 175 miles. In this way, the crew crossed the metropolitan area from one navigable body of water to another.

"The ropes hadn't stretched yet," Marr said. "They rode down so far on the back, and my back really hurt." Even though he knew that photographers were snapping pictures of the voyageurs as they started their long portage, he said, "I told myself I just can't do this." He finally dropped his load to shift the weight. He dropped it so awkwardly that it gave some observers the mistaken belief that he had simply collapsed under the packs he carried.

But he wasn't alone, and one by one the men all shifted their bundles higher and more securely. The men used tumplines to carry their gear. The five-inch-wide leather straps stretched across the forehead and attached to the packs with a rope. The connections put the loads high on the back and distributed the weight to the head, neck and shoulders.

Not only did loads have to be balanced, but so did the heights of voyageurs carrying canoes. It took a while before it occurred to the fellows that two people could carry a canoe more easily than three, because the third guy threw the balance off. The portagers trudged like a line of baby elephants along the streets and sidewalks. They moved ponderously under their loads, stepping slowly and leaning forward, swaying slightly and looking down at the heels of the man ahead. There was nothing romantic about the work. It was drudgery, and long days of it ground the men down. No Dr. Scholl's pads cushioned the footfalls of thin-soled moccasins hitting the pavement, many hundreds of steps every hour, several thousands of steps every day.

In fact, many of the guys went barefoot at first to save their moccasins, which were not designed for concrete pavement and asphalt roads. Arches ached constantly. When blisters began to develop, the fellows put the moccasins back on, but the attempt to save their feet was largely in vain. Only John went the entire distance without putting on moccasins, admitting that he had been too lazy to make the eleven pairs each crewman was supposed to make and meant to conserve the few he did make.

With heads down, it was not surprising that someone missed a turn and found himself alone on a Toronto street. John Fialko got lost the first day, drifting at least a couple of blocks away from the portage route and walking perhaps a mile out of his way. Hobart had said to go on Old Mill Road but had meant Old Mill Drive. When John raised his eyes and looked around for other voyageurs, he realized that he was alone. Eventually, someone from the Quebec embassy picked him up. Typical of John, he never complained about the extra distance he had to walk or the freight he had to carry. For him, it all went with the territory.

"Anyone who says they like portaging is either a liar or crazy," said Bill Mason, the noted Canadian naturalist. "Portaging is like hitting yourself on the head with a hammer: It feels so good when you stop."

The portage gave the young men a physical test beyond any they had attempted before. But the portage was also one of many psychological tests the guys also had to face on their journey. The number of poses each traveler walked and the relative weight that each man carried sometimes led to cross words between companions or unspoken but simmering resentment. Despite their psychological exercises and the warnings of their trainers, the voyageurs were even less prepared for the mental strain than they were the physical.

Watts didn't feel resentment. He felt guilt. He suffered from a congenital condition that produced varicose veins. The valves in his veins failed to pump blood as they should, and he had to undergo a procedure called vascular vein stripping. Following medical advice, he wrapped his legs to move blood more efficiently out of his legs. The bandages were wrapped tightly at the ankles and more loosely as the bandages wound higher. During the portages his legs ached more acutely than they would have had he been healthy. After the first pose, Watts dropped his load and guarded the canoes and baggage as his mates went back for a second and, often, a third load. His contribution was valuable, but it was easy to feel useless.

"I felt I wasn't helping anyone here," he said.

People who had watched the crew struggle through town all day stopped by with gifts of apples, coffee, and hot chocolate. Despite this bounty, the first dinner the weary travelers had on the portage that night was pea soup and hot dogs. The first night, Palmer and Baumgartner actually pitched their tent near the three voyageur shelters, one for each module. Citizens who visited the encampment saw the girls living in a tent so near to the boys and asked, "Do your mothers know you're traveling with all these young men?" While the girls said they did, the parents of Toronto refused to let that go and insisted that the girls spend the night in warm beds in their homes.

The girls surrendered to the siren song of modern comforts and let authenticity be damned. In doing so, they helped to create a network of sympathizers who phoned each other and spread the word that these Americans were carrying the torch for their own history, the history of Canada. The girls never had to sleep in a tent in Toronto again, and the boys received a hero's welcome wherever they went.

The people of Toronto stepped up big time. Not only did the people allow the expedition to camp in their yards and use their bathrooms, but they also cooked and baked for them, fetched all manner of refreshments to fill their stomachs, ease their aching feet, and otherwise welcome them. In one suburb the crew portaged past a fence where a man was visible only above the bridge of his nose. He spoke to them in a heavy Sicilian accent. As the men tried to explain what they were doing, a small pair of hands grasped the top edge of the fence. Once the travelers explained their mission, one of the hands disappeared for a moment, then it popped back up holding out a ripe tomato. In another town, a small boy said he didn't have enough money to buy doughnuts for everyone, but he could offer each voyageur one-third of a doughnut.

These American voyageurs were their heritage, their history come to life, and they took in these visitors as one hopes Americans would have welcomed Canadians reenacting wagon trains up the Oregon Trail. The morning of the second day, a representative from the Quebec government came by and asked what kind of foods the crew needed. He later brought candy bars, cheese, two cases of beer, a case of Cokes, and oatmeal.

A seventeenth-century voyageur parade through a heavily urban area naturally attracted attention. The *Toronto Star* ran a two-page spread on the visitors from another era. Every day, it seemed, a photographer from one news outlet or another snapped photos or ran video as the men snaked their way north across the city. If notoriety equaled fame, the Elgin contingent had found it. Man and boy, they began to think themselves famous, their Andy Warhol fifteen minutes drawing out for months to come.

The second day, a Saturday, the portage continued up Jane Street, one of Toronto's busiest thoroughfares. "Hey, did you guys miss the twentieth century?" one passerby called out.

The crew camped the second night in Smythe Park in the borough of York, still without permission and again without water or restrooms. Lieberman's dad and brother showed up with "care packages" from home, so much that his boat mates shared the treasure with the rest of the crew.

Lesieutre wrote his girlfriend, Annie: "We end up walking about 10 hours; when we get in, everyone is so tired. We eat & hit the hay. The people we meet are just great; following us around—'Can we carry something?'—giving us water and lemonade and food items. You get pretty tired of pea &/or bean soup. Homesickness has set in; not homesickness, but you-sickness. I just wander around late at night—playing my harmonica and thinking of you . . . All I meet are strangers and these 22 other guys—day in and day out. They're not encouraging—'At U of I? She'll find someone else,' etc."

After two relatively short hauls the first two days, the portage on Sunday the 13th was four and a half miles long, some of it uphill. The long day concluded only after dark around 9:15 in Strathburn Park. A man named Gordon Kerr saw a segment on the expedition on television and donated a McDonald's fast food meal, a most welcome dinner for the weary travelers.

"That's 27 miles of walking! & it took us 11½ hours to do it," Braun wrote. "It was a grueling day. That's the day when my feet and arches really went to hell. I could hardly walk without collapsing."

Another four miles took the voyageurs to Rowntree Mills Park. No one had suspected that Marr turned eighteen that day until everyone had bedded down for the night. Then Garcia called out, "Get up, everyone. It's [Marr's] birthday." The crew mercilessly dragged Marr out of his sleeping bag and tossed him, according to their custom.

The crew left Toronto itself on Tuesday, Sept. 15, marching three and a half miles by 8:00 p.m. to Fundale Park in Woodbridge. It was literally a day of ups and downs. Bardwell wrote, "Got off the main highway today. Went down and up a hill and valley which we almost needed ropes to handle, and I did it with a double load and nearly killed myself."

Daily, it seemed, the liaison women made a mountain of peanut butter sandwiches, but more was always needed. On the 14th the voyageurs had waited forty-five minutes at their appointed lunch stop while the liaison team went to buy three loaves of bread, but the buyers decided to do some extended shopping. The travelers were not pleased, and they complained again the next morning when the liaison team, which was late in bringing breakfast, brought only individual packets of oatmeal—a fraction of what the guys normally ate. Together it didn't fill the bowl and scarcely provided enough fuel to start walking the day's mileage. Men and boys whose caloric requirements were so high knew only that they were not getting what they needed. As tempers frayed among the crew, the liaison team became an easy target for their anger.

The crew performed Tuesday night at the Boyd Conservation Center, where schoolchildren come for a week of outdoor education workshops. The nature center had a profound impact on Palmer, who began at that time to dream of a post-expedition future working at such an educational center, perhaps in the States.

A light but steady rain trailed the crew to the Humber Trails Conservation Area. The boys looked like wraiths from another world, wearing ponchos as they trudged through the mist. They began to see markers for the Toronto Carry Place, 1615–1793. This had been the very portage made by the voyageurs two and three centuries earlier. Rain had soaked the wood available for kindling at dinner time, which was delayed. Then it rained all night.

Every night the crew dropped in their tracks from exhaustion. Carry, rest, carry, lunch, carry, rest, carry, drop—the pattern was the same day after day. At night, only the need to start a fire, raise a shelter, and eat kept their muscles moving.

While spending time with the boys during the day, Baumgartner checked in with Jan and Scavuzzo throughout the portage. The two women stayed in a hotel near the waterfront, keeping an eye on Father Loran, whose painful back kept him in the *Haida's* sick bay during the entire portage. At the end of the trip, the expedition had moved into the countryside and stayed on the grounds of grand homes, even mansions. At this point Jan and Scavuzzo emerged from the city and sought lodgings in those homes. Palmer said that this embarrassed the girls, who had been grateful for the charity of strangers, people they did not intend to impose on further.

The expedition camped in the front yard of retired contractor Harold Groves on Sept. 18. He had a pool and one of the largest collections of Indian paintings and artifacts in Canada. Fred and Meryl Leslie, a couple whom the crew had met in Brighton and who had followed the voyageurs nearly every day since then, made the boys a spaghetti dinner that night, and the crew celebrated Fredenburg's nineteenth birthday.

Fred Leslie was a glass blower at the University of Toronto who had let Bardwell store all the expedition gear from his van at their house. Their sixteen-year-old daughter said they were trying to save enough money to meet the expedition in New Orleans. It was rare to see anyone twice during the expedition, so the Leslies stood out in the minds of all the voyageurs. The mayor of King Township followed up their dinner with homemade apple pie and a case of cold beer. In a little more than a month the fellows had received a bottle of brandy, ten or so bottles of wine, maybe a dozen cases of beer, and a couple of cases of soft drinks.

The movable feast careened over rolling hills and gravel roads past split-rail fences to the backyard of Bob Pittendreigh's Twin Acres, where the crew took a rain day—and showers. The mayor of King Township baked for the crew both days—muffins and apple pies—and in a refrain that would become all too common during the long journey to the Gulf, said she was sorry that she and her staff did not have more notice of their arrival. The portage finally ended at the north branch of the Holland River Canal on Sept. 21 at Duval's onion and carrot farm.

The kindness of the people they met humbled the voyageurs. Canadians had let the crew camp on their lawns, drive stakes and dig fire pits, and generally make themselves at home. Then they cooked and baked and served their visitors: homemade soup, banana bread, chili, pies, cakes, coffee, beer, hot chocolate, tea, and cookies. The people of Ontario had reconstructions, facsimiles of forts and missions of long ago. But they had nothing like the living past moving among them, and they responded hungrily to this reminder of who they had been, of who, at bottom, they believed themselves to be. Canadians were a rugged people who had tamed the land, fiercely independent of mind and generous of spirit. La Salle: Expedition II was a museum's wax tableau come to life, stepping out of a glass-encased exhibit and calling on its audience to take part in the hearty, challenging life of the voyageur. No admission fee had been asked but the pleasure of their company.

The final push to the Holland Canal was accompanied by a brief rain shower, then a shimmering double rainbow before a violent icy downpour. On the last day of the portage, Fialko came up lame, slipping on a wet hill and dropping a canoe on his foot. A Toronto doctor diagnosed inflammation but no break. Foot problems plagued the entire group. Blisters were common. Bunions had formed. Arches had crumbled like ancient ruins, but in days, not centuries. Foster had gone through half of his moccasins by the end of the march, but the long, rough haul had cost everybody some portion of footwear. To fill holes or shore up soles to support aching arches, the boys had become great scavengers. Some used carpet remnants or bits of cardboard, but fistfuls of grass provided a softness underfoot that worked better than anything else.

There were casualties of other types. Father Loran joined the crew Sunday and said mass, then left the following day, unable to shoulder the loads of the portage. Foster picked up body lice. Wilson's feet were cracked and blistered. Cox fought plantar fasciitis in his flat feet. Surprisingly, the barefoot DiFulvio's feet didn't betray him, but he came down with flu just before the end of the portage. He also had an allergic reaction to something that resulted in a rash on his side.

Ironically, the suffering that infused the expedition had bestowed upon it legitimacy that paddling up the St. Lawrence had not. Dean reported that the Chicago papers had become much more interested in the voyage after the Toronto portage. The genuine nature of the trip and the willingness of the boys to trudge miles and miles through pain had lent them a new credibility, as if the coverage over the previous two years had merely been an indulgent nod to a quixotic notion.

For more than a generation, the Toronto portage was remembered by those who walked it as one of the hardest parts of the journey. At least the worst was over, they thought at the time. Except for a few miles between the St. Joseph and Kankakee rivers, the rest of the trip was on water. They could return to the romantic life of the voyageur, the relaxation of the campfire, and the beauty of nature. Before the Bicentennial year ended, however, weather would cruelly smash their expectations. Arctic conditions would frost their vision, and the men of La Salle: Expedition II would have hundreds more miles of hiking ahead of them.

SO LONG TO CIVILIZATION

(Sept. 22–29) To Sainte-Marie among the Hurons

The crew had looked forward to the serenity of Georgian Bay. It was the leg of the voyage believed to be most like the primitive world shared by the Native Americans and the fur traders of La Salle's Canada. Few towns lined the north shore. Ironically, it was the crowd around them that kept the crew from leaving Duval's before eleven o'clock on the morning of Sept. 22. The canoes made good time despite the rain, paddling down the narrow canal for two hours before reaching the Bradford marina for lunch. Wind, rain, and temperatures in the low thirties made it one of the colder lunches the travelers had eaten in a while.

There would be no more than three rendezvous with the expedition for resupply in Georgian Bay, so the liaison team planned early for what the crew would need. In late July they contacted Marty Garafolo, an independent grocer in Chicago's southern suburbs. Stillwagon and Cox's wife, Pam, drew up a list of goods the guys would need to sustain themselves away from civilization for several weeks. It included 50 pounds each of salt, lard, and onions; 100 pounds of sweet potatoes; 200 pounds each of dried corn, dried peas, dried fruit, and wheat flour; 250 pounds of corn meal; 400 pounds of dried beans; 2 pounds of bullion; 50 gallons of maple syrup; and enough powder to mix 100 gallons each of Tang orange drink (no, not exactly authentic voyageur fare) and hot chocolate, and 120 gallons of milk. Except for the corn, Marty was able to obtain everything for $600.

The canoes paddle past Sainte-Marie among the Hurons, a replica of the wilderness fort that sheltered a quarter of the population of New France in the days of La Salle. The center for historical education gives the people of Canada a window on their voyageur heritage.

The expedition took five days to travel from the vegetable farm on the Holland Canal to Port Severn on Georgian Bay. The canoes traveled down the north branch of the canal and moved through cattails and marsh grass into Cooks Bay on Lake Simcoe, called Lake Toronto in an earlier century. Twenty-seven miles after they began, the voyageurs made camp at the end of the first day in the front yard of a summer cottage owned by Gordon Kern. The cottage was closed. The night was especially chilly and rainy. Only after the wind died down did the crew make a run for it the next day. A violent rainstorm caught the paddlers midway across the bay, but the sun was shining by the time they made Big Bay Point on Kempenfelt Bay, seven miles from Barrie. The wind blew up to thirty miles per hour.

Wind-bound there Sept. 23, the boys saw Kempenfelt Bay as an ocean in squall, with wall-to-wall whitecaps and a howling wind. Busses took the voyageurs into Barrie. A crowd of five hundred was ready for them, and TV and radio stations had reporters and equipment to record the moment. Campbell dressed himself up with odds and ends for the occasion, putting on two sashes, adding a tail on his pouches and a feather in his cap. Cox, who noticed that there were also several pieces of wool sewn onto Campbell's outfit to hold it all together, commented that he looked as though he'd picked up roadkill along the way. The observation became a nickname that stuck. Several days later in a mock ceremony, Dean knighted Campbell with a dead fish and dubbed him "Road Kill."

The next day the canoes were ahead of schedule when they were held up just before entering Orillia. Reid met with the crew to tell them that their relations with the liaison team were so bad that Jan and Scavuzzo were talking about going home. The two women had tired of what they heard as constant criticism without a single word of praise for their contributions to the voyage. Reid said that there could be no expedition without the liaison team. Whether the crew saw the women as sensitive or emotional was beside the point, Reid told the guys. The crew would have to learn to live with their moods. The crew clearly indicated that they shouldn't be expected to walk on eggshells to avoid hurting feelings. But the difficult relationship continued in Orillia.

The liaison team had not provided firewood, Cox reported in his journal, and did not know where to find any. A city official told Reid that residents would have prepared a meal for the guys but the liaison team told them—apparently without checking—that the voyageurs would rather fix their own. Before leaving a hockey rink where the guys were able to shower, Stillwagon also learned that their dinner that night would not have any meat because the liaison team had decided on its own that the group had had plenty the night before. Chastised by Stillwagon, the women took off to get meat—inadvertently taking the group's guitar with them. This delayed the voyageurs' performance at the band shell. But when the liaison team returned to camp, the guitar was not in the van. After the show, Stillwagon talked to a man who'd written articles on hypothermia. He asked Palmer for the tape recorder so that he could interview the fellow. She went to get it but came back with empty hands. Someone had forgotten to pack it.

"It's so ironic that the day we have our meeting about helping the L team, they can fuck up so badly," Braun said in his journal. Despite all that, a restaurant owner had seen the voyageurs and offered the guys a dinner at his Ossawippi Express Dining Cars after ten that night—steaks and potatoes, mushrooms and carrots, and dessert.

On Saturday, Sept. 25, the expedition left Lake Couchiching and entered Sparrow Lake. Ten miles into this leg, the group entered the Trent Canal. The landscape altered along the canal. No cottages appeared. No trash littered the shore to reveal the carelessness of civilized man. The seasons had begun to shift during the Toronto portage. Now all along the rocky cliffs above the Severn River trees exploded in a splash of yellow, orange, and bright red. Dean boarded a canoe to take photographs on the twenty-six-mile stretch and got a real taste for the life of a voyageur. His shoulder and back were really hurting by the end of the day, but he enjoyed the experience.

"I preferred so much to be out there [on the water]," he said. "I went into the canoes anytime I could. I preferred to throw a bag in the snow or sleep in the shelter to sleeping in a motel." Whether to take photos or to take the place of a sick voyageur, Dean frequently became as much a member of the crew as he was a member of the liaison team. He must have felt like a traveler between two worlds, because a chasm had developed between the teams.

The crew "thought we weren't doing our job," Baumgartner wrote her family in a long letter on Sept. 25. "In fact, it grew to the point where crew members made snide & sarcastic remarks about Jan and Marlena both to their faces & behind their backs. . . . I've finally gotten to know Jan and Marlena & love them both dearly. I saw all the paperwork they had to contend with and helped them by doing what I could. Eventually, as I spent more time with them, I could feel tenseness toward me from the guys, kind of a distrustfulness—very frustrating. So while Cathy was praised (they could SEE what she did all day), we were cut down because of our absence. I finally got infuriated with Clif [Wilson] & John

[DiFulvio] and had a nice long 'discussion' on what the liaison team function was. Not long afterwards, John got sick and had to be with us. In 3 days' time, he changed his tune and promises never to badmouth us again."

While individuals were sometimes able to walk a mile in the shoes of the liaison team, snide remarks remained a staple of conversation throughout the journey, spiking every time the liaison team couldn't meet the crew, drove off unwittingly with equipment the crew considered important, failed to double-check advance arrangements with local officials, or failed through oversight or inadequate funds to provide for crew food requirements. Sometimes the criticism was warranted. Sometimes it was not. The L team's frequent absence from campsites came at the cost of face time that might have helped the relationship with the men and boys, and not only from a public relations point of view. Right up to the launch in Montreal, Lieberman and Baumgartner had been dating.

"I haven't seen much of Marc lately, as I've been busy elsewhere, and we've resorted to a quick wink once in awhile," Baumgartner told her parents. "Not what you'd call your basic boyfriend/girlfriend relationship, but we keep smiling!"

While the support team was able to stay in hotels in the big cities and motels in smaller communities, their accommodations were sometimes almost as Spartan as the crew's. Along the Severn River, the team spent three nights on the second floor of an old farmhouse. It had a solitary light bulb, three broken windows, and no heat. Downstairs, the house featured broken furniture, a burned-out stove, and a hole that offered a quick drop in the dark through the floor and into the basement.

Sometimes just getting to such rustic rooms proved hard enough. One night Palmer accepted an invitation to stay with a local family overnight. When she left with them, she didn't realize that she'd taken with her the only keys to the van, which was ninety minutes away from Baumgartner's lodging for the night. Baumgartner had to persuade Reid and Gross to hotwire the van. The procedure, however, left the heater, defroster, and windshield wipers unavailable for use, so Baumgartner had to wipe the condensation off the windshield from time to time. Whatever lodging the liaison team had, however, must have seemed like a palace to Father Loran. After spending twelve days on the *Haida* in Toronto during the portage, he had tried paddling again and spent just one day in the canoe before seeking sanctuary again with the support team.

"Father Loran was in the canoes 1 day . . . and is back with us, poor man," wrote Baumgartner. "He told me if it happens much more he's leaving for good. Although I hope he doesn't, he's gotten soft and pampered—always a beer in one hand, a cigarette in the other."

The travelers moved under a railroad bridge in a fog on Monday the 27th, and into the eastern reaches of Georgian Bay. They fired muskets as they passed. In a rarity, all of them discharged successfully.

The crew's next stop was Sainte-Marie among the Hurons, a modern re-creation of the historic Jesuit mission, where they were met by Jesuit priests from the Martyrs' Shrine. In 1648 the wooden fort was home to sixty-six Frenchmen, one-fifth of the European population of New France. The following year it was burned and abandoned in the face of mounting attacks by the warlike Iroquois. The mission fort serves as a history classroom for Canadian schoolchildren to experience the life of priests, Indians, and voyageurs alike. In 1976 the mission preserved the authenticity of the experience by forgoing electricity. After Doug Cole, the director, gave them a tour of the grounds, the Elgin contingent gathered in the Indian chapel, where Father Loran and a local priest conducted mass. Then the voyageurs warmed themselves at a hearth in the Upright, or Pillared, Building within the stockade and dined by candlelight.

Stillwagon took the opportunity to write Rowena, thanking her for the wool pants he had received and remembering each of their children—Jeff's hopes to join crew at Purdue, Andy's stepping up to take responsibility at home and at school, Diana's interests in diving and gymnastics, and Anissa's concerns with scouting. "Tell Anissa I enjoyed her letter very much & that I hope she sells a lot of Brownie cookies. Tell her it's OK to wear her uniform to school, that everyone else in her class will want to wear one then, too!" he wrote. Stillwagon also kept his eye on fund-raising efforts for La Salle II, suggesting contact with local libraries to run a La Salle week or with schools to have a La Salle poster week.

After dinner the Americans gave a show for three hundred people in the lobby of the mission. They were thanked by a standing ovation. When the crowd dwindled to a scant number, Hess and Campbell joined the Radical Five in conversation at a little fire they built in a bark-covered tepee in the Indian village at one end of the mission.

The twentieth century seemed far away from the mission fort, but the expedition problems remained close by. Hobart and Cox turned aside at the museum to talk with Dean. The young journalist had become involved in the expedition on a personal level. His articles and photos of the La Salle: Expedition II had been used by newspapers across the country and boosted the voyage's profile and credibility. Without Bob Osborn to film the trip as he had the Tri-centennial voyage, Dean's pictures had become the true visual chronicle of the Bicentennial paddle. However, Dean was broke and his bills were piling up. At the same time, Northwestern University was holding up his master's degree until he made good on his unpaid school bills. Dean had shown increasing disaffection with the Lewis brothers. Rather than provide cash for photo expenses, Reid had criticized the quality of Dean's photos, he said. Hobart and Cox feared that a valuable part of the expedition would be lost, and they encouraged Dean to remain with the expedition.

On Tuesday, Sept. 28, the group took a van and two cars to the first of three elementary schools for presentations. The youngsters loved to join in, singing, "Oui, oui, oui! Non, non, non!" in the chorus of the drinking song, "*Chevaliers de la Table Ronde.*" Their shouts provided a wall of high-pitched noise, followed by the strong male punch line, *Goûtons voir si le vin est bon*: "Let's taste to see if the wine is good." And so it went joyfully on through seven stanzas, the children's thunderous chorus reaching a crescendo. That evening the voyageurs performed for about two hundred people at the entrance to the mission museum. They received a scroll that welcomed the Americans into the wilderness. Phone calls had come in all day from people hoping to get the travelers to perform, and they were told they could be booked solid if they stayed the week.

After-dinner conversation turned serious, as the Brauns brought Reid questions that had emerged at the parents' meeting at the Wilsons' home back in Elgin. The parents wanted to know the financial situation. Perry Lewis said the expedition had $10,000 in cash, and that it cost $5,000 a month to sustain operations. The fact that others were questioning his financial stewardship bothered Reid, and he expressed frustration that people didn't trust him. He wondered aloud if they wanted him to borrow even more money.

The Brauns said the parents had set up a committee in Elgin to raise $20,000. Among the families on the committee were the Wilsons, Brauns, Lesieutres, and DiFulvios. U-46 Superintendent Paul Lawrence was a cochair of the committee, and members of the school board kicked into the kitty being collected. The Elgin Junior Women's Club was also taking part in the effort. The parent meeting also touched on tall tales from the Elgin rumor mill.

"We are not behind & everyone is OK," Campbell wrote home in a Sept. 30 postcard. "Please let people know this!"

The liaison team had other problems. The van was to have been picked up from the body shop. But Jan called to tell Reid that the insurance adjuster had still not arrived, so nothing had been done to repair the van.

During a wind-bound day of rest at the mission, guides brought school groups over to watch the voyageurs darn socks, patch clothing, and repair equipment. The boys fielded questions expertly. Impressed by the Americans' knowledge of the voyageur experience, Cole said he would brave the hassle he knew he would get from government to give priority hiring to any of the boys who wanted to work at the mission the following summer. Bardwell was really interested. Cole also made dinner for his visitors that last night. Bill Parker, an Indian at Sainte-Marie, told the voyageurs that the place where they had crossed from Big Bay Point to Gall Park near Barrie was the exact spot the Hurons used to use. He said they left tobacco and other gifts on Gull Rock for the spirits that dwelled there. Part devil, the spirits could do either good or bad deeds, depending on how you treated them. Parker also said that the Gitchie Manitou, or god, lived on the Manitoulin Islands.

Superstition figured heavily in the seventeenth-century world, and not only for Native Americans. Less than a decade after La Salle's men reached the Gulf of Mexico, witch hunts ripped open the gullible community of Salem, Massachusetts. Like the Puritans, the French voyageurs were simple people. If the Indians told them that monsters lurked in the waters and woods along their route, the voyageurs believed them. If French gossip told them that their boss was dead or bankrupt, La Salle's men believed it. And they deserted him in droves.

Stillwagon, Fialko, and Ken returned from Toronto, where they checked on ground covers, mittens, heavy wool underwear, waist-high waders for the bow men, and rubber rain gear to protect legs. The consensus was to buy most of the gear, despite a lack of authenticity. Mr. Lewis would send the $1,100 or so needed for the liaison team to purchase it that week. The liaison team also rented a cottage in Perry Sound, two days' paddle away, where they planned to bring the boys' personal bags.

After dinner the guys met to discuss equipment and what to expect in Georgian Bay. An emphasis was placed on authenticity. They decided that no one could use a telephone. Only Hobart, Watts, and Fialko would see the maps. No one would know the time except Reid, who would keep track of it as an experiment to see how closely the crew could follow their fifty-minute paddle/ten-minute rest routine by feel. The crew also agreed to eat only two meals a day—a late breakfast and dinner at the end of the day. Books were allowed, but authenticity hounds like Ken were not pleased. Afterward Cole, who had an extensive background in group dynamics, told Stillwagon it was one of the finest sessions he'd ever seen, and wished his staff could have seen the crew at work. He also said he'd never heard a group attempting so true a re-creation and thought the group was correct to obtain some modern equipment. He called the expedition one of the finest groups he'd ever seen. He said that going back in time was a real joy. In wishing them luck, he gave the travelers four beaver skins and a large deer hide for an exploit robe.

Fredenburg's parents had sent him a skunk-skin hat to wear. He cut off the tail and affixed it to the back of his canoe. Somehow the skunk tail "flag" was apt for Fredenburg, who went by the French voyageur name Pierre You. His comrades loved shortening it to P.U.—a nickname that would have suited every one of the voyageurs on any given day of the journey.

THE WILDERNESS IN FALL

(Sept. 30–Oct. 22) Georgian Bay and Lake Huron

The expedition left the mission on the last day of September, paddling twenty miles to Split Rock Island. At one point a man from Cincinnati, Ohio, emerged from his cabin as they passed and waved a Bicentennial American flag. That night a spectacular sunset graced the campsite. Even after Cole's "fisherman's surprise" the night before, the guys accepted their pea soup and bannock bread as the price of the light show. As they ate, a half moon rose into a clear sky, and the stars raced into the darkness overhead. A sense of peace enveloped the shelters. Something new had come over the voyageurs—liberty. There were no spectators. Without them, the guys welcomed a release from social expectation.

The boys had been told that this would be the part of the journey most like the natural world through which La Salle's voyageurs themselves had traveled. But it was decidedly not the same universe of circumstances.

The voyageurs of the 1680s were a rough lot in a lawless world. They paddled and tramped many hundreds of miles from the narrow strand of hovels that passed for French civilization on the St. Lawrence. They lived among savage peoples who lived for war and used torture as entertainment. Many New World Frenchmen could neither read nor write, though they could speak native languages and dialects and sing French folk songs. They coupled with Indian women, drank and swore as they pleased, and generally lived each day as if it were their last—because it might have been.

Landing canoes in rough water outside Blind River on Georgian Bay takes all hands, (L–R), Steve Marr, Chuck Campbell, Gary Braun, Bob Kulick (behind), Clif Wilson, Mark Fredenburg, George Lesieutre (behind), Ken Lewis, and Rich Gross standing.

The voyageurs of the 1970s were suburban boys raised in a world of rules. They had rarely been far from civilization, even while camping. Their neighbors and teachers expected adolescent nonsense, perhaps, but never far outside the bounds of acceptable behavior. All of them could not only read and write, but they had a much more extensive library of entertainment after three centuries of invention. Their daily lives were not all about survival and self-gratification. Most of the lads had futures that involved college or skilled trades and a return to a complicated but comfortable world.

Did the young travelers of the twentieth century sit around the campfire asking themselves how the original voyageurs might have felt? Not exactly. They had studied the voyageurs for two years and continually told audiences about their lifestyle. Sure, these young men complained about their aches and pains of the day, sang songs, and tried to keep their moccasins dry. But they didn't worry, as the originals did, about taking an arrow at the next village on their itinerary. They didn't imagine how to set a trap for beaver or use a musket to bring down a deer.

In the quiet of the Canadian wilderness, the travelers' thoughts turned inward toward family, school, the past, the future, the widening gyre of the world and one's place in it. When the awesome questions overwhelmed them, the voyageurs turned to the fellowship of song or the solitary comfort of books. Among the favorites passed around were the novels of Joseph Wambaugh and Saul Bellow and the personal essays of Hunter S. Thompson. Others included *North Dallas Forty*, *I Heard the Owl Call My Name*, and *The Spandau Diaries* of Nazi war criminal Albert Speer.

The 1976 voyageurs quickly molded themselves to the 1681 lifestyle they had chosen.

The food they carried consisted of things that wouldn't spoil—flour, oatmeal, peas, and beans. By now the days of "crunchy" beans were behind them. The cooks had learned to soak the beans in cooking pots full of water during the day. Five and a half hours more brought them to Kilbear Provincial Park on Perry Sound, thirty-five miles along the coast from Sainte-Marie among the Hurons and a day ahead of schedule. Again, the multicolored foliage surrounded the travelers. Again, the moon and stars appeared in a crystal clear sky. As they had on Lake Ontario, the crew drank directly from the bay. In one place where their paddles finally lay quietly across their knees, the boys heard echoes, their last three words clearly bouncing back to them.

With no public appearances scheduled, no interviews to do, no performances to give, the paddling and the camping were everything. The fleet made excellent time and greater distances. Hobart's navigation suffered somewhat because the maps he used had not been updated since 1926. Georgian Bay contains tens of thousands of small islands. Many of those the enterprise encountered didn't appear on the maps, and large portions of the map were marked, "Not Explored."

"We have to set up camp on solid granite for about a month—the

Canadian Shield sticking up—that's all Georgian Bay is," Lesieutre wrote Annie on Oct. 1. The expedition was thirty miles north of Midland in Parry Sound. "We use rocks to set up instead of stakes! Granite is fun, fun, fun to sleep on. Actually, it's OK." He described the rapid advance of the canoes, as well. "Water conditions were near ideal. The 1st three hours we had following seas, and after brunch (for lack of a better name), we had zero wind. We go about 6½ mph on glass like that. It's really something to see. We've gotten quite a bit stronger from when we left; we're quite the men, aren't we? We ate Georgian Bay alive today, really cooked up the water!" New kinds of wildlife appeared along the shore, in the water, and at campsites. Small rattlesnakes seemed to slither around them with startling frequency. Once they saw a mink. The voyageurs spied at least three large beaver dams and a heron, and droppings showed the bears' diet included berries. For many it was the sight and sound of the loons that clung to their memory.

"Once you've heard the call of a loon, you'll never forget it," Cox wrote. "But once again words fail me when I try to describe the sound. It was both inviting, somewhat lonely, and very haunting. It was always interesting to see one bobbing up and down on the water. It was especially interesting to see them early in the morning or at dusk. Maybe that's why the call sounded so lonely to me, since we usually saw them alone. But it was very haunting when you heard their call but couldn't see them. It was almost like they were watching us."

The boys' personality quirks emerged in relief during the longer hours in camp. Paul Simon's "Fifty Ways to Leave Your Lover" had come out in 1975, and the rhyming pattern produced by such lyrics as "make a new plan, Stan" and "hop on the bus, Gus" had given Fredenburg's lexicon such phrases as "Stand back, Jack" and "Be cool, fool." Garcia served as cook for his module and had become very exacting about how things should be done. Tomato slices had to be the same size and arranged in a pattern. Salads couldn't be served before the dinner. And Foster came in for Garcia's ire once for "butchering" a potato. Gross liked to talk, and if no one was around, he'd talk to trees or rocks or himself. His response to things he liked was, "Wow!" His answer to things he didn't was, "*Bad merde.*"

The adults had their own odd characteristics. Confronted with a stormy morning, Ken would often head down to the beach and strike a pose. With his arms folded across his chest and one hand gently stroking his beard, he'd stare at the water for a long time before announcing, "I see a corridor."

Another quirk developed among the *milieu*. It had to do with their seating. Seats fore and aft were built into the canoes, but the guys in the middle sat on makeshift seats that were designed to look like fur bales. A square-bottomed bale did not sit motionless on the curved bottom of a canoe, and comfort was important to men trying to keep from falling over while stroking through sometimes difficult waters as many as 25,000 times a day. So *milieu* paddlers prepared their faux bales so they were just right. They collected little pieces of driftwood to shim up the bales for the right height and pitch. Losing these bits of driftwood sometimes became occasion for arguments. If they fell onto the beach and a companion unwittingly picked them up while gathering tinder and wood for the campfire, all hell could break loose.

"We made it through eight months with our personal space the distance between our shoulders," Ken said. "We got finicky about getting into a proper position." Balance was important and personal. "It could make the difference between an easy day and a miserable day. It seems supremely trivial, but at the same time it was critical. We learned to guard our pieces of driftwood with our lives."

When the crew stopped for lunch on Head Island on Oct. 3, Stillwagon took the time to write to Rowena and describe the majesty of the pristine land through which they traveled.

"The weather has been a miracle. Fr. [Loran] says it's because of St. John Brabeouf, Terry [Cox] says it's because of the Gitchee Manitou—take your pick. . . . This is beautiful country. I would say about 60% color change in the leaves & we hardly see a cottage anymore. Of course we've been drinking the H2O right from the lake for several days now. There is nothing to pitch our camp on but granite &

quartz & moss. It's surprising how comfortable a slab of stone is for sleeping. Last night I got up during the nite & could not believe how the stars looked. I've never seen a clearer sky."

Hess's mother, who had rented a motorboat, found the crew on Head Island, where a three-cabin resort stood out of sight from the water. The managers said that Champlain and La Salle themselves had been to the island. The excited hoteliers insisted that the crew sign the guest book.

When the enterprise passed the mouth of the French River, the travelers were reminded that the seventeenth-century voyageurs would take the Ottawa River to French River then follow the setting sun through Thunder Bay to points west. During the two years of training, Fialko had had a recurring dream of Georgian Bay. In his dream, he was a seventeenth-century voyageur and the rocks, woods, and waters imprinted themselves on his mind.

"I had these déjà vu things to the extent of paddling through the rapids with a guy named Pierre, who was my bow man," Fialko said. "It was probably because we'd done so much research." One day in Georgian Bay, he was asked to take the lead. As he steered his canoe out from behind an island, he said, "I knew exactly where I was. This was the French River" as he had seen it in his dreams, right down to "The Chickens," a group of rocks in the water.

West of the French River the travelers paddled in rough water unprotected by land forms. A strong wind from the south made paddling difficult on Oct. 5–6, but sounds like a crashing sea rocked the travelers to sleep each night. Cold and wet, members of the expedition pitched their dwellings in front of Bert Duchesne's Mahzenazing River Lodge on the 6th. A building being torn down offered plenty of firewood, but Father Loran told Reid that night that he simply couldn't take the cold and was ready to go home. For others, the region was a piece of heaven. They camped in a lovely pine forest.

"No sign of humans ever being here," Lesieutre wrote Annie in a letter mailed a week later. "There's nothing like sneaking up to a flock of 400+ ducks and seeing and hearing them take off . . . or the woods or . . . it's so beautiful here . . . You've just got to see the autumn up here sometime. It's indescribably beautiful."

Gorse threw a line in the water to help supplement their diet. The crew had not seen the liaison group for days and the cooks were rationing, giving each voyageur a cup of pea soup for dinner. Gorse reeled in seven five-inch perch and a foot-long northern. That night the sky clouded over and the rain poured down more heavily than any of the crew had experienced on the trip.

The next morning Mrs. Duchesne brought the boys four large loaves of bread, three jars of apple jelly, and a bag of cookies for breakfast, all of it homemade. Rain had slacked off and the water was calm. When the canoes emerged from the granite bluffs of the Voyageur Channel, the Killarney Mountains appeared on their right, the first mountains Gorse had ever seen. They appeared to be capped by snow. What the boys thought was snow, however, turned out to be sunlight glinting off quartz.

A northerly wind caught the crew suddenly that afternoon, and unprotected hands rapidly turned very cold. But the liaison team caught up with them that night. Between the rain the night before and the cold winds that afternoon, the team had worried greatly about the crew's safety. Scavuzzo, who could reasonably be expected to dislike the young men for their snide comments, talked of taking a plane up to look for them. Now everyone received rain pants and capote bags. Half the crew got diver's gloves, and three of the l'avants got hip-high waders. The rest of the gear was expected to arrive Oct. 15, when the red van was supposed to be ready to drive again. After the liaison team left, Hess picked up several splinters in his eye while chopping wood. Reid took him to a local clinic, which recommended that he be taken to the hospital in Sudbury. Fortunately, Reid was able to call Jan, who brought the green van back to pick up the patient. Together with other illnesses, Hess was hospitalized three times before he left Canada.

In other news that night, Reid told Stillwagon that his father, Mr. Lewis, had received a bill for $4,000. Mr. Lewis said that if he paid it, the expedition's corporation would be out of money. Father

Loran left camp to stay with the local Catholic priest. Father Loran was expected to leave the expedition at St. Ignace near the Straits of Mackinac. *The Canadian Readers Digest* (circulation eleven million) planned to fly a reporter up to see the crew in Blind River.

Gray clouds and a cold wind sent the crew on its way Friday, Oct. 8. In four hours they made it to Little Current on Manitoulin Island. Reid phoned the hospital from a local store to check on Hess. He'd had his eye patched and been told to rest. The store's owner, a Mr. Turner, invited the expedition to camp in his front yard. Turner had sailed on a ship in the Arctic, and was to be named Commodore of the Great Lakes Sailing Association on Dec. 14th in Chicago. Turner sent fresh pies and coffee to the camp that evening and warm muffins and coffee the next morning. At his home, the adults sat and talked downstairs while the teens were let into a room with a stereo, a refrigerator full of beer, and a television. The TV was left untouched. Instead, the boys drank and listened to music. Later several of the canoeists talked around the fire about school and teaching. Kulick said he thought he might want to become an elementary schoolteacher someday. When the chat ended around midnight, a full moon beamed down on Georgian Bay.

From Little Current, La Salle II traveled into the North Channel of Lake Huron. By now the crew was used to the cold, but Dean, traveling in Stillwagon's canoe, shivered for hours as they got under way. Strong winds and choppy seas increased his discomfort, and the canoes put in at privately held Schreiber Island, twenty-nine acres of rocky terrain. The owners, who arrived just minutes ahead of the voyageurs, had purchased the island and its eight buildings, formerly an Indian arts and crafts center, for $40,000 and planned to take out the water lines and electricity. The new owners had heard weather reports that overnight winds would reach fifty miles an hour. This raised the prospect of turning the canoes directly into the prevailing wind, a northwest gale, and trying to paddle across three miles of open water to reach the mainland.

The voyageurs' hands turned icy in the frigid Canadian wind the next day. Morning temperatures were scarcely above freezing.

Paddlers who had the thick diver's gloves discovered that they were too stiff for effective paddling and could not be managed more than a few minutes at a time. Lieberman described it to a friend.

"I can't believe how the weather changes at the drop of a hat out here," Lieberman wrote. "One day it is fifty degrees and warm, and the next it's freezing. We were hoping that the god of the area, Tichee Manitou [sic], would have a little compassion for a meek bunch of voyageurs who just want to get off his turf!"

When they stopped for breakfast, a pickup truck came roaring down a dirt road. Two Native Americans jumped out with rifles and demanded to know who the visitors were and explain what they were doing on their reservation. When the expedition was explained, one of the Indians smiled, said he'd heard about the band of voyageurs, and wished them luck. The Indians had not carried weapons to be threatening. They had simply been out hunting.

The canoes traveled twenty-four miles against the wind that day, but the crew made a mistake, waiting until an hour before sunset to begin looking for a campsite. When none could be found, the crew had to make do, landing at a spot where only one canoe at a time could come ashore. The site itself was little more than a beach covered in rocks. The shelters were still being set up and wood cut for the fire when darkness fell like a stone.

Dean continued to deal with the cold. With the milieu taking up the faux bales for seats in the canoe, he sat lower than others, but he wore jeans, not woolen pants, and his flannel shirt, if wet, offered little protection from the chill. Almost as soon as camp was set up, Dean would turn in. One morning the others found him huddled under a canoe as part of a shelter. He was covered in frost. When asked why he wasn't in one of the low-slung, tent-like shelters, he laughed.

"It's impossible to stay inside. You have no idea what it smells like in there," he answered. The sleeping bags had by then acquired a particularly pungent aroma. With beans a constant part of the voyageur diet, the resulting gas constantly pervaded the tent as well. Dean was apparently no stranger to emissions in the motel room, either. Father Loran, who often spent time as his roommate, had stomach problems, including ulcers.

In the camp shelters, the smell and the noise of the farting often came accompanied by a chorus of usually incoherent mumbles and shouts from men who talked in their sleep.

"When I was a boy," Watts said, "my parents would walk in while I was dead asleep. They'd ask me a question, and I would answer them as if I were awake. I never knew about it until they'd tell me later."

Once Ken woke without quite knowing what was real and what was a dream. The occasion came shortly after the crew had seen their first rattler. As guys awoke, Ken whispered that no one should make any sudden movement because he had a rattler crawling in his bag. It turned out that he'd worn all of his clothes to bed and was sweating profusely when he awoke. The snake turned out to be a coil of rope. He may have dreamed of a snake and wakened in a semi-panic.

En route to Blind River, Father Loran didn't paddle a stroke. At the meal break, he told Stillwagon he was through—just had no energy. He said it was all he could do to keep warm.

"I must say he was a pitiful-looking sight just sitting there so stoic, looking haggard and staring straight ahead," Cox wrote in his journal. "This last week has been a living hell for him. We'd do him more harm than good if we try to talk him into staying. He wasn't exactly living a lifestyle that prepared him for this—as if any of us were."

After lunch on the 10th, the canoes ran through three-foot waves that slugged them broadside. Progress was slow. Soon the three-foot waves became four- and five-foot swells that both scared and exhilarated the canoeists almost as much as the fury of Sand Banks and Wicked Point. Landing posed similar problems, too. The canoes surfed in, racing toward a small sandy beach surrounded by a rocky coast. Every canoe had at least a foot of water in it as it ran aground and pitched sideways. Everyone already ashore dragged each canoe in then turned around to assist the next one.

"It's often easy to be bored and complacent in the course of a good day, but a day like today you're locked and loaded and all systems are go," Cox observed in his journal. "You can feel your body come alive. You really feel like you're working to your full potential. . . . It's so damn easy to just sleepwalk through life, or a typical paddling day. Daydreaming is easy, and maybe even rewarding at times. But this . . . People probably thought I was nuts, but I felt so good I started yelling and screaming about how much I was loving it."

Ken, whose gung-ho attitude was by now well-known, surprised no one by asking Hobart why the canoes being thrown about were putting in. And having reached shore, he asked why the crew couldn't launch and head back out into the maelstrom.

The crew had developed a keen efficiency. Everyone knew his role, and the guys quickly went to work in modules as soon as the boats were safely ashore. In no time at all, three fires were started, three wood hawks were collecting wood, three tents were quickly pitched, and clothes and gear were hung to dry on lines. The wilderness clothes dryer required some tending, as gloves sometimes dropped into the flames and sparks could burn holes in shirts if people weren't careful.

The principal of the Blind River high school, enrollment seven hundred, came out to the campsite Monday night. It was Canadian Thanksgiving (Oct. 11). The school's bus picked the travelers up the next day and brought them in for a performance. After lunch the crew went to two social studies classrooms. Every voyageur was so well versed in the material that presentations went smoothly. There was no competition for attention, no grandstanding. However, at the second stop that day, a 9th grade class on Canadian history, a girl said she smelled the guys as they came in. The principal later suggested that the boys bathe. The water of Georgian Bay had been crystal clear, easily drinkable as it was. But it had been much too cold to induce anyone to bathe. The showers at Blind River were their first since Orillia, eighteen days earlier.

Stillwagon took the voyageurs down to the nurse's office for a weigh-in after their showers. Marr had lost forty-one pounds, and Cox, who was shorter than most, and wiry, had shed nearly ten since Quebec. On the other hand, Kulick now weighed 171 after packing on 15 pounds. Stillwagon said the crew split into roughly equal thirds—some had lost weight, some had gained, and others had stayed the same. But in all cases, there was more muscle.

Wilson and Watts had begun to notice something new going on in the group dynamics of the crew itself. Tempers were becoming shorter, they said. Away from the crowds who had followed them in the first part of their trip, the men had been living now with themselves alone. With fewer distractions, everyone's flaws, as every other man saw them, became sharply focused.

"Tempers were always flaring," Bardwell observed, "Hobart, Cox, and Stillwagon always wanting to stop and Reid and Ken always wanting to go on. Boy, those guys would go out in a tornado with a tidal wave to boot, but that's behind us and it is nothing but experiences to draw off of." The entire stretch from Blind River to St. Ignace irritated Bardwell, who also didn't care for cornmeal and insisted there was no way to cook beans to make them taste good.

Baumgartner, who began one of her long letters home on Oct. 10, finally finished it two days later. The Elgin rumors that had arrived at Sainte-Marie among the Hurons had disturbed her, and the chatter among crew members regarding Reid could only have added to her frustration. She had something to get off her chest.

"I've become close to Reid also and he confides things in me as well as Jan," she wrote. "I've heard about the hassles with some of the parents at the meetings. If anyone ever asks you if I've said anything or what you think on such a matter, I just want you to know how I feel. Reid Lewis is one of the most determined men I've met. He's not in the least underhanded about what he does. (He is <u>certainly</u> not mishandling money trying to be reimbursed for the J&M Expedition.) He is baffled and hurt, even frustrated at attitudes taken against him. He's all for teamwork & effort, and wants to say he did <u>everything</u> he could to make this expedition go. I stand behind him . . . I don't know how he stays personable doing not only the physical labor of paddling but having the mental strain of money constantly harassing him. Perhaps this will help you understand how I feel. I hope so . . ."

While the crew was in Georgian Bay, the liaison team had few opportunities to connect with them. The long absences made Baumgartner anxious and "a little touchy." While that was not an unusual feeling among both groups, she felt it much more keenly because of her relationship with Lieberman. Like other young women who have had earlier relationships come apart on them, Baumgartner wanted to take her time with this relationship, which she valued highly. Impulsive, like most young men, Lieberman only knew that he wanted her in his life. He did not see the shoals; he saw only calm waters and felt only a fair wind at his back.

"It was so strange to see Marc again," Baumgartner said. "Perhaps I'd lost a clear mental picture of him. Mom, I like him an awful lot. I'm not willing to say I 'love' him yet, 'cause I don't know what that is. I've been wrong once. I don't look forward to another mistake. Unfortunately, I still think a lot about Dave, something I'm trying to overcome. Marc is scaring me a little, making plans for college, plans for saving money, plans for where to live and priorities for us after we're 'married.' He says he prefers marriage only after he can support me with his income, probably another 5 years, certainly after college. That's fine because in that time we'll either grow closer or break apart. Again he upset me by saying (first thing after 6 days of absence), 'Let's get engaged.' I don't want things rushed, or any mistakes made."

Wednesday, Oct. 13 dawned in an eerie fog as the temperature rose into the fifties. Again the canoes faced into the wind, this time coming out of the west, and the waves drenched the l'avants immediately. The boats swung back into Blind River, where they stayed through the following day. The new campsite in a small park next to a hospital and elementary school attracted many visitors, some bearing gifts of food—venison, berries, pickles, milk, muffins, sweet rolls, cookies, and hot chocolate. One couple living nearby let the crew use their toilets.

Father Loran decided not to go home but instead to travel with the liaison team. He would be out of the canoes until Peoria or St. Louis, the crew was told. Father Loran became Dean's roommate when he was out of the canoes, which was often, and Dean always suspected the depth of Father Loran's devotion. One night when the good father had had a few drinks and was less guarded about his responses, he offered some insight into his past and how it had affected his present situation. Loran had been born into a large farming family in the Plains and spent his childhood during Dust Bowl and Depression days. The priesthood offered food, shelter, easy work, and lifelong security. He preferred the Franciscans, he told Dean, because the Jesuits had too many responsibilities and worked too hard. The padre's decision to quit the canoes did not sit well with other members of the liaison team.

"If Father's with us, it's like having a dead weight," Baumgartner said, echoing a refrain common to the canoeists. "He can't really *do* anything, and we can't fool around with him or tease him. I know that's terrible of me, yet it's sadly true. He's of no *real* use to us, and that's what he *doesn't* want."

The wind kicked up four- to six-foot waves on Friday, Oct. 15, an otherwise lovely day. The canoes came ashore after only two and a half miles. Stillwagon, Reid, and Watts hitched a ride with a hunter into nearby Thessalon after Watts broke a tooth on a piece of tough bannock bread. A dentist in town pulled it out.

Jan called the auto shop to confirm that the red van was ready for pickup and was told that it wouldn't be ready until Monday. The L team had counted on the van to carry equipment being stored in a nearby cottage. Instead, they would have to cram it into the green van and a Volvo. It also meant that, unless the liaison team moved its operation four days' paddle down the shore to St. Ignace, that it would be an eight-hour drive from Little Current to meet the crew.

Since Bardwell had replaced Father Loran in the canoes, Baumgartner had taken over the job of working with Hobart to determine when and where the support group was to meet the crew.

"As mom will tell you, Father Loran has given up the crew life," she wrote her father on Oct. 15. "For a 54-year-old stubborn man, I think he's lasted admirably long! . . . Father snores like thunder and is terribly opinionated. Ah, well . . ."

Perhaps remembering the beer cans she had seen washed up along the shore earlier in the trip, Baumgartner also wrote to her brother Rod on the 16th, hoping to make him more conscious of his own environment.

"Rod, there is something you can do to help the expedition," she wrote. "You see, back in 1681 there was no pollution—no car exhaust, no industries, no garbage . . . Everything was wild and free, clean and pure. Our voyageurs are trying to tell people that if we try, we can make our situation better—We can clean up our environment. It would be really helpful if you picked up trash you find on the street or in a yard, on a sidewalk, and put it in a trash can. That way, you can be a part of our whole expedition. I hope you'll consider doing that, Rod."

Reid roused the sleepers in the dark at six on Saturday, Oct. 16, shuffling from shelter to shelter across the frosted earth. The boats hit the water as the sun came up, but dawn offered little relief from the cold. Fingertips froze in the scuba mittens. On the lake, a flake settled, then more until light snow flurries whirled around the canoes. It was the first of several days of flurries. The twenty-seven-mile day closed with four miles of stroking over waves three to four feet high and an hour-long search for a suitable landing. Again, camp was not set up till after dark.

The expedition crossed into the United States the next day. Paddling literally from sunup to sundown, the crew passed DeTour Village, Michigan, two days ahead of schedule. The liaison team had finally picked up the red van. Now that Bardwell had become a full member of the crew, Baumgartner took responsibility for the repaired vehicle.

"Marlena dislikes driving it with a passion & I LOVE it, so it's like my baby now," a happy Baumgartner wrote to her family. "I cleaned the whole inside & outside, windows, packed it myself w/

sound equip. & luggage—all because I feel almost like it's mine! . . . [I'm] so glad this expedition came along. I'm learning responsibility & discipline. I'll respect school obligations much more readily . . . and [I hope] strive for the highest, best I can do. As Reid would say, 'Then I can say I've tried everything. I gave it my all.'"

Riding together in one of the vans, Baumgartner and Palmer looked at each other as they crossed the border and tried to smile but burst into tears instead.

"Canada has been such an important part in this whole expedition, not to mention our home for well over 2 months," Baumgartner wrote her family. "The people were great. I'll never forget ANY of them."

Three ore boats held up progress, but Sunday was still another twenty-five-mile day. Three rabbits, a gift from a DeTour resident, went into the vegetable barley soup prepared by Braun. A girl at a bar where the crew used the bathrooms gave them a case of Cokes. Hobart topped off the feast with bannock and pineapples. Temperatures bottomed out overnight at twenty-seven degrees. Dean reported that the forecasted low for their second night in the States was something in the teens.

Meanwhile, toes were becoming sore with cold for lack of movement during hours of paddling, and heels were becoming sore with overuse as they braced paddlers on every stroke. Unlaundered sleeping bags were not only foul but increasingly inadequate to insulate against the cold the campers were now experiencing. Instead of closing with zippers, the bags used snaps that let in the frigid air. Illness also stalked the crew. Several had sniffles, and Hobart had a serious cold. Stillwagon thought the crew's diet and the cold also took a toll on energy levels. A lot of guys emerged from the North Channel dreaming of food. Stillwagon said he had a dream in which hamburgers danced across the horizon.

The tour of Georgian Bay and the North Channel saw no large gatherings. Towns were few, and those the expedition came across were small. Blind River's population of 4,000 dwarfed Little Current (1,200), Killarney (500), and DeTour Village (300). People managed to find the celebrated time travelers regardless of solitude, but from now on, the demands on La Salle II to perform would grow by the day. Instead of seeing two or three individuals, the men would be in front of and surrounded by two or three hundred. The excitement of "fame" would replace the wonder of nature. The crew would now have performances to give. They would have to watch their language and their actions. They would have to become socially appropriate. Another thousand miles of that would have the voyageurs again yearning for privacy, perhaps understanding that there's a price to pay for any way of life.

With the support team expecting to meet the crew in St. Ignace, Baumgartner anticipated a rendezvous with Lieberman. They had not seen each other since Blind River, and she touched on her ambivalence again in a letter home.

"Marc is just fine, I think. It's been 8 days since I've seen him so I can't say for sure . . . I don't know if I'm looking forward to seeing him tomorrow. Probably more hesitant since I know exactly how he'll act, what he'll say, and how much I wish we didn't have to worry about it."

The crew entered St. Ignace riding the coattails of a rain that turned into a blinding snowstorm. A TV crew from Sault Ste. Marie filmed enough to put three minutes of their landing on the air, ghosts emerging from the snow. The big, flat flakes turned into biting hail after the landing, but many friends and relatives were on hand to greet the voyageurs onshore. Hobart's parents, his aunt, and brother had come. Braun's girlfriend, Lora, and her father and brother were there. Campbell's parents and Reid's had arrived. Fialko's fiancée, Linda, had also come, and he raced up the gunnels when he saw her, dashing past his startled boat mates. Each person got some kind of present, ranging from venison stew and cherry pies to warm socks and gloves.

Excitement doubled the next day when the voyageurs bussed in for a presentation at the high school. The St. Ignace Saints, a team not known as a football power, were celebrating Homecoming. Elementary schools had brought in their enrollment as well. After the assembly, the visitors divided into groups of three or four to visit classrooms for an hour. This was followed by hot showers and an all-you-can-eat lunch at the cafeteria, where some of the girls asked the guys to come to the homecoming dance that night. More classrooms were visited over the next three hours. The kids listened well and asked a lot of questions about the voyageurs and their history before a pep rally in the gymnasium.

When the marching band came down the hallway toward the gym playing "When the Saints Come Marching In," Hobart marched in with them, playing the tuba. He sat with the band throughout the assembly, and screamed his guts out. The Homecoming Parade cranked up at 6:30, and the crew arrived just as it was starting. They were placed right behind the band and became a big hit, especially when they fired off their muskets. The voyageurs excused themselves to give a show at a local church, but they rushed over to the football game immediately afterward. The principal persuaded Watts to fire his musket as the home team pulled off a victory.

KNOCKING ON
DEATH'S DOOR, PART 2

(Oct. 23–Nov. 4) Michigan Shore and Washington Island

A foreboding settled over the members of La Salle: Expedition II on Saturday, Oct. 23. Their canoes moved under the Mackinac Bridge and into Lake Michigan. Only a few days remained along the northern shore, the leeward shore, where the coastline was protected from the wind. Then the small craft would encounter long stretches away from land as the unpredictable winter winds of the Great Lakes toyed with them.

"After passing through the Straits of Mackinac, the trip really seemed to change," said Clif Wilson. "The feeling that the travel was more dangerous was a constant companion. Colder, windier, more open water as we went from island to island."

As the crew paddled its way down Lake Michigan's western shore, an eerie echo of trouble rose up the pop music charts. On Nov. 10, 1975, a storm on Lake Superior had sunk an iron ore freighter and killed all twenty-nine men aboard. Two weeks later *Newsweek* magazine ran "The Cruelest Month," an article about the violent storms of November on the Great Lakes. The article inspired Canadian songwriter Gordon Lightfoot to write "The Wreck of the *Edmund Fitzgerald*," which was climbing the Billboard Top 40 list almost a year after the fatal foundering itself. The song warns of a lake that never gives up her dead and the gloomy skies of November.

"We know how bad Lake Michigan can be—especially in December," Cox wrote in his journal. "We're all hoping for a mild November/December, but it's not looking good. I think I can safely say this will be the most dangerous part of the trip."

La Salle: Expedition II paddles past Mackinac Bridge into Lake Michigan in October. The winds rise and the temperatures plummet as the canoes struggle toward a date with destiny.

High above Mackinac, the danger had already found expedition photographer Barton Dean taking aerial shots of the voyageurs passing under the bridge. Dean rode in a Cessna 180, a small plane flown, in Dean's words, by "a crazy bush pilot in buckskins and a coonskin cap." When they got about five hundred feet above the bridge supports, the pilot had Dean remove the door on his side of the plane for a better view. Then, without warning, he threw the plane into a wing-over slip, a maneuver the craft wasn't designed for, and dived straight for the water saying, "OK, shoot."

"My best recollection is that I was too busy praying to push the shutter button on my camera," Dean said. "Then I heard him say the last words you want to hear from a pilot: 'Oh, shit.'"

Apparently, the plane had been "customized" by rerouting the control cables from their normal location (beneath the floor panel) to the surface of the floor itself—right beneath Dean's feet. As he clung for dear life to his seat, Dean had unknowingly jammed his feet against those very control cables, thus preventing the pilot from coming out of the dive. Hanging sideways over the open door as the water raced toward him, Dean looked up at the pilot, who was wrestling for control, unable to stop plummeting. The lake was coming up fast.

In the last few hundred feet of a long dive, the pilot realized the problem and yelled at Dean to lift his feet. The plane pulled out of the dive with seconds to spare, and the pilot showed Dean proudly that he had done so without spilling a drop of the beer he was drinking.

"It's getting cold up here and making it very difficult to write," Lesieutre wrote Annie near Epoufette. "We are acclimating & getting used to it, but my moccasins are frozen every morning . . . and it hasn't gotten over 50 in quite a few days."

By Wednesday the crew was in Manistique on Michigan's Upper Peninsula. A strong wind whipped the sand across the campsite. Simply walking became difficult, and Kulick and DiFulvio had to rig a stronger system to keep the shelter up. Snow continued to accumulate.

Some of the boys decided to have a snowball fight in their encampment at Manistique Township Park. Among them was Hess, who had hurt his foot stepping on a sharp rock in St. Ignace. In the frenzy of dodging and throwing here, he stumbled over a large rock which helped hold down the shelter. When the crew decided to walk down the nearby train tracks into town, Hess struggled. He had made a cane for himself but still moved slowly, painfully. Lieberman and Kulick took turns carrying Hess on their backs. The guy dubbed "a walking accident" had actually broken his foot. As the crew spent Friday making presentations to local groups in town, Hess was taken to have his foot put in a cast.

In Manistique, the expedition passed the thousand-mile mark and the crew visited local schools. "Elementary kids are truly amazing," Cox observed. "They can follow a really intelligent question with the weirdest/strangest/most off-the-wall thing you've ever heard. One boy very seriously asked us if we'd seen many dead animals. I don't know if he was happy or sad when we told him we had."

At the high school, the girls flocked around the voyageurs, sometimes whistling at them. The guys found the heat too much indoors and went out to the front of the school to cool off. The second floor was lined with girls staring down at them. When one of the crew came up to the second floor, he was mobbed by girls pouring out of their room while girls in the room directly across the hall waved out their window at other voyageurs. One teacher said she was glad she had no teenage girls of her own.

Wind held up the canoes at Manistique, but the expedition pressed on that Saturday to Little Harbor, more than twenty miles away. Light rain kept up all day. Late that night as Hobart and Cox, the last wakeful adults, slipped into their sleeping bags, a trio of drunken teenage boys dropped by the camp and said what a hit the voyageurs had been to the folks in Manistique. At 2:00 a.m. the last bit of Daylight Savings Time slipped away. On Sunday, Oct. 31, Father Loran celebrated Mass.

Since returning to the States, the crew was now on the clock, with deadlines to meet, but the canoes did not take off till 9:00 a.m. The canoes covered roughly twenty miles that day, and the north wind allowed the fellows a rare opportunity to deploy the sails across the open water. At the end of this leg of the trip, the canoes put into a small bay on Summer Island, where the Jolliet-Marquette expedition had camped in 1973. The teams went to work, collecting wood for a fire, preparing to cook, securing the canoes, and setting up shelter.

After dinner Campbell refused to let Halloween pass without a few hijinks. Lacking a costume, he made do with his own capote, a colorful poncho-like wrap each crewman had made from the heavy woolen blankets purchased on a shopping trip to Canada. Racing around the camp trick-or-treating, Campbell became The Flasher, suddenly opening his capote when he got a cookie. Lieberman joined in, fashioning a mask from a scrap of material and becoming the Lone Ranger.

Gradually, slumber settled over the voyageur camp on Summer Island. In fact, the travelers lay unknowingly at a curious confluence of time and space. The voyageurs slept peacefully ashore while on nearby shoals it's believed La Salle's ship *Le Griffon*, the first ship to sail above Niagara Falls, lay under water where it went down in a storm in 1679.

Beyond that spot of land lay Death's Door, the stretch of water between Washington Island and Wisconsin's Door County, a spike of the mainland slicing Green Bay from Lake Michigan like a knife. Death's Door lay open for the voyageurs as they entered the most dangerous month for Lake Michigan travelers. Fate would stop them before they stroked through it, and there would be a toll to pay.

The snoring in his own tent shook Kulick awake early Monday morning. He noticed that his contact lenses had frozen, but the pre-dawn sky was alive, sparkling with stars. The men paddled another nineteen miles to Washington Island, crossing into Wisconsin. The day was sunny, and the wind came out of the southwest toward the canoes. Camp was made at Jackson Harbor on the island's north side, a forested shoreline across a strait from the smaller Rock Island. Landfall came around 3:00 p.m., at least three days before the voyageurs were expected. The early landing had presented the crew with a chance to rest and renew themselves.

"It was nice out and we had some daylight" left that day, Wilson remembers. "We screwed around. We built a fire down by the water, read books, ran around and checked the place out. It does seem like we were always either restless or tired. That day, we were restless."

Shortly after the canoes came ashore, Dean found a tavern in the woods of the island's interior. Nelsen's Hall was named for its former owner, Tom Nelsen, who died at age ninety in the apartment where he resided above the bar. The pub had stayed in business during Prohibition because Nelsen, who had a lifelong love affair with bitters and drank them every day, obtained a pharmacy license and sold the bar staple as a medicine. Some folks have said Nelsen continues to haunt the tavern, changing stations on the radio, treading the stairs audibly at night, and sometimes jarring patrons by appearing before them in the women's restroom. After surviving the bar's ritual initiation of drinking bitters straight (no chaser), Dean talked with some of the island residents at the bar.

"I recall one of the locals telling me that the straits between the southeast tip of the island and the southern tip of land that forms Green Bay was called *Porte du Mort* by the French explorers, because so many of them had drowned trying to cross it. The problem was the wind and the relative shallowness of the bay. The combination generates very large waves in a very short time," Dean reported. According to the legend, "You have to wait for the devil [wind] to turn his back [reverse direction and knock down the waves] before you can run through the door."

On Nov. 2 the men were invited to the home of Thor Williamson, a principal resident of the island. He lent the La Salle group his International Harvester Travelall to get back and forth on the island and the use of his piano to practice songs for the performance scheduled for Thursday at the local school. That evening, Cox stayed up till midnight in Williamson's car, listening to election returns that turned a peanut farmer from Georgia into President Jimmy Carter.

Wilson remembers wind delaying departure. The Death's Door passage to the Wisconsin mainland was on everyone's mind.

"I don't remember how long we stayed put," he recalled. "I just remember that we weren't very good at that. Lots of pent-up energy, and we were more than a little afraid of making that crossing. A decision was made that we could not paddle across the pass, still too rough, but we could move our camp to another site on Washington Island and be in a better position to make the crossing when the weather improved. We packed up and left much later than our normal dawn start. But I sort of knew we were only planning to paddle for a couple of hours and go to a new camp."

It was a calm morning as Nov. 4 dawned. Hess had returned to duty holding his plastered foot high like a white flag over the gunnel to protect it from lake water. He took a flurry of kidding about it with good humor. For the first time on the expedition, a thin layer of ice had formed along the shoreline. It wasn't much, but it was ice, and the voyageurs had to break it before they could launch. The men pushed off into the channel, paddling down the eastern shore just before 8:00. They were already late.

The schedule called for the crew to leave at 6:30 and arrive at the town on the south side of the island, six miles away, by 8:30. Half the adults—Reid, Hobart, and John—had taken Thor Williamson's car to check conditions at a number of points along the coast. They reported that there would be rough water for a mile or two before they found smooth water. The initial calm helped the men get under way, but not until 7:45.

"Some days the all-important rhythm of the four paddlers together would come very easy, and some days it felt like you were out of synch all day," said Wilson. "On this particular day, it came easy. We weren't having any problems, and we were running a little ahead of the pack, which was unusual. We frequently had trouble keeping up."

As the day's brief paddle began, the wind picked up. Rapidly, a strong northwest wind swept over the island, creating choppy water that curled and foamed in the reef off shore. Waves obscured the long view, but some saw whitecaps dancing far out in the lake.

"As soon as we got on the water, the travel was tough," said Wilson, the l'avant. "The waves weren't rolling. They were choppy and big. Plenty of water coming in and the ride in the bow was very wet. Nothing really unusual, though. We had all experienced it before, and we were making good progress." Behind Wilson in the canoe, Foster and Garcia sat in the milieu and Watts held the long paddle of the gouvernail.

About a mile and a half out of Jackson Harbor, the canoes rounded a point of land and headed south, and the whole expedition went sideways—literally. The northwest wind shifted suddenly and strongly out of the northeast, quickly building to thirty miles per hour. The six canoes had been in the calmer lee of the island. Now they were immediately exposed to waves six feet high and coming at them broadside. The waves rolled under the canoes and broke over the gunnels. The water rushed off an arc of shallows so fast that it joined the wind in forcing the canoes toward the shore.

In the St. Joseph, Fialko and Bardwell both pulled as hard as they could against the waves and Marr and Sohn stroked with all their might, but for fifty yards or so the canoe ran inland at speeds four times faster than normal. Everyone faced the same struggle. The surf tossed the light craft around and became especially wild as the canoes came within half a mile of Hog Island. Hog itself was scarcely more than a sharp rise of ground several hundred yards off the northeast shoulder of Washington Island. The little bump in the watery road stretched roughly a hundred yards down its length and no more than 80 yards across. There was no true beach. Brown weeds, dead bracken, and small trees covered the rocky outcropping, and an escarpment ten feet high ran along its middle like the dorsal ridge of a razorback hog.

In the Frontenac, Hobart had turned around to see Ken bailing furiously in the Fleur de Lys, which Fredenburg, Hess, and Lesieutre were trying desperately to keep from foundering. Fredenburg had seen Watts guide his craft toward the left, outside Hog Island. When he tried to follow that lead, however, he caught a breaker broadside. As Ken had tried to push the water out, their canoe was rocked by two or three more breakers. The waves raced at them astern, raising the rear of the canoe first.

"We were paddling our asses off, but we were unable to break this pattern of swells," Fredenburg said. As a wave lifted the canoe, it broke on a shoal underneath the Fleur de Lys. The stern dropped into a trough and the canoe instantly filled with water. The lake poured over the gunnels, and the canoe became a bathtub. A keg floated away from the canoe, and Ken yelled out that they were sinking. Hess was terrified that his leg cast and heavy clothes would certainly drag him straight to the bottom, life jacket and all. In a moment Hobart had swung the Frontenac around and its crew paddled to their aid. Hobart and Cox managed to get the attention of the adult gouvernails, Fialko in the St. Joseph and Stillwagon in the Montreal. They and their crews also turned quickly to aid Fredenburg, whose canoe was about fifty yards away.

In L'Illinois, Gross had seen what was happening and shouted, "They're over!" Reid told Kulick to start unlashing gear in case they had to pick up survivors. DiFulvio had maneuvered L'Illinois to one side of the Fleur de Lys by the time the others got there. The stricken craft was filled with water, and the crew was doing everything possible to keep from tipping over. Hess paddled while nearly prone, his cast-encased foot in the air to keep it dry. Ken cracked jokes, trying to keep the mood light even on the cusp of disaster. It may have helped, but Lesieutre looked grim.

The Montreal raced to shore to start a fire, knowing that the men's wet clothes would create hypothermic conditions. They would need to strip the clothes off and keep warm. The sinking canoe was bracketed by L'Illinois and the Frontenac, with the St. Joseph bringing up the rear. As Stillwagon's Montreal canoe touched land, the Frontenac peeled away to lend a hand and the St. Joseph moved up to take its place and keep the struggling canoe bracketed. The bows were pointed toward shore, the canoes moving with the wind now. There was less fear of capsizing.

By the time the canoes reached shore, the Fleur de Lys was virtually under water, its stern submerged four feet below the surface. Naturally, the men in that canoe were soaked. They bailed out the water, then they peeled off their clothes. Everyone hit the beach to find anything that would burn. Cox chopped bigger pieces of wood, Campbell gathered twigs to start a fire, and everyone hauled in wood.

Fredenburg's crew had to drag their canoe onshore. But by that time a fire was blazing, warm capotes were out, and soup was being heated. It may have been only then that many of the voyageurs realized something else was not right.

"I don't know how we got this careless," Ken recalled. "We

noticed there were only five canoes. Then we looked out from the shore and couldn't see any canoes on the lake." Watts's was missing.

"Well, you're in their module," Reid said to John. "Why don't you see if you can find 'em?" Then Reid and Hobart dashed off to notify the authorities and find help.

"We thought that they had gone behind the island and kept on going," said Fialko. He gathered his boat mates together—Bardwell, Marr, and Sohn—and headed back out into the lake. "We paddled out there expecting them to come passing beyond the island where we could see them, but there was nobody there. So we went from one end of the island to the other and not really around it, because they had breakers on the shoals there. We just couldn't locate them. It was kind of scary. Then we tried to land, but we couldn't, due to the surf breaking around the island."

Meanwhile, the television crew from the local CBS affiliate came by. They had been waiting in town at the other end of the island when Reid called Williamson to explain the setback. Spectators had followed the film crew down to the shore where the crew had been warming up—and worrying.

"The liaison team immediately contacted the Coast Guard to see if they could launch a cutter," Dean recalled. "But they told us they had pulled all of their boats out of the water for the winter. Reid and I ran around the island in a van. We went racing down the cottages along the south side of Washington Island. We managed to locate the one local boat owner who hadn't yet stored his boat for the winter and convinced this brave soul to take us out on the lake despite ten-foot waves and thirty-eight-degree water."

Even after the situation had been explained to him, Al Thornton, the captain of the twenty-five-foot cabin cruiser, clearly did not welcome the chance to be a hero. He said he would try his best but couldn't guarantee anything. Hobart agreed to stay behind to monitor radio traffic from the boat. As soon as the boat hit the harbor mouth, the waves crested at fifteen feet and were irregular in makeup and direction. Water washed over the stern. One fifteen-footer dropped the boat in a teeth-rattling crash.

"Reid and I set out with him for Hog Island, hoping against hope that the crew had somehow made it to the only land between Washington Island and the Wisconsin coast—and their only chance of survival," Dean said. The cabin cruiser got a mile and a half out of harbor when a huge wave raised the boat to its crest, and the men aboard looked over the side into the twenty-foot trough at a rock the size of a house. "For the second time in a matter of weeks, I thought I was a goner," Dean said. "If the boat smashed on the rock or capsized, there was no hope of rescue." He added that he was never as scared as he was in those breakers.

The boat slid down the face of the wave, riding up again as the succeeding wave filled part of the trough. The boat's depth gauge, leaping in every crest and plummeting in every trough, showed the hull missed the rock by less than three feet. Thornton felt the close call was enough and decided to run back to harbor.

"Reid and I protested, but he told us to forget about Hog Island—we'd be lucky to make it back to shore. With the wind at our backs, waves crashed over the stern the whole way home, nearly swamping us, Dean recalled, saying Thornton "went way above and beyond the call."

On the way back, the pilot of a news helicopter flying over the area kept radio contact with Reid on the cabin cruiser.

"We're over Hog Island," the pilot reported. Nervous seconds passed. "There's no sign of life."

Aboard the cabin cruiser, the mood became somber.

"We see a submerged canoe about a half a mile out and drifting with the wind." The reporter again paused for several seconds. "There's no sign of survivors."

When he heard those words, Reid said, "my heart dropped." Reid asked the pilot to pass over Hog Island and see if he could spot anyone there.

"The island appears to be deserted," the pilot radioed back.

"I think we all assumed the worst at that point," Dean recalled.

But only moments later, the helicopter reporter relayed some good news:

"Wait! We definitely see smoke coming up from the island!"

The Louisiana, the same canoe that had lagged behind in the early days on the St. Lawrence, had actually out-stroked the others. Watts had gauged his choices. He could have set his course to the inside of Hog Island and braved the rough water being kicked up in the shallows. Instead, he steered to the outside, where he would lose protection from the wind but where deeper water would preserve the boat from the shoals.

"No one else said a thing. It was his call and he knew what he was doing," Wilson said. "That was one of the enduring beauties of the trip. If it was your job, it really was up to you. Not like real life at all. But it sure worked in that setting."

Trouble multiplied as soon as they had committed to the outside route. Watts said he turned back to see everyone else heading for shore, and he yelled for Foster, Wilson, and Garcia to turn around. As they did, the canoe was hit broadside by the wind-whipped lake. The water spilled over the gunnels as the wave rolled the canoe and threw the boys under. The water temperature was later reported to be 39.8 degrees Fahrenheit.

"We got heavy, we got sideways, and then we capsized," Wilson said. "What a shock the cold water was! First, it was on my lap, and then we were in it. I remember two thoughts from that moment very clearly. The first was that we were all dead. The second was that the hot chocolate powder I had hidden in my pouch was probably wrecked. That was the first time in my life I'd ever considered dying, you know, and the mind-boggling aspect is that we were in the water, we were upside down, we couldn't see anybody for any kind of assistance, and [after coming up] we were just looking across these cold waves," Wilson remembered. They popped up, gasping more from cold than for air. They counted heads. Then they clasped hands over the hull.

Wilson wore waders, and the high boots rapidly filled with water. He yelled that he couldn't get them off. Watts and Garcia held him up as Wilson kept a death grip on the canoe, though the water pressures equalized and Wilson later said more was made about the waders than was warranted.

No one panicked. Only Watts spoke. He told the guys to cut

away all the gear to make the canoe lighter. He said they would stay with the canoe. Though they were floating, Watts said that he could touch bottom, so they would be fine.

"I believed him," said Wilson. "I think Foster and Garcia did, too. We started walking. So it was push up, plant, and then pull toward Hog Island. Not many words were exchanged, but we worked together on a task we had never practiced before—or even conceived of—in concert."

The shoals were little more than five feet deep, but the frequent swells pulled them up off the lake bottom and swept over their heads. As they fell back into the trough, the quartet tiptoed toward Hog, pushing the canoe until the next swell lifted them up. After each crashing wave, the men took a head count. Each swell pushed them farther south toward the edge of the tiny oasis in the frigid water. The shore was no more than two hundred yards away, but the cold rushed upon them faster than the shore. The water gradually fell from their necks to their chests to their waists, then to their knees. They barely made the tip of the island before the waves could carry them out into the lake and possible death.

As the four got to the shallows, they tried to right the canoe, but their attempt was feeble. Wracked by the cold, they could barely stand. Their bodies shook. Their hands trembled. Small motor functions completely disappeared. They wanted to save their craft. They could not. They dragged themselves onto the island and let the lake take the canoe.

"We were really cold, really not thinking very clearly. But I do remember that for a moment we felt like gods," Wilson said. "We lived. The rush was overwhelming."

Watts directed his crew to strip off their wet clothes and get into the sleeping bags in pairs, Watts with Garcia and Wilson with Foster. Inside the bags they shook with the cold. They prayed that whatever body heat they had would combat the effects of the near-freezing water. Garcia was suffering the most from the cold. He said he felt that he was going into hypothermia shortly after they reached Hog. He couldn't untie his sleeping bag or function at all.

Watts was already taking the blame for their difficulties, but the others wouldn't hear of it.

Foster appeared to be the least affected by the cold. Little time passed before Watts suggested that he go looking for help. Foster left the relative warmth of his cocoon and climbed back out of the sleeping bag. There were five other canoes out there. Maybe they were in the same kind of trouble. Maybe they were looking for him and his comrades. He had to find out.

Meanwhile, the St. Joseph landed on the lee side of Hog Island. Sohn rushed into the brush and up the hogback. Peering over the escarpment, he saw Watts and Wilson and Garcia lying in their sleeping bags and shivering with cold. "Buckwheat" called over his shoulder for Fialko and the others, but he didn't wait for them. He rushed down to the rocky shore and tried to start a fire with waterproof matches. That effort failed. He found the signal flares and tried to start a fire with them. The lake water had soaked them, too.

Watts, who had been one of the six voyageurs to have a musket, offered gunpowder that had hung in a capped horn around his neck. Sohn pulled out his fire-starting kit. Each of the voyageurs was equipped with flint and steel. He struck the steel and flint over the instant tinder Watts had given him and immediately kindled a flame. It was the smoke from that small fire that the helicopter pilot reported by radio to Reid and Dean as they headed back to port.

While Sohn was kindling the fire, a wave nearly smashed the St. Joseph on the rocks. Fialko and Bardwell fought to keep their canoe intact. When it was steady, Bardwell followed Sohn's call from the other side of the island.

Within a few minutes, Foster returned to the shore where fire now flared. Bardwell had worked his way through the jungle of bracken to the small fire Sohn had built. Unable to form a coherent sentence, Garcia was judged in most immediate need of evacuation. Bardwell took one arm and Wilson took the other, and together they maneuvered Garcia back across Hog to the St. Joseph, which rocked in the water at the base of the rocky ledge four to six feet high. One look at Garcia told Fialko that he had to take him back as soon as he could. He left Bardwell with the survivors before beginning the difficult paddle to Washington Island with the news.

Waiting on shore, the voyageurs strained to see over the choppy waves. With binoculars, they saw Fialko's canoe, but Gorse thought he saw Watts's canoe behind the St. Joseph, and sinking. News crews and law enforcement officials crowded the beach. Everyone told the voyageurs not to go back out. How could they not go? If they didn't, who else would? There was no one else.

The comrades quickly responded. Stillwagon, Gorse, Lieberman, and Braun leaped into a canoe and raced out to meet them. DiFulvio, Kulick, and Gross joined Cox in a second canoe and pushed out, paddling quickly to catch up. Ken was wild to join the hunt for the missing men, but others restrained him. He was practically blue with cold himself, having stayed in the shallows to help guide the others onto the shore. He had stripped down to his boxer shorts and needed to stay by the fire to warm up. Several of the canoeists, already out on the water, realized they had left without their mittens, and they knew they would regret that rashness in the chilled waters and the arctic air.

As they approached him, Fialko told the outbound canoeists that the missing men were safe on the opposite side of Hog Island. Stillwagon's canoe went on to the rugged shore but found nothing but jagged rocks and shoals on the north and south sides of Hog. With no place to land, Braun, the l'avant, got out to hold the canoe, struggling in the wind to balance himself on the rocks. Cox's canoe hung offshore about fifty yards and tried to hold position. A few minutes later—what seemed an eternity to Cox and his mates offshore—Bardwell and Wilson emerged from the brush, leading Foster. As soon as Foster stumbled into the canoe, Stillwagon headed back toward the big island. Cox's group then maneuvered into shore and took on Wilson. Wilson's friend Kulick made room for him in his canoe.

"Clif was shaking terribly, and I could see the fear—no, terror—in his eyes," Kulick recorded in his journal. "I asked him if he was

OK and in a shaky voice [he] said, 'I've never been so scared in my life . . . I'm going to have nightmares about it. . . . It was really a strange feeling to have the thought cross your mind that you're going to die.'"

On shore, Fialko had put together a fresh crew and returned to Hog for Bardwell, Sohn, and Watts. They all came ashore with TV cameras rolling.

"You know, people were being as funny as they could all the way back so that they could keep [us] poor, sick suckers laughing, and they were successful," Wilson said. "Right before we landed, Terry said, 'Hey, listen. Before you make your big TV debut you might want to wipe the snot off your face.' I came out, the cameras came down [to the water]: 'Here's one of the disaster victims coming in now . . .' and I was just laughing hysterically. I was out of control. It was funny, and that was on Green Bay TV: 'Here's one of them. So that is just one of the . . . the crew is a *strong* group of people'"— who apparently laughed in the face of disaster.

Watts was distraught, though. He viewed the near disaster as his fault, based on his decision, and he wept. His canoe mates would have none of this, but he was inconsolable. His reaction reflected the sense of responsibility each of the voyageurs felt for the others, and the accountability that each felt naturally belonged to him, whether for good or ill.

The capsizing shifted the entire paradigm of activity for the liaison team. Jan and Scavuzzo had been fielding a number of requests for schedule changes from social and civic organizations further along the route. Baumgartner and Palmer had focused on accommodating those requests. Now, suddenly, they were thrust into a liaison between the expedition and the voyageurs' families seeking word of their situation. Thanks to media from Green Bay, this was easier than it would be later. At least two television stations were filming the scene of survival on Washington Island's east coast.

Between the film crews and spectators, the voyageurs themselves found it hard to move about the camp. Those who had remained on shore had built a fire and prepared some food—oatmeal and chicken noodle soup. Despite his good humor after the icy plunge through the waves, Wilson shook uncontrollably.

"He was cold, so cold," Marr said.

Hobart and Reid returned around eleven o'clock that morning. Hobart and Watts responded to a report that the damaged canoe was drifting along the shore in the next bay to the south. About half an hour later, a resident drove several crew members a mile down the coast to try to find the missing boat. They found the canoe through the woods in a little inlet nearby. Hog's rocks had smashed the bow. All the pitch had come off. Half a gunnel cap was torn off, along with much of the lashing. A hole had been punched in the side, and the shell was cracked wide open. Though they scavenged for lost equipment, they didn't find any; but when they came back they learned that others had found some of it washed up on the shore even farther south.

At camp, Reid gathered the crew together and asked if the guys were up for making a presentation at the island school where they had been due to arrive at 9:30. The school had a hundred students in grades K-12, and the senior class consisted of six girls. The decision to perform was unanimous, and they ran through script number two at 2:45 that afternoon. Howard Platt had driven up with three friends. Platt had followed the progress of the expedition and had joined them with a friend around their campfire the previous week. Platt couldn't believe that the same individuals who had survived a nearly fatal disaster only hours earlier were able to put on a show. In his journal, Cox commented, "Howard, we're damn near professionals. The show must go on."

Members of the expedition, however, remember that the best line of the day was delivered as they rode the bus to the school that afternoon. The young men who had endured so much that morning sat in their seats, nodding with exhaustion. Among them were the survivors of the capsized canoe. Foster's head hung low. Deep in thought, he played back the morning's events and mulled what might have been. Suddenly, he raised his head, opened his eyes, and said, "Well, I'm tired of thinking about death. I think I'll brush my hair." And he began to drag the bristles of the brush through his tangled, storm-tossed web.

After the show, the crew took showers at the community center and got ready for the scheduled 5:00 p.m. fish boil. On an island of 500 residents, 115 tickets had been sold. All the proceeds went to the expedition. The food tasted especially good to the voyageurs, who feasted on whitefish, slaw, potatoes, onions, and "Thor's famous doughnuts." Someone had brought a small TV, and the men watched themselves on the six o'clock news out of Green Bay. Then they performed the skits and songs of script number one for the fish boil audience at 6:30. But their day was not yet over.

At 9:00 that night the expedition met in a small library to discuss the day's events. The men agreed that they had observed safety in leaving that morning. The wind shifted only after the boats were on the water, and the canoes generally stayed close to one shore or another. Among other important realizations were these:

- The canoes needed to stay close enough to remain in voice contact.
- Everything in the canoes must be lashed down.
- In a capsizing, the crew must stay with the canoe and push rather than pull it to shore.
- No waders should be worn in the canoes. They should be removed immediately.
- Beware of loaded questions from the media. Reporters like to play the blame game.
- Rescue groups need to be prepared for the elements. Several of the voyageurs had rushed out to Hog Island without mittens.

"Today was our roughest day, but it was probably our most rewarding day," Cox observed. "We came close to tragedy but are now closer to really being a unified group. I have never been so damn proud of a group of people or been so proud of being a member of a group. Today's events have . . . certainly made men out of a few teenage boys, and old men out of a few adults."

Fialko, the expedition's armorer, didn't want to leave the crew but said he would drive the battered canoe back to the Chicagoland Canoe Base for repairs. He said he would go alone, but Cox insisted that someone go with him, at least to help Fialko drive. Gorse volunteered to ride shotgun. Both men knew that someone had to take care of the damaged canoe, but it was hard to leave the rest of the guys. They didn't feel guilty, exactly. But it did feel as though something was missing.

"It felt like we were playing hooky," said Fialko. "We were talking about that on the way down. It felt good to get back."

The shattered boat was loaded on a truck and driven back to Chicago. By the time it got there, Frese had gathered a crew who worked overnight to repair the damages. They put it on a flatbed and sent it back to Death's Door, where it arrived on Sunday—a three-day turnaround. No one could tell that the canoe had been damaged at all. The crew successfully launched on Monday, Nov. 8, having spent a week on Washington Island. The paddle through Death's Door that day proceeded peacefully. Few of the voyageurs missed the irony.

Though he did not believe it at the time, Watts had passed a test of leadership that week. He had shown himself to be decisive. But he had also displayed flexibility, a positive attitude toward problem solving, and a responsibility toward those who depended on him. His calm demeanor under pressure helped steady his crewmates and allowed them to function together effectively in an emergency situation, as they were trained to do.

Foster's concern for others, both near and far, had lifted him out of a relatively warm, comfortable sleeping bag to look for voyageurs lost in a storm. And he did so even though he himself was shivering flotsam on a stony crag in the middle of a raging gale. His strength of will and strength of character continued to be a rock upon which the team of La Salle: Expedition II would depend.

Wilson and Garcia had emerged from their ordeal relatively unscathed. They had endured. Their ability to deal calmly under pressure speeded their maturity as men. They had reason to bless the Providence that had brought them through the storm. But a much sterner test awaited both of them hundreds of miles beyond Washington Island.

And for the voyageurs treading in La Salle's footsteps, the way would not become easier. The breath of winter was closing about them.

Hard rivers lay ahead.

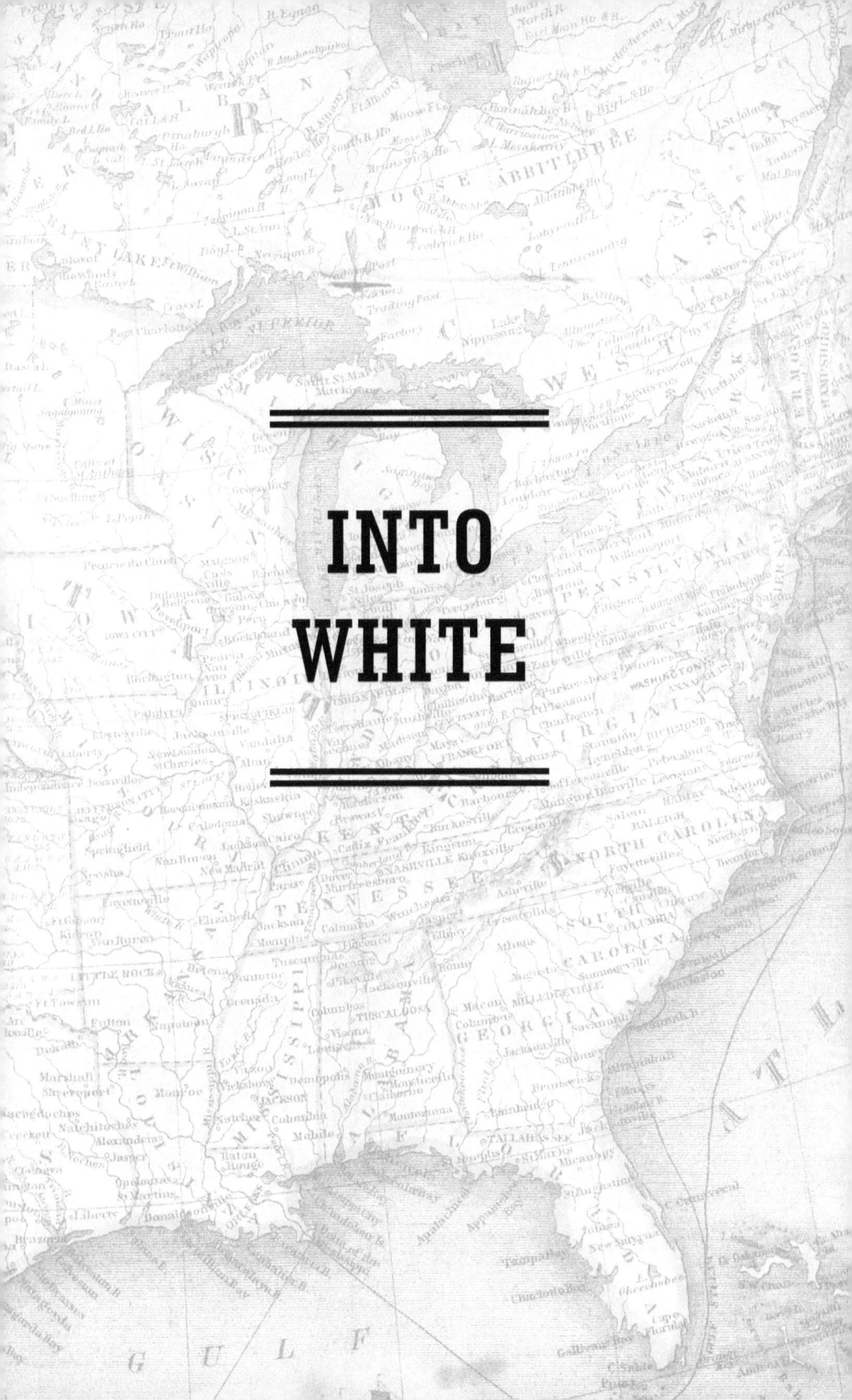

INTO WHITE

THE AUTUMN WINDS BLOW CHILLY AND COLD

(Nov. 5–25) Wisconsin

While waiting for their chance to leave Washington Island, the men kept busy with school visits and project work. A naturalist who raised hawks came by the campsite the night of Nov. 5 with three cheesecakes for the crew. Only Hobart, Cox, Lesieutre, Garcia, Fredenburg, and Braun were up at the time. They told the Hawk Lady that they would eat one and save the other two for breakfast. But the first one simply whetted their appetites. After they finished the second one, they decided it would be silly to leave one cheesecake for the whole crew for breakfast, so they ate the third one as well. When it came to food, it seemed like it was every man for himself.

Many parents came up over the weekend, shaken by the scare the previous week. Saturday's ferry ride to the mainland illustrated the danger perfectly. The seas were too high to land at Gilles Park, the usual dock, so the ferry headed for North Point, where the families were all gathered.

An overnight snow and a brutal wind greeted the campers on Sunday. Both Gilles Park and North Point were closed, so a third spot was chosen for the ferry to embark for Washington Island. In the seventy-five minutes it took the ferry to make the forty-five-minute trip, Pam Cox's Honda was covered in ice from the frozen spray blown off the lake. Sometime during the week, the overnight temperature fell to nine degrees above zero, the coldest reading in the nation.

Up by five o'clock Monday, Nov. 8, the crew caught a small break in the weather around seven, and made more than seventeen miles. Nevertheless, they paddled through skim ice on the lake. The temperature was in single digits, and wherever a drop of lake water hit, it froze. By the time the canoes put in, icicles hung off the gunnels, shirtsleeves were covered with a frozen film, and mittens were fringed with frost. Moccasins froze to the pavement as the men walked. Fialko and Gorse rejoined the crew that evening, singing for a small group at Sturgeon Bay High School. It was snowing again when the men got back to camp and the night was cold, even in capotes.

Doug Sohn hacks through the Lake Michigan ice as crewmates (from left) Steve Marr, Bill Watts, and John Fialko power through the floes and slush in front of the Baha'i Temple in Wilmette.

The crisis at Hog Island had put the enterprise in the public eye. The crew had been on TV five days in a row, and local radio was mentioning them every hour. In Manitowoc people appeared along the lakeshore every few minutes, waving and taking pictures. Hundreds of people awaited their arrival at the YMCA.

In the area Monday, the group visited four schools; At more than one, it seemed that girls were impressed when Gross was introduced. Perhaps it was his hair—long and curly, a sort of Afro style.

The crew left the area reluctantly on Nov. 16 and within a couple of hours ran into trouble. An old pier had been torn down about seven or eight miles down the coast, leaving old, mostly submerged pilings. Though the voyageurs had been warned about them, they had a difficult time seeing them. The sun off the water created a glare that even shaded and squinted eyes couldn't defeat. Finally, the pilings were spotted between the boats and the shoreline less than a quarter mile away. The posts were barely visible above the surface.

Suddenly, Hobart's canoe found itself surrounded by pilings, one of which lifted the prow into the air and left it balancing precariously six inches out of the water. Gorse and Cox crawled toward the stern to try to ease the bow off the old wood, but the boat wouldn't budge. Hobart threw Stillwagon the canoe's painter, and Stillwagon gently pulled the boat off the post without tipping the boat over, but the piling had punched a fist-sized hole in the canoe, and it was taking on water. After the trio bailed out five inches of water while getting to shore, Gorse and Fialko repaired the damage in less than a couple of hours.

With little time left on the water before the men had to make camp, the expedition came ashore in Cleveland, Wisconsin, population two hundred. It seemed as if the whole town came down to see the crew land at this unexpected stop, and one woman summed up the bonhomie by saying, "Who'd ever think this could happen to Cleveland, Wisconsin?" A case of Pabst Blue Ribbon beer was already waiting before the first canoe touched land, courtesy of the local tavern owner. Another man brought in a pick-up truck full of firewood for the camp. A member of the Jaycees sent them off the next morning with dried backpacking food.

A couple of days later the crew stopped for lunch near a house that displayed a big banner reading, "Bienvenue, Voyageurs." The voyageurs arrived that afternoon in a flotsam of algae at Port Washington. Variations in arrival estimates led a reporter for the *Milwaukee Journal* to quip that the crew showed "all the dependability of Amtrak." More than a hundred people braved the raw conditions to wait for them, including fifth and sixth graders who had to be back on the school bus within half an hour. Just as expectations dimmed, the canoes came into view, hugging the shoreline. Then the men swung out into the lake and back again, six abreast. After a few musket shots, the voyageurs lifted their paddles in salute, gave a shout, and began to sing, digging for shore as the crowd erupted in applause.

Reid Lewis shows mock surprise as Rich Gross lifts a pair of young students and Sid Bardwell (left) and Sam Hess look on. In addition to more than 500 performances, voyageurs visited hundreds of classrooms, hospitals, and nursing homes along the route.

After the peace of Georgian Bay, the constant presence of people around the voyageur camp, particularly after the publicity surrounding the Hog Island incident, began to take a toll on some of the men. Living in a fishbowl was not for everyone, and the trip provided a two-edged sword. On one hand, the expedition called for people to come see their French heritage, to reach out and touch their history in a real way. On the other, the physical demands of pulling a wooden paddle through water for hours at a time demanded some rest off the water, and that was hard to find.

A throng of more than six hundred people gathered at Vernon Park in Mequon to cheer the expedition to shore. Miraculously, the muskets all went off in greeting, echoing against the 120-foot bluffs. But even in good weather the quarter-mile climb uphill to the campsite took a lot of effort for men used to using their arms and backs—and not their legs. Forty feet up the slope, Gorse stretched a leg a bit too far and both legs went out from under him. He held on for a moment before he lost his grip and twisted in the air, bounced off the hill, and landed safely on his feet, surprising himself and drawing laughs from his crewmates.

Sohn and Wilson expected to spend the night in a kind of makeshift lean-to under one of the canoes to guard the gear on the beach. At night, however, the water rose suddenly. Wilson, sleeping soundly, awoke to find his feet wet, and the two guards had to scramble to drag the gear uphill or watch it wash away. By the time they alerted the crew and moved the spare gear up the hillside, the beach was gone. The next morning the east wind blew the surf into waves pounding the bluffs. The men made three fires, and the spray put out all three.

"I looked out over the lake last night and it looked alive," Cox recorded. "With the gentle rollers it was almost like it was breathing. But today it was angry and cruel with whitecaps as far as you could see. As nasty as the wind and waves were, they changed the color of the water. It was almost beautiful, as long as you're not in the mood to challenge it."

The men chose not to challenge it Sunday. At dinner that night at the K of C hall, the voyageurs were back to eat and sing. Father Loran was back to say mass. And Dr. Brown was back with a sign out, selling La Salle mementoes. The wind increased the next day, with breakers hitting the beach again. The canoes didn't leave until two o'clock. Two and a half hours later, the men had gone ten miles. It was already dark, and only two men were at the landing site. But they quickly telephoned local media, and soon all kinds of people showed up bearing gifts. Another twenty-six miles brought the expedition back on schedule in Racine, but ice covered the canoes and gear bags. The thermometer read twenty degrees. The canoes had passed a couple of coal-fired power plants, and the air and water coming into town was awful. Only 150 people turned out to hear the voyageurs perform at the Senior Citizens Drop-In Center in the state's third largest city.

Thanksgiving Day brought a battle again with Lake Michigan. The men fought the wind and waves for six hours, soaked to the skin and chilled to the bone. Only the fact that the temperature rose into the fifties kept that leg from Racine to Kenosha from becoming unbearable. And even though there was a sandy beach about three hundred yards north of the landing site, the canoes came ashore at the narrow, rocky Southport beach, where half of the canoes were damaged. More than a hundred people gave up their Thanksgiving football to come watch the crew land. Stillwagon's wife, Rowena, and their four children were there as well. A family living across the street invited the campers in for a holiday feast. Overnight the temperature plummeted from near sixty to below freezing.

The voyageurs paddled the eleven miles to Zion, Illinois, in ninety minutes the day after Thanksgiving. They didn't dare stop, because the waves would have prevented re-launching. The liaison team did not meet them at Illinois Beach State Park, the prearranged landing site. The temperature dropped to at least ten degrees below zero before the camp was set up.

The dinner that night at a senior citizens community center provided the first in a series of forums sponsored by the Illinois Humanities Council. This one was on the history of Zion. The council had pledged $20,000 to the expedition in exchange for participation in the forums, but La Salle II had to pay for the venue, the set-up, and the speakers. A month after the Zion forum, the voyageurs learned that they would realize only $8,000 of the $20,000 the council had pledged. In the minds of many, the forums scarcely profited the La Salle enterprise, and they obligated the voyageurs individually and collectively.

For men used to strenuous physical activity in the cold, the forums were sedentary and oppressively warm, and most of the men found the forums boring. Their stomachs full, their activity in pause mode, they often lapsed into a torpor. During the evening, a patron asked Reid a question, which he directed to Stillwagon. However, surgeon "Jean Michel" was sitting in the back of the room sound asleep.

Hess's parents had driven into Zion to see their son and make sure he was all right after his latest medical needs. They brought with them four turkey sandwiches—leftovers from their Thanksgiving dinner. "Don't bring them out!" Hess cried, looking around him to see if anyone had noticed the food. He knew that they would immediately become expedition "property" if seen and be divided into twenty-four equal bites and consumed posthaste by the entire group. Hess ate all four that same night, to keep them out of "enemy" hands.

The younger men looked forward to sleeping in on the programmed weather day, Saturday, Nov. 27, but Stillwagon woke everyone up by sweeping snow off the shelter and resetting the tent stakes. Reid hoped the weather day presented an opportunity to resolve the conflict between the crew and the liaison team. To be sure, it was mostly a conflict between Hobart and Cox on the one side and Jan and Scavuzzo on the other, but each pair of adults had adherents. The two groups had been at odds almost constantly from Day One, though some voyageurs had no idea that the rift was a chasm. The meeting buried the hatchet all right—into the collective psyche of the liaison team. Reid tried to play the role of peacemaker. Knowing that the session would be emotional, Reid tried to keep the discussion from becoming a verbal free-for-all. He asked the crew of each canoe to pick a representative to speak. That limitation achieved order but stoked resentment, too.

"Reid tried to hold off both sides at the same time and all that," said Wilson. "There were lots of problems with the liaison team that stemmed back for four months. The problems had never been talked about with the liaison team. But it was always the feeling of the crew that . . . there was no value in talking about things that happened so long ago. I think, in this particular case, it would have been of value to go over some things that were old." The conversation began well enough, but attitudes of both the support team and the voyageurs had hardened by this point.

Scavuzzo tried to explain that the canoeists did not understand the land team's problems, but her voice was drowned in the two-hour blood-letting. Afterward, Cox asked Dean about the liaison problems, and Dean said the women were making the best of a bad situation. In Waukegan the windchill factor was seven below zero. Reid called another meeting after dinner to discuss the earlier session with the liaison team. Neither Jan nor Scavuzzo had any interest in dealing with anyone but the Lewis brothers, Reid said. Father Loran threatened to quit the expedition if the women quit, which failed to intimidate any of the voyageurs.

The wind chill reached minus-twenty-two on Nov. 29. The air was so cold that fog rose from the chilly but relatively warm lake and made it hard to see a canoe fifty feet ahead. As the expedition approached Chicago, the eerie mist was a frequent companion, and the cold began to produce slush in the water as the lake shifted from liquid to solid. The men had to drag ropes along the bottoms of the canoes to scrape the slush off the hull. When the crew appeared in a schoolhouse that morning, so much ice melted off the men's clothes that Bardwell said Fialko "would have to start treading water" if he stood in the same spot too long.

The time on the water had shortened. The men spent no more than a couple of hours of paddling a day. Over the next week, the expedition would visit the wealthy suburbs along Chicago's North Shore, and the reception would be as warm as the air was cold. In Lake Forest, the men visited schools before returning to the campsite, where photographers from the *Sun-Times* and *Daily News* waited for them. At the campsite the crew lit a huge bonfire.

Sometime during the trip a few of the campers had created a

Once-a-Month Club, deciding to go for a plunge in the nearest lake or river once a month, regardless of weather conditions. Campbell, Lesieutre, and Gorse chose this extremely cold night to have their midnight swim. They stripped off every bit of clothing as the embers flew from the bonfire into the November dark. Then they raced across the campsite, dashed down a stony embankment, and quick-stepped across the gravel-covered apron of Lake Michigan before plunging headfirst into the dark water. Instantly, the men leaped out of the liquid ice as if on fire. The trio turned and frantically retreated almost as fast as they had come, using the bonfire as their beacon. But they overlooked something important. While they could see the drop-off and the water easily by the firelight, they could not see the stony embankment rising before them in the darkness as they raced back up the beach. Their eyes were all on the fire.

Gorse led the assault, slamming unexpectedly into the embankment. The pebbles along the escarpment immediately stuck to his wet chest, stomach, and legs. The lake water acted like glue as it turned to ice on his body, freezing the pebbles in place. Campbell, trailing Gorse up from the lake, heard him say, "Ooof!" as the collision knocked the air out of him. But Campbell and Lesieutre had slowed when they realized that ice forming on the soles of their feet had picked up pebbles over the ground. The bottoms of their feet, now stony with the little rocks, ran roughly over the sand beyond the water's edge, making for a difficult and uneven stride, slowing them down even before the embankment. Only after they crawled back to the campfire did they find enough warmth to melt the stones from their soles.

In Highland Park, the water at Park Avenue Beach on the last day of November was as slushy as a snow cone. Morning temperatures hovered around zero, and the wind chill measured eighteen degrees below. After the men visited schools during the day, Lieberman's aunt and uncle hosted the crew for dinner in a lovely home with a magnificent spiral staircase. A voyageur performance accompanied another of the council forums in Lake Forest, this one on preserving the local lakefront. But ominous signs began to appear on the lake. Ice had built up to three feet in places. It obliterated the beach and extended farther out over the lake during the wind-bound days in Highland Park.

As many as eight hundred people received the crew in Winnetka. Behind the voyageurs at a local school appearance, the children had draped a large map they had made of the United States showing La Salle's route. A local family hosted the travelers and about 120 others at their home. Kulick spent much of the evening talking with Loris Miller, ninety-three, who had given $10,000 to the expedition. Miller told Kulick that he had traveled north to canoe the backwoods alone, carrying only a bag of oats with him, trapping and fishing for the rest of his food.

In Wilmette the ice had grown so thick and extensive that the crew had to chop their way into the only natural harbor on the North Shore. Again several hundred people were on hand to say hello, some with hot chocolate and candy. After camp was set up, some of the men walked over to the beautiful Baha'i Temple there on the lakeshore. Ice froze the voyageurs into Wilmette Harbor the next day, and they couldn't chop their way out, though they tried for a couple of hours. Instead, the parks department sent over a backhoe to clear an entrance of about one hundred feet along the shore. The ice was four feet thick. Snow filled the air as the canoes moved through a fog out into the lake. The canoes moved through floes of ice that had formed in rings, then drifted together into sheets. Only a mile and a half away, Evanston's landing spot had ice a foot thick. Again, the site had to be cleared for them to land. The mercury simply plunged deeper and deeper.

"The cold just seeps through the bag and liner and you wake up chilled," Cox wrote at the time. "You can feel it all around you, and there's not a damn thing you can do about it."

The crew had learned to protect their hands while paddling in the freezing waters, though. By wearing two pairs of mittens, a voyageur could dip the backs of the outside mittens in the water. The water on the surface would rapidly turn to ice and insulate the mitten underneath. The hands stayed relatively warm. Even so, the men's hands looked like iron, cured to a gunmetal gray by the constant cold. The veins and muscles underneath looked like cables twisted beneath a hard metallic surface.

Finally, the day came for the voyageurs to return to Elgin, to greet old friends and to show that the expedition was alive and well. The bus picked them up Dec. 7 and took them to Larkin High for breakfast. The men performed before opening the floor for questions, but there were none. At least the French Club gave them a check for $201.48. The crowd at Elgin High, by contrast, was very enthusiastic and asked a lot of questions. Some clubs there raised more than $500 for the enterprise. The crew performed for the Kiwanis Club at lunch, then traveled to Central Middle School and visited one of Pam Cox's classes. The Coxes spent the late afternoon together at home, "almost like I hadn't been gone since August 2. I played a little [John] Prine and Waylon [Jennings]. . . . God, but it felt good to be home."

Capacity at Hemmens Auditorium was twelve hundred, but the house was packed at 7:30 for another voyageur performance. The crew ran onto the stage to a thunderous standing ovation. The men got back to the campsite by midnight. The warmth of the crowd was gone. Home already seemed far away, and the night was cold.

OLD MAN WINTER

(Dec. 8–31) The Chicago Portage

On his discovery of the Mississippi River in 1673, Louis Jolliet paddled down the western side of Lake Michigan. Eight years later on his way to the Gulf of Mexico, La Salle might have followed either the western or eastern lakeshore. It is not known which. However, Reid's group deliberately chose the western shore because it was much more populous, and La Salle: Expedition II was about bringing French heritage to more Americans. At least the route *could* have been La Salle's.

The route's authenticity became less clear in Chicago. Fearing armed Spaniards near the Arkansas River, Jolliet turned north. He took the Illinois, Des Plaines, and Chicago Rivers to Lake Michigan. On his way to the Gulf in 1681, La Salle paused at the mouth of the St. Joseph River in Michigan and cached supplies. Then he had followed the lakeshore south and reversed Jolliet's path along the Chicago and Des Plaines to the Illinois, though the frozen rivers forced him to drag his canoes hundreds of miles on sledges until the water ran freely again.

The modern voyageurs followed the shoreline through northern Indiana and southern Michigan all right, but when they headed south again it was not toward Chicago. Instead, the crew followed the St. Joseph and Kankakee toward the Illinois. This was the route La Salle had followed when he first came to Illinois country in 1679, which was authentically La Salle's but not authentically 1681's. Again, the rationale was to reach people, specifically those who had helped Dave Upton support the expedition in that region.

The National Bank of Paris planned an outdoor gourmet feast for the voyageurs Wednesday, Dec. 8, at Adler Planetarium. The banquet tent was to include white linen tablecloths and crystal glassware. The event was slated to begin at 2:00 p.m., with a cocktail reception for La Salle II donors to follow. Frese set up a campsite there for the crew, with tepees and plenty of firewood. Reid told a Channel 2 mini-cam photographer and a public relations firm hired by the bank that the crew would have canoes in the water by noon.

As La Salle II awoke that morning, however, Lake Michigan was a block of ice five inches thick. The windchill factor registered seventeen degrees below zero and the lake appeared to be solid as far as the eye could see. Stunned by conditions, Reid briefly thought about moving off the lake and using La Salle's true route of 1681, but there was the bank's dinner to be considered.

After battling across the Northwestern University campus and braving the ice shelf and frigid water for hours, six lonesome canoes move south along the lakeshore as darkness envelops Chicago.

After scouting the situation, an opening in the ice was found at the south end of the Northwestern University campus. At ten o'clock Stillwagon stirred the waiting voyageurs for a portage. Six toboggans were obtained to carry the thousands of pounds of gear in the canoes, saving an extra trip. Then the men hauled their canoes and the loaded toboggans a mile and a half across the campus, through a parking lot, and over a plowed field.

The men put the gear back into the canoes and shoved off into Lake Michigan a bit after two o'clock. They still had to paddle about fourteen miles to reach their destination. The men first headed well out into the lake, away from the ice-choked shore. Then they turned south around the jagged edge of the ice shelf and past floes. The dinner was postponed for two hours, though it was still unlikely the crew would arrive on time at the 12th Street beach next to the planetarium, even by the revised time. Ever the optimist, Reid believed the men could travel the distance before dark, but plans were made to stop at Belmont Harbor—roughly half way—if they couldn't. By four that afternoon, the canoes had only made Belmont Harbor, but there was still no place to put in. An hour later the men saw their best opportunity to claw for shore. Even then there was a sheet of ice between the voyageurs and the raised shoreline.

Cold descended with the darkness. Twilight fell over the city. The lights of Chicago gleamed at men hacking through the ice. When they made the breakwater, the Wednesday evening rush hour flew by just above them on Lake Shore Drive. The men threw their bundles over the five-foot wall before struggling to climb up to the twentieth century on their own. La Salle II had already fought the current on the St. Lawrence and the waves of Wicked Point, slogged over the concrete and through the rains of the Toronto portage, and survived the terror of Washington Island and the brutal cold of the Wisconsin shore. But in a post-expedition note to his journal, Fialko said of Belmont Harbor, "This was the beginning of our trials."

Reid left as soon as the canoes landed and was gone an hour, trying to get a bus to take the men to the dinner. But Channel 2 arrived, and the men were forced to remain outside while the reporter interviewed Reid. By the time the bus had collected the chilled voyageurs and arrived at the destination, the cocktail party was all but over. No gourmet meal awaited them; that dinner had been canceled. As a consolation, the crew was given a nice restaurant meal to make up for it. Observers indoors said that the temperature in the room dropped perceptibly when the crew walked in.

Back at camp, Cox asked to address the crew, who had heard him all day angrily protest decisions that he thought put the crew in jeopardy in order to please the Chicago media and potential donors. Recalling the harrowing events of the day, he said he thought that the expedition was more media conscious than safety oriented and that too few people were making the most important decisions, often hastily. Clearly aiming his comments at Reid, Cox said he didn't think much had been learned from Washington Island and that nothing would be until someone was seriously hurt. He threatened to leave the expedition if things didn't change. Not everyone agreed with Cox's assessment, however, and the discussion dragged on till 2:00 a.m. without a real resolution. Meanwhile, Dean had problems of his own.

"By the time we reached Chicago," he said, "my cameras were shot. I wasn't getting paid. I went to my camera shop and got an estimate to get the cameras tuned up. The estimate was $165." The cameras had sand in them. The metering and focus were off. From Chicago on, the focus and exposure were set entirely by guesswork.

Sleeping in on Dec. 9, the travelers awoke to the local CBS and ABC crews filming as they got dressed in their voyageur clothing. A school appearance had been canceled, so the men took a bus to La Salle National Bank for lunch and a short performance for a small crowd in the bank's lobby. In the afternoon, they went to the Chicago Academy of Science to see the voyageur exhibit that Dr. William Beecher and his staff had put together, a quartet of manikins in period dress and in various poses around an old birch-bark canoe Frese had provided. The Chicago Historical Society welcomed the voyageurs after dinner, but there were fewer than fifty people in the audience. By contrast, eight hundred elementary school students packed the Museum of Science and Industry as the voyageurs performed and another forum was held. The subject was technology, and most of the material was way over the heads of the children.

By this time the Coast Guard had reported that Lake Michigan was eighty percent covered with ice three miles out from shore. That ice was up to three inches thick and extended all the way east to Gary, Indiana. From there to St. Joseph, Michigan, one to three inches of ice covered twenty percent of the lake as far out as two miles. Two groups were sent to scout conditions; they saw the Chicago River (open); the Des Plaines River (frozen solid); the St. Joseph River near south end of Lake Michigan (frozen in spots); and the Kankakee River (open).

On the 11th, the crew held a meeting and cast votes for their preferred route. In a close outcome, the voyageurs chose the river route down the Chicago to the Des Plaines to seek navigable water to the Illinois. That way would chop hundreds of miles off the scheduled route. Surprisingly, Cox and Reid both voted for the lake option. There were several problems with the river route. First, it would suspend the itinerary for weeks. Second, it would bypass both Indiana and Michigan, which had been so supportive under the leadership of Dave Upton. Even Cox said they would have to reschedule appearances in Valparaiso and Michigan City. Third, the river route would depart from authenticity, since the crew would never touch land in Michigan or Indiana, as La Salle did.

Despite the vote, Reid and others persuaded the crew that authenticity and commitments in two states trumped convenience. To gain the crew's cooperation, he said that public appearances would be set aside until the canoes were off the lake. The river option was not abandoned, exactly. But Reid's assurances led the crew to put it in their back pocket as a viable option. The meeting completely muddied not only the question of "what we decided" but also who decided what.

"I really do believe the lake will be OK to travel on," Fialko wrote in his journal. "But I also believe that we'll be behind schedule, due to the weather." After surviving Sand Banks and the Door of Death, the teenagers still felt invincible. Ken had a tremendous desire to prove himself and push himself to the limit. He even talked in Chicago one evening about paddling directly across the lake to St. Joe, passing the south shore by traveling around the solid ice shelf at its elbow. There the Hawk, the fierce Chicago wind, had blown the water into ragged rocks of ice and sharp stalagmites well out on the lake.

"They were talking about chipping handholds or footholds into the ice shelf," Marr said. "It really scared me." He fled from the conversation with Ken and asked to speak to Reid about it. But as soon as Marr began to talk, he said, Ken burst into the conversation, yelling angrily. "I lost it. I started crying," Marr said. "To his credit," he added, Ken stopped his rant when he saw how Marr had reacted. Ken calmed immediately and tried to comfort the young man. "We worked it out," Marr said. But safety considerations really did make a difference, and the notion of cutting across Lake Michigan was scrapped.

Kulick wrote his first entry in the official journal in eight days. He had written diligently throughout the trip, trying to put something on paper every day, but he realized that he was trying to record everything and was getting bogged down in details. The journal had suffered, Kulick believed, because it had not captured enough of his own feelings and reactions and those of the crew. He would have only three entries over the next three weeks. In the first of these, on Dec. 15, he admitted he would rather talk to people he met than spend his free time, as Cox did, writing so extensively. Tellingly, most of the official journal covers the first half of the expedition. Less than twenty percent discusses the second half.

The canoes finally left Chicago on Sunday, Dec. 12, a rare sunny day when temperatures rose above freezing. Slowed by ice at first, the crew got a northwest wind and put in at the Calumet Beach Coast Guard station nearly eighteen miles away. The men passed through the sulfurous air of Whiting, Indiana, and the dirty air around Inland Steel. By the time the crew made landfall, their faces were covered in soot.

When the crew awoke in the darkness early Tuesday, they felt a strong wind blowing out into the lake. As the light grew on the eastern horizon, they could see the waves crashing two miles out. Few were eager to test the water.

"The L'avants Local 105 went on strike!" Braun recorded in his journal. "But as always we were ignored and we went anyway!"

The canoes moved down the coast until shore ice and conditions on the lake forced the crew to put in. The seven-mile struggle against the wind and waves from Calumet Beach took six hours.

Stillwagon's three-man crew found themselves fighting thirty-five-mile-per-hour offshore winds and three-foot waves to pass through the giant gates at the US Steel plant in East Chicago. The gates presented a breakwater that rose seven feet high and stretched many hundreds of yards into the lake. As hard as the crew tried to paddle the length of the gates and into shore, the wind pushed the canoe further away. Braun had the job of securing a position at the end of the long gate and lining the craft into a sheltered place where the men could beach the canoe. Standing in his slick-soled moccasins on the icy gunnel of his canoe, Braun had to time the waves so that he could leap at their crest from his narrow, slippery perch and reach the gate's top, an eighteen-inch, ice-glazed precipice. Once there, he pulled with all his might against the gale, the weight of the canoe and his crewmates and their five hundred pounds of cargo—and prayed that he wouldn't slide off and tumble into the stunningly cold water.

"I haven't had any good times for 2 or 3 weeks as a whole, & I'm just really fed up with this whole thing," Braun wrote in his journal after the ordeal. He expressed his depression and his dissatisfaction with some of the adults. "Oh, the hell with it. I'm going to bed . . . Happy fucking birthday, Jean du [Lignon]." It was Braun's nineteenth birthday. It was also the first day he began to question what he was doing.

The crew set up camp next to the East Chicago Yacht Club. Later that day the crew made appearances in Crown Point, Indiana, at the Rotary Club and local schools. At a dinner that evening at

Crown Point High School, Principal Paul Gorgas introduced Cox as a 1959 graduate of the high school.

"The trip has really aged me, but you're making it worse. I was a '65 grad," Cox replied.

"Yes," Gorgas quipped, "but you were supposed to graduate in '59." Cox appreciated the joke at his expense.

December 15 was a beautiful day: fifty degrees and a light westerly wind, a perfect day for paddling. Instead the crew spent the day making appearances in Valparaiso and Michigan City, Indiana. Hobart told Reid it would be stupid not to travel on a day like that, and many of the teenagers agreed. But Reid said the expedition had made commitments to towns that had worked hard to host them. His position did not sit well with Cox, however, who recalled what he thought was Reid's agreement to bypass some towns and reschedule them only after reaching the St. Joseph River, where the travelers would finally be off the lake.

Kulick, who had resolved to record less minutiae and write more about crew feelings and reactions, made his first entry since Dec. 10. He noted that "things have been growing steadily tenser lately—I think since Chicago, mostly between Babouef [Cox] and Reid." But almost everyone was upset about the lack of travel on a beautiful day.

"I'm still a bit depressed from the actions of late by certain asinine individuals!" Braun wrote that night. Recalling the terror of US Steel, he added, "Tomorrow hopefully there will at least be someone checking out the landing site. Also, just found out that the weather and wind was shifting to the NW at 15–20 mph!" Braun had reached his limit in at least one sense. The next day he wrote, "Dec. 16, Thurs." and crossed it out as the journal sputtered to a close nearly four months early. His last entry was: "Dec. 26 Sun. Forget it!"

"We didn't paddle yesterday because of 'commitments' made to Valparaiso and Michigan City that couldn't be canceled. Bullshit," Campbell wrote Dec. 16 in his journal. "In Chicago at Belmont Harbor when we said we were going the lake route we said we would cancel all showings until we got off the lake."

Even the usually even-tempered, level-headed, team-oriented Lesieutre had reached a breaking point. His letter to Annie that night showed how deeply and adversely the entire crew had been affected by Reid's decision:

> "Today it was fifty degrees, light winds. We could have made at least twenty miles, but no . . . Reid had set up a performance at Valparaiso U. . . . We had a meeting less than a week ago and 'decided' to go the lake—if we canned the itinerary until we were off the lake. We would go as far as we could when we could. The actual vote was 13–10 rivers (!) until we said we would shit-can the schedule and make time. . . . Needless to say, I'm not the only voyageur on the crew [who feels this way]. The expedition morale is, by my estimation, at an all-time low. Guys would have gone home if they hadn't put in 2 years of hard work into it."

Wind-bound at the yacht club from Tuesday through Saturday, Dec. 14–18, the crew continued to bicker. At a meeting on the 16th, several of the men griped about Reid's leadership, particularly his apparent about-face on bypassing towns for now and rescheduling appearances there. Reid said that people misunderstood him when he said he would call ahead to reschedule, that he only had St. Joseph in mind. He said that the crew seemed to be taking the towns for granted, and Cox growled that Reid had lied and was taking the crew for granted. Privately, Reid bristled at being called a liar and expressed concern that the crew was splintering. That evening, though, members of the yacht club brought in at least three cases of beer and fed the jukebox upstairs as perhaps fifteen of the crew enjoyed some unauthorized time off.

"It is the first time I have seen real smiles on our faces since about a month ago," Campbell wrote in his journal. "Reid may think we are rebelling, but right now I don't care."

Halfway through the expedition, some of the voyageurs had tired of the daily grind. The men had been told to expect this, but the reality was so much harder than they had foreseen. Privately, a few expressed to each other a readiness to return to normal living. Some longed to see their families. Others simply needed a break from the cold, the wet clothes, the fatigue, the smelly sleeping bags, and the expectations that living in a fishbowl lay upon them as performers who were always "on." And perhaps they needed a break from each other.

For some, the expedition had stopped being fun, yet no one considered leaving the enterprise. Their families and friends had contributed money. There were hundreds, perhaps thousands, of people who cared whether they completed their journey. And there was the foxhole, that narrow trench of fiberglass that had seen them through so much already. Had one person left, perhaps many would have followed. But no one wanted to be the first to quit, to abandon the unstated obligation of each man to the others in his canoe.

The spread of ice across Lake Michigan now forced the crew to face the same choices they had voted on Dec. 11: the lake route or the river route. The St. Joseph was freezing, and the Kankakee was already frozen once it crossed into Illinois. If camp were made along the river route, the crew would take a bus back east to scheduled appearances in several towns along the original route, despite the lack of authenticity. Which was worse: arriving late by canoe or on time by bus? A final decision was postponed until the enterprise reached Indiana Dunes State Park. At that point, the canoes would be roughly halfway between St. Joseph, Michigan, and the Chicago River. In another discussion on Dec. 17, the crew decided to continue the original route. However, Lake Michigan had frozen from shore to shore for only the third time in a century, and there was no way the men could paddle through the ice. Finally, the men decided to do what La Salle would have done—take only what they needed and start walking until they hit open water.

"That was a big compromise" with authenticity, Braun observed. La Salle did not walk along the southern end of the lake. That was true. But if the great explorer had faced the same conditions this group faced, some argued, he would have portaged here as he did on other occasions when conditions warranted it. It would be an eighty-mile hike to St. Joseph, but at least they wouldn't have to drag the canoes or heavy equipment, as La Salle did. Upton agreed to transport the canoes and heavier gear to St. Joseph and put it all in storage, pending their arrival.

Back in Michigan City, Indiana, a Boy Scout troop bivouacked next to the voyageur camp across from the armory in Washington Park. Each group cooked a meal. Then the men and boys exchanged foods. The Scouts got peas and beans, of course. The voyageurs supped on muskrat stew and raccoon, which turned out to be moist, like dark turkey meat. Afterward, Michelle White, the head of the Indiana Bicentennial Committee, gave each man a pin, a coin minted by the state, and a state flag. Michigan City declared the day La Salle II Day, and Reid gave White the scroll from the Quebec government.

The sun barely peeks through swirling snow as a motorist zips past voyageurs dragging their canoes on sledges down a Midwestern road.

Stillwagon, Hobart, and Watts took out the red van on Dec. 18 to scout a route to hike. Sgt. Opinker of the East Chicago Police Department showed them an abandoned road they could follow that paralleled the main road. He also helped get permission for the men to walk through properties owned by Union Carbide, a cement plant, and the local gas and electricity provider, the Northern Indiana Public Service Company. At US Steel's Gary Works, the daughter of the head of security was dating Stillwagon's son Andy (whom she later married), and the official arranged for escorts through the plant, a huge complex seven miles long that employed 38,000 people. A security guard there told Kulick that the company had halted operations on the loading dock, at a cost of $30,000, to let the crew pass. Upton's friend Bill Gorman set up dinner for the men that night.

The men didn't change clothes the next morning. "We took the rails at the end of the lake" and began walking, Sohn recalled. "Dick [Stillwagon] knew the area like the back of his hand, and we went from park to park to park along the shore."

The hike began with twelve miles on Sunday, Dec. 19, under sunny skies, though a ship in the harbor had five feet of ice piled up on its bow. The men stopped to eat at the end of the steel plant. They continued along the beach to Marquette Park. Without their six canoes to set up three modules, the crew made only one shelter that night. It consisted of two tarpaulins hoisted on thirteen paddles, ten on the outside and three in the middle. The crew called it their "circus tent," and it would be their traveling home for most of the next two months. At two in the morning, the wind gusted up to sixty-three miles per hour and lifted the center paddles completely off the ground. The seam between tarps separated and half of the shelter collapsed. The snow that had accumulated on the tarp covered the men underneath as well.

"Guys were running around in their underwear to try to put it back up again," Marr recalled. The mad scramble to reset the tent took place in a stiff wind that, together with the temperature, had thrown the windchill factor down to minus thirty-five.

During another twelve miles along three highways to Dune Acres, Indiana, the caravan of snowmen missed highway US 12, extending the portage farther than planned. Frozen ground made planting tent stakes almost impossible.

From their line of march along US 12 to St. Joseph, the crew was bussed each night to appearance commitments in different locations ahead of them: Michigan City, Indiana; and New Buffalo and Bridgman, Michigan.

Portaging through a light snowfall continued twelve miles on the shortest day of the year to Washington Park in Michigan City. The Michigan City harbor was completely frozen, and the beach had nearly disappeared. Ice extended hundreds of yards into the lake and even stacked up six to eight feet high in places. Gorman followed the travelers and persuaded a friend of his to feed them lunch. Later that night Gorman arranged for a party in a home in front of the campsite with pizza and beer. Songs rang through the house, but afterward the snow fell again, a gale blew, and the lake roared loudly. Whitecaps spangled the dark water far out on the lake. The temperature was seventeen degrees, but Dean said he had heard that the wind chill was minus thirty-three. The circus tent would not hold out the cold, and a few simply stayed up all night rather than trying for a few hours of fitful slumber.

In Bridgman, Upton secured a campsite behind a Texaco station. During the day Watts was taken to a doctor. He had experienced poor circulation in his feet, and they were killing him. Stillwagon thought it might be a stress fracture. It turned out to be a stretched tendon and ligaments, for which the recovery time would be even longer.

The voyageurs rose before dawn on Christmas Eve. Bussed to South Bend, the men visited three hospitals and four nursing homes, where residents' faces lit up when they heard the French paddling songs. That night while waiting for midnight mass at Notre Dame University, the much-maligned liaison team entertained the men who had so often criticized them. The team put on a skit, a parody of one of the voyageur presentations, and everyone enjoyed the show. Somehow, the heavenly peace of a season of hope had descended on a voyageur band much in need of each other's goodwill.

The men finally returned to camp, a silent night at 3:00 a.m. Shepherds who had kept watch over the Elgin flock had come like angels: There was a basket of fruit from a local 4-H club. The Magi had also come: A small Christmas tree had been put up near the shelter, lights and all. And there were tidings of great joy: A note in the bathroom let the guys know that the phone would be available that morning for anyone who wanted to call home. The neon sign by now was dark, but the symbolism was unmistakable: The Star of Texaco held its steady place above the deep and dreamless sleep of the voyageurs.

Parents met their sons at the Catholic Church Youth Center at noon Christmas Day. Upton invited everyone over to his home on a lake that afternoon.

Conditions did not change after the holiday. Snow fell in bitterly cold air, but the crew finally made it around the edge of Lake Michigan to St. Joseph on foot and a week late. There they found open water and made camp. But the St. Joseph River, which the adults were told a year earlier never froze before the end of January, froze overnight. The plan had been to take the St. Joe south again through South Bend and a short portage to the Kankakee, but the cold had changed the calculus again. Together the group decided to keep walking south to Berrien Springs to see if the situation might change.

The monotony of walking led the men to entertain themselves, some with thoughts of food, others with thoughts of home. A few created a world out of roadside attractions. Wilson, Kulick, Lieberman, and Gorse continued to walk as a group, but they now chose to call themselves the Mediators.

"We talked almost without stopping throughout the day—no easy thing to maintain, but we were consciously committed to it," Wilson remembered. "It was way better than thinking about your feet, or your load, or the damn wind. In order to hear what was being said we stayed very close to each other. We would rotate the lead guy, and the other three could just follow and talk. It was a pretty good way to travel. This verbal jag developed many different sub-stories and lines of bullshit. The most notable grew out of the Frank Lloyd Wright Inn."

As the expedition crept through St. Joseph, the men passed the Snowflake Motel, a dilapidated structure that claimed in a sign to have been designed by renowned architect Frank Lloyd Wright. Built in 1962 and actually designed by Wright's son-in-law, William

Wesley Peter, its fifty-six rooms were arranged in six V-shaped units that formed a six-pointed snowflake. It had saw-toothed roofs and skeletal geodesic domes made of rubber tubing. (The motel fell into disrepair and was demolished in 2006.) As the men passed the motel in 1977, it assumed mythic proportions.

"We created a club. It was called the Frank Lloyd Wright Inn and Supper Club," Wilson said. "We gave it by-laws, membership requirements, hazing rituals, annual meetings, a history, a future—all of it. We discussed famous people that could be [allowed] in and those that would never make the cut. Four people, seven to eight hours a day. The volume of crap that could be created was unlimited. The idea of talking all day to take your mind off the physical strain and the boredom was surprisingly effective."

They adopted the Chicago Bears fight song as their "hymn." Lieberman was named High Mediator, with everyone else as "para-Mediators"—whatever that meant. Each Mediator had charge of some aspect of the imaginary supper club: Kulick was major domo of the restaurant; Wilson had charge of entertainment; Lieberman held the keys to the liquor cabinet; and Gorse was to secure the presence of "four loose girls."

Fantasies like that kept spirits up as the expedition stumbled across southern Michigan, but the trek had taken its toll by the time the men limped into Berrien Springs, sick and lame. Gross was ill. Foster had rubbed his thighs raw and could barely walk. Watts was out with his tendon problem. Reid's knee was swollen, and Stillwagon thought "La Salle" might have strained a tendon. Campbell and Fialko checked the river and came back saying it was frozen all the way to Niles, Michigan. On the way down Highway 33, a few semitrailer trucks nearly swept the marchers away. One car almost rear-ended a guy who had slowed down to gawk at the odd characters. At the sound of screeching brakes, Braun, Lesieutre, and Stillwagon jumped into a ditch just in time. A two-car police escort brought them into town, sirens screaming.

The men spent a memorable evening at Tabor Hill Vineyards, owned by Len Olson. Olson had served the adults wine the night before after their meeting at the Holiday Inn in St. Joseph and became entranced by the men's epic adventure. Olson had quit steel sales in 1968 to open a winery in Buchanan, about ten miles south of Berrien Springs. On July 14, 1972, the business had sold its first bottle of wine. Francophiles like the La Salle crew understood the significance of that date. It was Bastille Day, French Independence Day. Two years later President Gerald Ford, a Michigan man, made some of Olson's wine the first from the Midwest to grace the table at the White House. At Tabor Hill, Olson gave voyageurs a tour of the wine cellar and its carved wooden barrels. Olson showed pride in being the first to grow German grapes in Michigan and told a story about how he smuggled Riesling cuttings into the country through Canada in a bakery truck.

Olson had a surprise for his visitors. That afternoon he had made a special white wine, and he wanted the young men of La Salle II to name it. Given the unseasonably cold winter through which they traveled, Reid suggested "La Salle's Winter," in French, of course. Others wanted it called "The Voyageur's Winter," naturally in French. But no consensus was reached, so they all said they would decide the next day. Immediately, Olson said, "That's it! We'll call it We'll Decide Tomorrow"—*en français, naturellement.* And so *Decidons Demain* was born.

The voyageurs signed a paper with their French names to be used on the label on the back of the bottle. Wilson, perhaps having imbibed too much of the house blend, mistakenly wrote his real name instead. The others called his attention to the error, and he put down his French name, but his was the only 1976 name to "join" La Salle's original crew. Beneath the signatures, Olson added these words: "We met. We dined. We became friends. Dedicated to the free spirit of La Salle: Expedition II." Olson said he would make a thousand cases of the wine, sold in a wooden box branded with La Salle's own credo, *Toujours plus loin*—Always farther. Olson promised each of the men a case in New Orleans. The rest he expected to sell at $20 a bottle, keep $3.50 for his efforts, and donate the proceeds to the expedition.

The march continued Dec. 28 with skies pouring snow all day. The men perspired inside their wool garb and under their packs while stepping through the drifts. When they stopped moving forward, the chill was indescribable. As they marched into Niles, the men encountered an interesting fellow who said he had spent his whole life as a trapper. The man was headed to Baton Rouge, Louisiana, he said. He had run afoul of "my old lady" after spending the summer with another woman in Hudson Bay. The trapper told a story about coming back to the Lower Forty-eight from Alaska by hitchhiking and riding freight trains. He wore an elastic luggage strap as a belt, and he said he slept on top of the freight cars by hooking the belt to the brief metal bars that formed a catwalk on the roofs. He said he would look up the voyageurs when they got to Louisiana, though no one remembers seeing him again.

At Niles they made camp in snow three to four inches deep. Kulick, Gorse, Wilson, and Fialko took two hours to chop a hole in the river's thin ice thirty feet long and twelve feet wide. Overnight the snow continued as the mercury dropped to minus-six and the reported wind chill to nineteen below zero. The hole that they had made in the ice the day before had closed up. The voyageurs awoke to a river frozen solid for half a mile. Beyond that, chunks of ice blocked the river all the way to South Bend. With hope for a thaw downriver, though, the crew began work on a way to bring the canoes with them.

The Niles Parks Department opened a building, and Fialko recruited Gorse, Braun, Gross, and Fredenburg to help him build sledges while the other guys worked on repairs to clothes and moccasins. A local Scout troop helped the effort by cutting saplings fifteen to twenty feet long. The men used draw knives to cut mortises, or notches, in the logs. Then they secured cross-pieces by straps into a kind of horizontal ladder. In all, there were eight sledges, including two for gear. The men then loaded the sledges and prepared to drag them with tumplines across their chests.

The sledges moved out Dec. 30 over snow-packed roads and made good time. The curious seventeenth-century sight stopped traffic more than once en route to Pinhook Park in South Bend. The snow stopped and the sun came out. The temperature soared to seven above. On the last day of 1976, a Friday, roads remained relatively clear of traffic, but progress slowed when the sledges moved through Council Oak Cemetery, where snow had piled up in the wind, and the men had to double up to pull the sledges through the drifts. Things improved when the sledges returned to the roads, except where rock salt deiced the road and the sledges scraped noisily over exposed pavement. Pedestrians came out to the roadside to see the strange caravan. Ironically, a path had been cleared across an airport, but the voyageurs missed seeing it among the drifts. Winds gusting up to fifty miles an hour raged across the airport landscape.

"It looked and sounded like a scene out of *Dr. Zhivago*. My face was so iced up it ached," wrote Cox.

The Adventurers' Club of Chicago had planned a New Year's Eve bash in a converted garage in the woods at the Stunty Tree Farm in Walkerton. But when the men arrived at 8:00 p.m., there was no electricity—and no Adventurers' Club. The crew decided to see the old year out in style anyway. They broke out care packages from home and took up a collection, which Dean used to buy a case and a half of beer. The Adventurers did come at ten o'clock, with fried chicken, four gallons of grog, and three cases of soft drinks. Some of Ken's friends arrived to play music, and the party cranked up.

The party finally concluded early in the morning, and the voyageurs rode back "home" to the big top. The Bicentennial year came to a stunningly cold end.

BLOOD ON THE SHOULDER

(Jan. 1-13) Leaving the River

As 1976 turned into 1977, the voyageurs slept on Phil Coorman's farm. Most of the sleeping bags lay haphazardly in the big barn while a few of the men made their beds in the loft of a smaller barn on the property. Some snored softly, others loudly. At least one man screamed in his sleep.

A return to the water on Sunday, Jan. 2, turned out to be brief. Half an hour after entering the Kankakee, the river iced over again. Efforts to hack through ice six to eight inches thick were abandoned, and the explorers made camp again two hundred yards from the river. Temperatures rose into the twenties the next day under sunny skies. The canoes got a late start, finally hitting the water about 11:30. About thirty minutes later the boats crossed under a small wooden bridge. A man and a woman jumped off their new snowmobile to take pictures. But as she took snapshots, the man restarted the snowmobile, which was still in gear and took off. He hung on but hit the throttle instead of the brake. He yelled as he flew off the bridge, and he missed Fialko's canoe by less than a foot. When the snowmobile hit the shallow water the man's head bounced off the handlebars. He got up, ran ashore, and collapsed. Wilson got to him first and threw a capote over him. Stillwagon arrived shortly after that and attended to the gash on his forehead as the man's girlfriend calmly took pictures.

Voyageurs swing into action to help an injured man after his snowmobile lurched into drive and flew over the canoes and into a bank of the Kankakee River.

The expedition made six miles before ice stopped its progress. In the occasional attempts to hack through the ice, the crew lost a pair of axes. When the ice finally gave way, there was nothing to prevent the smooth wooden handles from sliding through their ice-slicked mittens and tired hands. As the paddles fell silent, the solitude of the Kankakee through rural Indiana put Cox in a poetic frame of mind.

"I love the silence," he wrote. "Beyond the snowy banks it's all farms, so there's not much going on this time of year. I love to just drift along and listen to the birds, and the breaking of the ice. It's amazing how every body of water we've been on has had its own distinct character and personality. The Kankakee certainly isn't anything like the St. Lawrence, or the Severn."

After another nice day and six more miles, the travelers bedded down next to the bridge at Highway 35. Again, Cox was in a poetic mood: "It's an absolutely beautiful night. The moon was nearly blood red when it came up. I stood out in the middle of a cornfield and watched it rise. As it got higher in the sky it went from red, to orange, to off white, to bright white. What a beautiful thing to watch, especially in near total silence."

Travel along the Kankakee River may have been lovely, but it was also painstakingly slow. The canoes navigated a meandering stream often hemmed in and sometimes covered over by ice. When the ice was less than two inches thick, the voyageurs discovered that the lead canoe could serve as an icebreaker. They would pull a loaded canoe over the ice cap and let the weight cave in the solid layer, revealing the water below. When the ice grew too thick to break with axes or the weight of canoes, the men would haul their canoes over the ice as they had in warmer months through shoals and against stiff winds along shorelines.

Sometimes the voyageurs would unload the canoes and make them light enough to carry from an ice-choked bend in the river to a stretch of open water. There the empty canoes would be returned to the water and reloaded, perhaps for a few hundred more yards before the whole ritual was performed again. While walking the banks of the Kankakee to line their canoes, the men also encountered bushes, brush, exposed roots, overhanging tree limbs, and deadfall along the banks that slowed progress to a crawl.

If the men moved onto the river to escape the hazards on shore, they found that the snow insulated the river ice and even melted it sometimes. The insulation was never enough to let the travelers slide their canoes into running water, but it was sometimes enough to weaken the ice and allow the men to fall through. This was such an ever-present danger that the voyageurs sat ten feet apart on the Kankakee River as a safety measure when they stopped to rest or eat. The ice gave way suddenly one day on the river, and Foster fell through. There was no bottom. His companions came to his rescue as they had at Hog Island. As cold as the air was when he got back on solid ground, Foster said, he felt oddly warmer with his clothes off than he did with them on while in the water.

La Salle II received an unexpected bit of help as it made its way along the Kankakee. A small private plane circled overhead before swooping low over the canoe caravan and dropping a note to tell the crew where the ice blocked their path downriver. A few minutes later the pilot swooped in again with another message.

Finally, the plane dropped a map dotted with red marks to show where the ice posed obstacles. The voyageurs still had to negotiate the hazards, but they now had a heads-up, a road map that let them anticipate problems.

The canoes often had to make their way around logs and limbs stuck in the mud in midstream. At one such spot, Lesieutre, the l'avant in the Fleur de Lys, yelled at his gouvernail, Fredenburg, to maneuver around a stump that threatened to punch a hole in their canoe. However, the channel was too narrow there and the current too quick to let Fredenburg do that, so Lesieutre himself avoided the inevitable collision, stopping the craft's forward progress. He reached out with his own paddle, stuck it toward the branch, and heard a sickening crack as the crunch of frozen wood snapped his paddle in two. Fredenburg offered a spare paddle, but Lesieutre flashed him an angry look. That paddle had been his companion for months, and you don't lose a friend without showing a sense of loss.

During some stretches of the Kankakee, the men experienced a sense of peace unencumbered by difficulties. As the canoes floated along in single file, the wind would die and the bare branches would cease rattling. The black-and-white landscape would slide by. Perhaps snow would float in big, slow-motion flakes around the canoe. The twitter of a bird marooned by the great migration south would punctuate the silence. Drifting quietly through the Indiana woods one day, the men in Fialko's canoe found themselves in such an idyll. Suddenly they realized that they were alone among the trees. The crew stopped and turned back to see if anything was the matter. The canoe behind them had snagged itself on a deer carcass left in the river and dragged it along, slowing every other canoe until the dead deer was cut loose.

Somewhere on the Kankakee portage, the travelers encountered an older gentleman with a raggedy appearance who asked if anyone among them was superstitious. The eccentric fellow was guided by the voyageurs along the line of march to Campbell for some reason.

"I'm looking for Road Kill," the man announced when he

found Campbell. He said he had a gift to bestow. He presented a mystified Campbell with a snapping turtle charm hung on a lanyard. "It won't bring you good luck," the man said, "but it will ward off bad luck."

The crew moved on to Tracy Methodist Church at Davis Station, where they stayed Jan. 6–7, nearly a week behind schedule. The men received a large dose of Hoosier hospitality in those days. People often cheered them on or brought them hot chocolate or McDonald's hamburgers. The folks from the Golden Arches also brought their own hamburgers to the feast. One woman driving by stopped next to Lieberman and Kulick, who were pulling a sledge full of gear, and asked, "What'd you like to have right now?" Flippantly avoiding the obvious, Lieberman replied, "A chocolate milk shake." About an hour later, the motorist returned—with chocolate milk shakes for everyone.

On Jan. 6 it snowed hard all day, but the expedition forged ahead several miles. The men moved like ghosts through the barren woods. It helped that someone had cut down trees along both sides of the stream in order to dredge the river. But the dead zone made a few of the voyageurs feel that something had been lost in the name of progress. The men also picked up a hitchhiker, one who offered no help but brought smiles to many faces. It was a stray dog. A local resident said it was named Schnapps. At first the crewmen called the dog Portage, but the name that stuck was *Suivant*, French for follower. When the men had dinner at an inn, Suivant waited outside the door for them to return. A few men brought back their T-bone with more than a morsel left on it. Suivant feasted that night, then joined the caravan south the next day. At rest stops, he would trot back along the line to say hello to every voyageur before returning to the head of the march.

On Jan. 7 a representative of the Army Corps of Engineers came by and gave the crew an ice report. He said that beyond navigable water nearby, the river was a skating rink, with ice three to nine inches thick all the way to the Indiana-Illinois line. The directors had originally scheduled fifteen days for the South Bend portage, but the expedition was already six days behind schedule. Even if the men covered ten miles a day on the Kankakee all the way to the Illinois River, as Reid thought they could, they would continue to fall behind schedule. With many of the towns along the route having made plans to greet the voyageurs, the delays created anxiety that the expedition would disappoint many people.

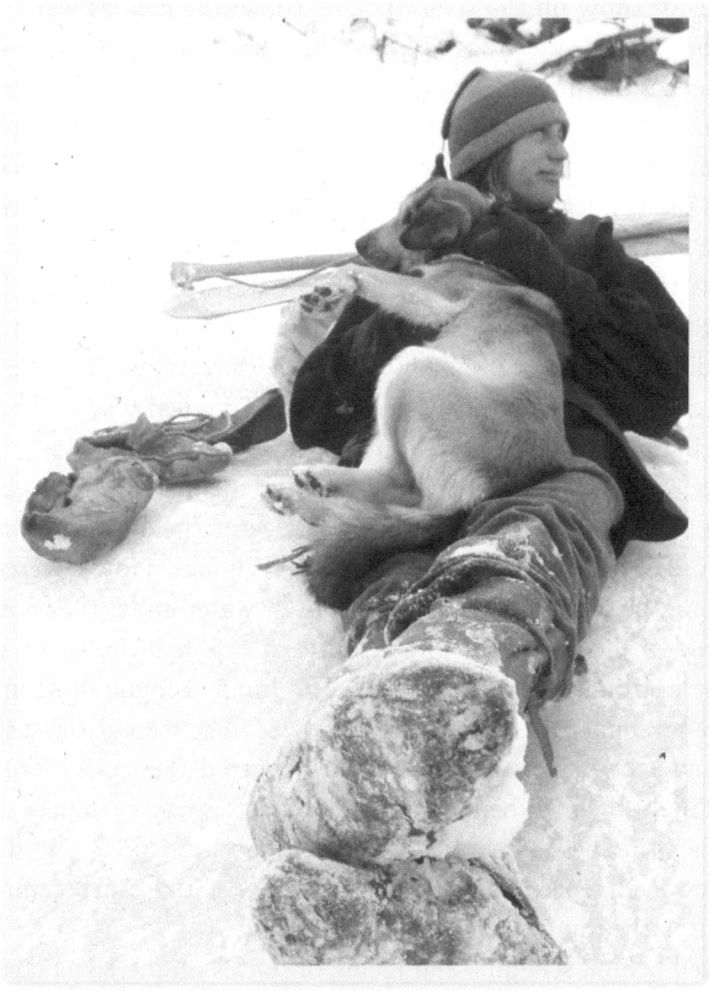

Sid Bardwell reclines in the snow with Suivant, the stray dog that adopted the voyageurs shortly before the crash at Hebron.

In addition, Hobart had found out that parts of the Illinois River were already frozen and closed to barge traffic. That raised the prospect of high water on the Mississippi and potentially dangerous ice floes. Foster was not alone in falling through the ice. The accident-prone Hess dropped through on Sunday morning, Jan. 9, when he and others went to check the river. It snowed heavily that day.

The sledges were next to impossible to pull through the eight inches of snow on the river on Jan. 10, so the canoes were taken off the sledges and dragged along their bottoms. It required seven voyageurs on tumplines to drag one canoe. By day's end the travelers had scarcely managed two and a half exhausting miles before camping on a levee road between the Kankakee and Yellow Rivers. Both the canoes and the sledges were raised on sticks to prevent being stuck to the ice. The forecast called for an overnight low of minus twenty and more snow. Classes were canceled for schools in Lowell and Shelby, where La Salle II performances had been scheduled. The crew decided to abandon the canoes altogether and ship them and their heavier gear ahead. The men would move on with light packs.

Tuesday, Jan. 11, dawned brightly, and the mercury rose steadily from an overnight low of twenty-two degrees below zero, peaking at three degrees above in the afternoon. Though snow covered the ground, the crew found several inches of water under the snow. By the end of the day's trek, chunks of ice a couple inches thick clung to the bottoms of everyone's feet. The Junior League in Momence prepared dinner for the crew that evening. The men also got showers and met the liaison team, who delivered their clean laundry. That night the men bedded down in a trio of massive tepees set up for them in Shelby by a black powder club headed by "Wild Bill" Voyles. Each tepee had a roaring fire whose smoke escaped through a vent in the top of the tent.

Well behind schedule and facing obstacles on the Kankakee, the crew decided that night to shift the portage from the river to the roads until the expedition reached the Illinois River. That way they could avoid a large horseshoe bend in the river and shorten their walk by more than thirty miles. The river route came with danger from shifting ice and tree-lined embankments. The roads were plowed and well-marked, with clear lines of sight in both directions.

The clearest sky greeted the crew as they left the river on the morning of Wednesday, Jan. 12. But the mercury registered ten degrees below zero, and a strong west wind blew into the men's faces as they trooped out of the woods toward the highway.

* * *

"I was walking off by myself," Foster recalled. "I was mad at Jorge [Garcia] and Steve [Marr] that day." The reason for his anger has been long forgotten, but his decision to walk on alone had far-reaching consequences for him. They headed west through the woods to the two-lane county road. The air was ten below and the wind was in their teeth. With light packs, however, the men had already gone six miles before stopping for lunch. The constant shuffle of legs in canvas or rough woolen pants usually led to serious chafing. To protect themselves, the men used Argo cornstarch as a talcum between their legs.

Wilson thought the traffic that day was light. He said an hour could go by without a single car in either direction. Fredenburg saw the traffic very differently. The highway was busy, he recalled, and punctuated by honking as vehicles passed the motley line of voyageurs. In fact, it was because of the number of cars on the road that he and Hess, walking with Hobart and Cox at the head of the line, chose to march well off the pavement. At some point the march came to a halt and the crew dropped their packs for a break. The men rubbed aching shoulders and sore feet. Their breath, still somewhat labored, steamed out into the cold. The four members of the Frank Lloyd Wright Supper Club sat on their packs and continued their fanciful plans while they passed around the box of cornstarch.

At 1:30 the men swung off County Road 900 and turned south onto the shoulder of northbound state Highway 2, also known there as US 231. They were fifteen miles south of Valparaiso and a mile and a half south of Hebron near a turnoff called Cemetery Road. It was a lonely place where headstones poked through the frozen earth in an unfenced graveyard not twenty yards from the highway. Hobart, Cox, Hess, and Fredenburg walked two hundred feet ahead of the others. A small truck appeared to slow as it went by; they felt a rush of air and heard the sound of screeching brakes and then the crash.

"By the time I got my pack off and turned around, I was witnessing a scene of utter chaos," said Cox. "People were yelling and screaming and running around as gear was scattered all over the area." All four of the men turned as one and ran back toward the trouble.

The anachronism of seventeenth-century canoe men marching along the shoulder of a twentieth-century highway certainly had drawn second looks from motorists all day. That was to be expected. As Alvin Lilley, aged sixty-nine, of Hebron drove his cattle truck toward the men, however, he had slowed for a longer, better look. Driving a semitrailer truck hauling a flatbed, thirty-three-year-old William Black of Virgie followed Lilley up Highway 2. Like Lilley, Black's eye was also drawn to the odd-looking pedestrians. He may have leaned forward to adjust the volume of his radio. He may have seen the cattle truck slow down, applied the brakes properly, and simply slid forward on unseen ice in the roadway. The semitrailer jackknifed and slammed into the cattle truck, pushing both onto the shoulder and grinding at high speed toward the voyageurs.

Trudging toward the disaster playing out on the road, Kulick looked up, saw the collision coming, and had just enough time to yell, "He's not going to make it!" before diving away from the shoulder. Gorse heard Black's horn and looked up long enough to see the trailer fishtail before rolling into the ditch beyond the shoulder. The tangled mass of steel hurtled into the column of travelers, taking out Marr, Wilson, Garcia, and Braun.

Near accidents had occurred several times during the journey. As Kulick rolled back to his knees and stood up, he thought this might simply be another. His comrades lay helter-skelter on the shoulder and along the ditch behind him, but no one seemed to be hurt. And then he saw Braun's backpack under the cattle truck. The sight shot adrenalin into his veins and he bolted toward the wreckage. Behind him Kulick could hear Reid's shaken cry, "My God! My God!"

"I looked up and I was looking at the grille of a white Ford farm truck," said Wilson. "I think it was less than two feet away. I remember two things from that moment with great clarity. There was no sound before the crash, probably because of the direction of the wind and the fact that I wasn't listening. The truck was white and had a chrome jet plane for a hood ornament that was exactly like the station wagon my mom drove when I was a kid. Then I got hit hard, I assume. I never lost consciousness. But I have no idea what it felt like to get hit like that, or what it was like to be thrown through the air or to hit the ground. It is as if that little snippet of tape has been removed: Never pictured it. Never dreamt about it. Nothing. The moment is gone. I'm thankful for that."

* * *

"The ground comes next," Wilson continued. "Just two things I was clear on again. The first was that I was one hurt cowboy, but I was not going to die. The second was that I was surrounded by snow, but that I was lying on some kind of big rock. I wanted the guys around me to get that damn thing out from under me. At first, they told me there was no rock. I just knew they were wrong and I REALLY wanted to be moved. NOW. They switched to a little lie. After our crew member responsible for medical stuff, Dick Stillwagon, had determined that the only thing to do with me was keep me still and wait for the ambulance, the crew members that stayed with me told me that I was in fact laying on a rock but that Stillwagon wanted me to stay still and I couldn't be moved. I bought that crap and started to settle down. Hard to say what the rock was. Probably a little of my pelvis and more of my back."

When people first got to Wilson, Cox recalled, he had a cut on his chin and was moaning about a dog. He lay on his back in a ditch running parallel to the road. The collision had thrown him there, up against a barbed wire fence. Today Wilson carries a scar on his chin, a constant reminder of Jan. 12, 1977.

Unlike Wilson, Marr remembers being hit. "I must have spun around," he said. "My leg was in the shape of an L between my knee and my ankle. I didn't feel any pain at all—until I tried to stick my leg out straight."

Marr's body lay on the shoulder, but his pack and his broken leg rested on the roadway. He knew he had a broken leg, and he asked that no one try to move him.

Garcia and Braun lay side by side behind the cattle truck. Garcia was obviously in great pain and bleeding from his head. Braun was on his stomach, with a sore leg. He also bled from a head wound but remained remarkably calm about the whole thing.

* * *

Stillwagon had seen the accident unfold. He'd watched Braun and Garcia get struck head-on and dragged under the cattle truck a good one hundred feet. Braun had been saved by the big cast iron pot on his back. When they were pulled out, however, Stillwagon thought Garcia was dying, drowning in his own blood; so he went into action immediately, giving Garcia first aid. Stillwagon yelled for warm clothing to protect the injured men. Out in the open, they were exposed to a wind chill of forty below.

Garcia kept saying he just wanted to go to sleep, but Stillwagon, fearing that he had internal injuries, refused to let that happen. At Stillwagon's urging, Garcia's friends kept talking to him to keep him conscious while they waited for an ambulance. Ken had held Garcia briefly and come away from the embrace without realizing that he had blood in his beard. He then turned to help Wilson, whose eyes widened dramatically when he saw the bloody beard.

Stillwagon recalled the Hebron accident as the most difficult situation in the entire trip, "seeing the crewmen lying in the snow, having seen some tumble under the truck, I knew they were dead!

They couldn't have survived. I'd promised Mr. Braun to bring Gary back, and now I had somehow failed. [I remember] asking a crewman, Marc Lieberman, I think, to sit with Steve Marr and not tell him his leg was broken . . . [There was] the feeling of near helplessness at making the judgment as to who to try to help first." Stillwagon determined that Garcia and Wilson, who had nearly lost their lives at Hog Island, were the most seriously hurt and had to be evacuated first.

Meanwhile, several of the crew tried to control traffic nearing the scene of the accident, yelling for cars and trucks to slow down. With adrenalin still rushing through him, Kulick was especially angry and hurling profanity-laced invective at passing motorists until Sohn and others told him to calm down. His rage quickly abated. Sohn had already had his moment of clarity. Watts had seen "Buckwheat" head toward one of the trucks "with fire in his eyes" before stopping halfway there when he realized there was nothing he could do.

Someone connected with the county coroner's office drove by, saw the carnage, and radioed the accident from the highway to emergency personnel. However, rapid response was hindered by the fact that an ambulance service in Hebron had been canceled the previous month when the state raised standards too high for many funeral homes to continue that service. The ambulance had to come from Valparaiso, and it didn't arrive for twenty minutes.

A crowd of onlookers had gathered by the time the first ambulance arrived. Among those who rushed to the scene were Lee and Marge Urbas, who owned the Colonial Inn restaurant across from Hebron High School. Lee was a volunteer firefighter, and he and Marge were trained in emergency medical techniques. They brought first aid supplies to the scene, including equipment for immobilizing limbs.

At first, the loyal dog, Suivant, wouldn't let anyone but the voyageurs near his injured friends, growling and howling at the paramedics until the crewmen quieted him. Two ambulances transported the injured to Porter Memorial Hospital in Valparaiso.

Hobart and Reid rode in the ambulances with the teens; later the rest of the crew was taken to the Colonial Inn.

"It was hard for me to comprehend—even after the guys were gone in the ambulance—what happened," Gorse said. "I didn't even sleep that night. It kept entering my mind: All the people that were hurt, and the fact that we were on the expedition and were supposed to be canoeing and were walking and all of a sudden these guys were going to the hospital because they were hit by trucks. And that was not seventeenth century."

Hess was shaken by the afternoon's event. All he could think of was how his mother might have reacted had he been injured in the wreck. For his part, "Road Kill" could ask the cosmic question of whether an eccentric old man's charm had saved him from harm.

* * *

For every one of the voyageurs, however, it was clear that a line had been crossed. At Sand Banks and Hog Island, their fate had always been in their hands. Against the terrible winter they had held their own, working together despite their differences. Now in one horrible moment their invincibility had been exposed; they were vulnerable. The entire episode was demoralizing.

Immediately after the accident, specific information was unavailable. This created a great deal of anxiety.

"The families all were concerned because, for a while, no one knew which kids were hurt," recalled Mrs. Gross. The support team was equally in the dark, however.

"We were contacted and told there was an accident," said Baumgartner. "The parents wanted to know what happened. *We* didn't know."

"When that truck hit our men, I was listening to my car radio," recalled Ken's wife, Judy. "It was the day before our anniversary. They cut into the regular program to report the accident. It felt like my heart stopped."

After a while Hobart returned from the hospital and gave a

report. He said Garcia had internal injuries and would be having surgery. Marr's broken leg was being set in a cast. Doctors were having trouble determining whether Wilson had a fractured wrist or a broken pelvis. They believed Braun had only cuts and scratches.

"It snowed every day around Valparaiso," Sohn observed. "They said if there weren't so much snow on the ground, it's likely there would have been much more serious injuries."

Reid remained at the hospital to monitor their condition. "Are they going to make it through the night? Are they going to be OK? That was my only thought," he remembered.

His brother called a meeting. Ken had two concerns: where the crew would camp that night and whether the men would give a show in Kankakee, where two hundred tickets had been sold for their performance. Unlike the crisis at Washington Island, however, the affected voyageurs were not merely cold after their accident. The crew would not perform that night. Ken attended alone. Tears flowed freely. Stillwagon wept at the meeting while saying that the hardest thing he'd ever done was to decide which of the injured should go to the hospital first.

* * *

"Stillwagon didn't owe anyone an explanation for his actions," Cox said. "He'd more than earned his salary today. Today was the day he had to take charge and make some tough decisions, and he did a great job." Cox shed tears privately in a stairwell himself, feeling a sense of helplessness and perhaps shared guilt in the decision to leave the river. "All of us know we made a mistake by selecting the route we took," he wrote.

Before leaving the Colonial, the voyageurs received an update from the hospital. Garcia was in critical condition with head trauma and a ruptured spleen. Marr had broken both of the lower bones in his left leg. Wilson had fractured a wrist, a leg, and his pelvis on both sides, and sustained back injuries. Braun had dislocated his collarbone and found breathing difficult, he said, though hospital workers had seen blood on his head and seemed more intent on X-raying his skull.

That night the voyageurs did not encamp on a rocky beach or a riverbank, a farmer's field or a frozen pier. They occupied the offices of Hebron High School, which hosted two basketball practices and a sports banquet the same night. It was the first time since they'd left Toronto that the crew slept indoors. Foster remembers a man dropping by with kernels of popping corn for the crew, then leaving quickly. The man, Foster swears, was Orville Redenbacher himself, the popcorn king appearing on TV commercials nationwide.

"I remember Reid coming back in [from the hospital], and we were all kind of leaning against the wall" in a hallway outside the offices, Sohn said. Reid addressed the crew and presented them with options. Ken remembers one option was to stop the expedition immediately. Another was to find replacements for the injured men and resume the trek. But the consensus among the crew was to continue the expedition, keeping open the places for the injured men in the hope that they could return. After all, it was not unusual for canoes to be maintained by three men instead of four, and no one wanted to abandon their task after all that they had come through and endured together. Braun, Marr, and Garcia's father told Reid at the hospital that the expedition should continue.

Ken had favored an outdoor encampment in Hebron and continuing the portage to protect the continuity and authenticity of the expedition. He was a minority of one, however. The crew decided to bus ahead to Wilmington, Illinois, near the confluence of the Kankakee and Illinois Rivers. The hope was that they could get back on schedule and that the Illinois would be more navigable than the Kankakee.

Braun rejoined the crew that night with his arm in a sling to protect his mending collarbone. He had four stitches in his head and a bruised sternum. He quickly returned to duty, but he relinquished his l'avant position in favor of a less strenuous milieu seat. Wilson was out for five weeks before returning.

Neither Garcia nor Marr ever got back in a voyageur canoe,

but neither man was ever replaced and both later rejoined the expedition as members of the liaison team. Marr returned in Memphis on March 2, and Garcia came back outside Greenville, Mississippi, on March 15.

"When I was in the hospital—you know, I'm not much of a letter writer—but I received letters from my peers, kids my age from Montreal to Indiana," Wilson said. "And for a kid to sit down and write a letter to something that had an impact on him of genuine concern about how things were going, that impressed me."

Elgin folks began to stream in. Pam and Rowena came with Pam's parents and Mrs. Lesieutre. Reporters from the *Elgin Courier-News* and the *Hammond Times* came in after hearing about the accident. Chicago TV stations had carried the news on the 5:00 p.m. report. The kid whose mother had had the voyageurs over for a Christmas party drove down from New Buffalo. John White, the Native American from Zion, called with good wishes. Someone who heard about the crash from Frese called all the way from the Yukon Territory.

The day after the accident the crew decompressed and took stock of the situation. It was a school day at Hebron High. Some of the crew remained in Hebron while the rest traveled by bus, leaving to an ovation from students and riding into a different world, it seemed. The snow-filled skies of Indiana gave way to a clear blue in Wilmington, where temperatures melted to a balmy thirty-one and open water gave a false impression. All reports, including those from the Army Corps of Engineers, indicated that the rivers were frozen as far as Peoria Lake, far down the Illinois River. At least the Izaak Walton League had already set up camp for the men on an island in the middle of the river and erected shelters with straw as a ground covering.

Dean drove Hobart and Watts upriver to examine conditions for paddling. On their way, Hobart discovered that October temperatures in the region had been the worst in fifty years. November had been the worst in 96 years, and December had been the worst in 104 years. Lake Erie was ninety-six percent frozen, and Lake

Michigan had frozen from shore to shore for only the third time in the twentieth century. January was expected to be another month of temperatures fifteen to seventeen degrees below normal.

After the accident, a local paper had run a story under the headline, "La Salle Voyageurs Forced to Give Tri-Creek Area Cold Shoulder." But the crew rescheduled and were bussed to Lowell, Indiana, for a show and dinner. In the voyageur presentation at the local high school that night Ken stood in for Wilson, and Fredenburg took on Marr's singing duties. The audience rose to their feet to cheer, lifting the men's spirits.

* * *

Hobart, Dean, Lesieutre, and Hess gathered around the campfire afterward with four or five members of the Izaak Walton League—"Ikes"—who had brought some beer. The travelers added some of their Tabor Hill wine to the mix. Len Olson had taken three cases to the hospital in Valparaiso as soon as he heard about the accident. The banter and singing went on into the small hours of Jan. 14. In many ways, the community and the sing-along had lifted a cloud from the crew and put the expedition back on track. During the days of trouble, Suivant became an indoor dog, kept by a Hebron mortician. At the camp one of the Ikes, Bill Gutshall, said he'd like to have the dog, and the crew voted to say *au revoir* to their mascot.

Heat from the discharge of Dresden nuclear power plant kept twenty miles of the Illinois River open west of the voyageur camp as far as Seneca, though fear of frostbite kept the men holed up for two days. Beyond that open water, the men faced a sixty-mile hike along the Illinois-Michigan Canal, which parallels the river to the twin cities of LaSalle-Peru. From there the Illinois was frozen, not just to Peoria Lake, but all the way to the Mississippi. Barges had tried to break the ice, but it had hardened into enormous jagged ice floes. A few barges had reportedly sunk even south of St. Louis. It would have been impossible to pull fragile canoes over the rough ice.

In balance with the weather report was some good news. Marr was released from the hospital. Wilson was transferred to a hospital in Elgin, though he was still in a great deal of pain. The word about Garcia traveled from Palmer through Hess to Cox, who reported that Garcia was very bitter about his situation and refused to see visitors or take any phone calls. Eventually, all the families whose boys were injured in Hebron would file lawsuits. Though the settlements were confidential, Wilson told some people that his paid for his college education.

The crew was divided on Saturday, Jan. 15. Some went back to Hebron to load canoes and gear. Half a dozen attended a ceremony in Kankakee, where a tree was planted in their honor. The rest stayed in camp with the gear they'd brought with them. In the afternoon, the crew moved up by bus to Channahon, a little north of Wilmington. The men made camp in a park close to the Illinois River, which steamed so fiercely that no one could see to the other side. On that day, record temperatures as low as twenty-one degrees below zero froze most of the remaining open water in the Midwest. The following night the wind chill surged to sixty-seven below.

The men of La Salle II had already portaged several times across many miles. Frustration, anger, and distrust had riven their unity and dogged their steps through every horrible walk. But every one of those was mere rehearsal for the march they now faced, dragging themselves hundreds of bitterly cold miles across the Illinois tundra.

More than three months remained in the journey of La Salle II, but the fun had drained out of the adventure. The frequent rain and snow, the illness, the intense cold, the public spotlight, the constant infighting, and the unremitting fatigue had taken an immense toll on the entire crew. Day after weary day, the work of putting one foot in front of another ended only with an expectation that authentic voyageurs would happily sing and act for sometimes sparse and occasionally disinterested audiences. The challenge was no longer to restore a sense of heritage or to invigorate a sense of conservation. It was not to show how modern youth could perform authentic tasks in authentic ways to duplicate the lifestyle of seventeenth-century explorers. By the time the crew reached open water again, their paramount desire would not be to live the adventure but simply to finish it.

HARD RIVERS

(Jan. 16–29) Across the Land of Lincoln

The Illinois River starts and ends in its namesake state, traveling west through LaSalle and Putnam Counties before it falls hundreds of miles roughly southwest across the midsection of Illinois. Before it empties into the Mississippi, the river's course carries it through a long series of lakes. Some form part of the river itself; others do not. The Michigan-Illinois Canal parallels the river, separated from it by a levee.

A solitary voyageur leans into the wind as he trudges over the ice along a frozen shore. Wind chills reached nearly eighty degrees below zero as impassable rivers forced the men to walk through a bitter winter across hundreds of miles of Midwest tundra.

As La Salle: Expedition II continued down the length of the river, the men frequently traveled through wetlands lying across their line of march. The ice there added to treacherous footing and offered obstacles on any given day. Virtually every member of the expedition found fragile ice somewhere and plunged a leg into freezing water up to his knee. However, the crew did not delay their departure because the river was icy or the wetlands menacing, but rather because the cold was so deep and the winds so strong.

At dawn in McKinley Woods in the Will County Forest Preserve District, the mercury on Jan. 16 read twenty-five degrees below zero with a windchill factor of sixty-five below. Chicago had broken its record low for that date. The next day promised to be even colder. It took Hess and Campbell forty-five minutes to get the morning fire started.

As cold as it was, the possibility of getting on the water held everyone's attention even more. Stillwagon and the Lewis brothers said they were ready to go if it were only themselves at risk. But Stillwagon said the crew should stay put, and the group voted not to try putting canoes on the river. Ken suggested the crew walk the canal that day, since Monday would be even colder, but no one took him seriously. They were bussed to a potluck dinner and presentation in Seneca that night before an audience of 250. Marr and his family came by, brightening the evening for his comrades. He said he hoped to rejoin the crew within a month, and he even participated in the night's performance.

The expedition was driven to Ottawa the next day, getting out before the bus reached town so the men could march in. It was the first time since the landing on Dec. 6 in Evanston that the crew had arrived in a town on schedule and under their own power. The cold caught up with the support team on the way, though, as Scavuzzo tried to make up time. Rolling down the highway, her van gradually seemed to lose speed. She shoved the gas pedal to the floorboard, but the van would not move faster than thirty-five to forty miles per hour. When she finally had the chance to have a mechanic look into the problem, it turned out that the gas line had frozen.

The cold gripped the entire Lower Forty-eight, it seemed. While the weather pattern kept the temperatures moderate in Alaska, a low-pressure trough in the East drew arctic air across the face of the Rocky Mountains. The blast gave the eastern two-thirds of the United States its coldest winter of the twentieth century. Jan. 18–21 was the coldest period ever recorded in Palm Beach County, Florida, hitting a low of twenty-seven on Jan. 20. South Florida experienced snowfall for the first time ever recorded, the National Weather Service said. Wind and temperatures ripped windows out of high-rise buildings in Chicago, and parts of Minnesota reported a wind chill of one hundred degrees below zero. Of course, most Americans were sleeping indoors during the brutal cold.

The expedition got under way under sunny skies on Jan. 18 for the first time on its own since the awful crash in Hebron. The crew intended to hike fifteen miles to the LaSalle-Peru area but stopped after nine miles because Utica scheduled activities that had not been on the itinerary. LaSalle-Peru apparently didn't budge on its itinerary, however, which meant the men had to encamp in Utica for events there and be bussed back and forth to LaSalle-Peru over the next two days for events there. Reid, Ken, Cox, and Lieberman passed a peace pipe with a Winnebago Indian named Hayne Sine during a ceremony at four o'clock. Sine prayed to the north, south, east, and west. The crew then smoked the calumet, too.

The day the country inaugurated Jimmy Carter as president, the men resumed their hike down the frozen Illinois River. The day was clear; bright sunshine glared off the crisp, white ground and nearly blinded the men. The canal no longer paralleled the river, so there was no towpath or levee to walk on. Away from highways and populated areas, the men moved over the river ice, along the river's banks, through woods and open fields. Only one road crossed their path all day, and the air temperature in the twenties seemed like a tropical heat wave to men used to high winds and subzero conditions. Their twisting path that day probably meant that the men covered more than the estimated fourteen miles of river. In the short days of the Midwest winter, the men spent the last hour of their march walking in the dark.

In some stretches of the Illinois River, high bluffs towered over the voyageurs. The desolate beauty of the region and its isolation reminded some of the travelers of Georgian Bay, though nothing of Canada compared to the unrelenting cold. Just as the last Ice Age exposed a land bridge between Asia and North America, the level of the Mississippi River had dropped as it froze, exposing more of the tree trunks along the banks. This affected one population especially: the beavers. Sohn saw a standing tree with roughly a dozen chew marks up and down the trunk as the beavers moved with the water level.

La Salle II encountered scores of barges marooned in place on the river. Two tugs seemed immune, however, as they broke the ice like glass in front of them and pushed two barges along. Where they passed, great shards of ice thrust outward with sharp edges that floated just above the surface and posed hazards to anyone along the shore. Every crew member had to watch his step or risk slashing his leg on a floe that might have seemed moored to the bank.

The expedition stopped for breakfast at a place in Peru called The Maples. Reid rented a Dodge maxi-van to carry the crew's bags for a month. The $480 cost covered travel for three thousand miles, but it could be driven only by someone twenty-two or older, which excused Baumgartner and Palmer.

Dr. Brown's effort to sell commemorative envelopes had born fruit in LaSalle-Peru. Seven hundred of the items had been sold, with proceeds going to the expedition. The crew also learned that Garcia would be released from the hospital on Jan. 22. Pam reported that Mrs. Garcia had called to say he was in a good mood. The weather forecast also brought the travelers good news. Temperatures were expected to continue in the balmy twenties for a few more days.

The expedition made camp about four miles short of the town of Hennepin, a community named for a priest who traveled through this part of the country with La Salle in the 1680s and, at La Salle's request, reconnoitered the Mississippi River at least as far north as Minneapolis, even before the great explorer reached the mouth of the Illinois. A potluck dinner at the Catholic youth center that night brought out a surprisingly large segment of the town, whose population was about four hundred at the time.

Expedition rules required canoes to stay together as much as possible on the water. No such rules governed the portages, where the men walked at different paces and spread out over time. During the walk from Hennepin, some struggled with foot problems—fallen arches, blisters, bunions, strained tendons. Sohn was ill with the first stages of flu and walking slowly. Gross and DiFulvio walked with him for company. Others required some kind of sustenance, like water or an orange, and stopped for a few moments to replenish fluids. Sometimes the route took the men through woods, where trees obscured their ability to see others walking faster or slower. By noon on Jan. 21, the hikers—one could hardly call them voyageurs now—were strung out over a distance of at least a mile. The first people got to the campsite in Henry at two o'clock. The last ones in didn't arrive for at least another hour. The gap between the head and the tail of the line was perceived by some as a safety concern.

"I can't remember how many times I've said we aren't safety conscious enough," Cox said. "Less than ten days after a near-fatal accident we've again resorted to being a leaderless dog-and-pony show. All I could think of was what would happen if the last guy twisted an ankle or knee on the jagged ice. It would be hours before anyone knew it." Cox resolved to look out for himself, dumping into a liaison vehicle all his gear but a poncho, capote, and ground pad, and adding snack items and a flashlight. But he also decided to keep his feelings to himself, funneling his anger and dissatisfaction into his journal.

When the group crossed the river into Henry, police blocked off both ends of the bridge and escorted the marchers to the other side. This, too, was a consequence of the incident in Hebron. At the Catholic church in Henry, so many residents had dressed up in elaborate outfits that the hall looked like a royal court. Madrigal singers and an orchestra entertained the visitors, who enjoyed a dinner of wild game and received ecology medallions. At camp afterward, a doctor came at Stillwagon's request to check out several of the men. Sohn could barely move his head because of a sore neck. Kulick and Cox were running temperatures. Ken, who had pushed himself on the day's march, had a chill but refused the physician's attentions.

The cold returned overnight, but the men slept late, since the walk to Lacon was only eight miles. Ken had been sick all night and was too sick to come to breakfast. He had been wearing all of his clothes on the portage instead of keeping most of them in his personal bags. He may have become overheated in his exertions to keep up with the leaders the day before. Sweat poured off his face as Stillwagon and Reid both told him to ride that day instead of walk. Almost immediately he rushed into a nearby building to throw up. With typical panache, however, he emerged whistling, trying to demonstrate his fitness for duty. Ken stayed with the trekkers, saying that he knew his own limits. Some of the men chose to admire his determination, others to ridicule his stubbornness. Sohn recognized his own need for rest and took the day off, his first day away from his comrades since the expedition began.

In Lacon, police again stopped traffic to let the crew cross the bridge. Marr met them at the crossing and seemed to be in great spirits, despite the news that his bones were not healing properly and he would have to have his leg broken again and reset. The expedition made camp next to the courthouse. Ken was pale and slept until dinnertime.

Police made the bridges safe for the voyageurs, but nothing could guarantee safety for the liaison team. Baumgartner, who drove up to 150 miles ahead of the voyageurs to help make arrangements for their campgrounds and performances, drove one of the vans. Scavuzzo, who hated driving, rode shotgun. One day they found themselves crossing a bridge over the Illinois River. At each end, long steel guardrails channeled traffic onto the two-lane bridge, where there were no shoulders. Sharon drove past the guardrails and onto the midsection of the bridge. There she saw a brace of eighteen-wheelers swing down the highway toward the opposite end of the bridge, one truck attempting to pass the other. Sharon had no time to turn around and no opportunity to stop and back up. And neither of the truck drivers appeared anxious to brake, fall behind the other, and clear the road for oncoming traffic.

They may not have seen the collision that was fast approaching, but Baumgartner did. Making an executive decision in a split second, the nineteen-year-old floored the accelerator and pushed the well-traveled van as hard as it could go toward the far guardrail. There was a chance that she could just make the far end of the span before she and Scavuzzo were crushed by the tons of steel hurtling toward them. Baumgartner entered the far guardrail area as the semitrailer trucks loomed large in her windshield, then she spun the steering wheel hard right just in time. The sides of the van shook from the cone of air blown off by the semis as Baumgartner kicked up stones from the gravel shoulder and skidded to a halt.

Dressed in buckskin and sporting a Mohawk haircut, local historian Dr. Baird Esme received the visitors in Chillicothe. It was the warmest day the men had seen in a while, but a strong wind in their faces made it seem colder. Ken walked again, though he lagged far behind the pack this time, plagued by diarrhea. Defending his brother's decision to continue on the trail, Reid told Bardwell that morning that people often improve their health by pushing themselves harder. Ken made his own defense in an interview with the *Elgin Courier-News*.

"Without the physical challenge of sleeping outdoors and fighting the weather and the water, we might just as well be a troop of actors," Ken said. "Our biggest responsibility, our biggest goal, is to educate, and we can only communicate with people when they know we are making sacrifices. If we compromise authenticity too much, then the people will no longer be excited and we might as well end the expedition."

In the minds of his fellow travelers, however, authenticity had already been compromised. It had suffered an enormous blow in Hebron with the shocking collision with modern times. The loss continued to be felt in the daily battle with weather, where choices had to be made between authentic reenactment and the need to take busses up and down the route to meet appearance commitments. The pageantry of paddling into a town was long gone.

"Everyone just wants to be paddling again," said Braun. "We've accepted the fact that we'll probably have to walk all the way to Memphis, and no one is about to give up. But there's a decline in enthusiasm. We're not down because of the weather or bad luck. It's just that we've had to compromise ourselves in order to keep on schedule."

Ken wasn't the only one hurting. Sohn's aches had moved from his neck down his spine to his waist. At the hospital nearby, he was diagnosed with flu and told to rest for the next four or five days. Kulick received a communication from Clif Wilson, who was still in the hospital in Elgin. Wilson joked that he was having a hard time keeping roommates because he insisted on keeping his window open. One rumor, later dispelled, was that his core temperature had dropped two degrees during his extended stay outdoors during the winter.

The night the crew camped in Chillicothe at Shore Acres Park, the rest of America witnessed the first of eight episodes of *Roots*, television's first true blockbuster TV miniseries. The finale garnered 71 percent of the TV audience, an estimated 130 million viewers, the highest-rated show ever. During the series run, La Salle II crewmen noticed that audiences were noticeably smaller than usual.

Temperatures broke into the mid-thirties on Monday, Jan. 24, though skies were uniformly gray. The men saw swans, and Stillwagon thought he saw a golden eagle. However, progress was slow. Wetlands surrounded an underground stream that fed into the river. The high temperatures made it impossible to walk on the ice for six or seven miles. Instead the men tromped through marshes and yards and over rocky beaches that reeked of dead fish. In other areas, both on and off the river, the men had to wade through deep snowdrifts.

Those leading the way ended the day with burrs and stickers on their clothes. Camp was established at a golf course between Peoria and Mossville before a cocktail reception for 125 guests invited by Peoria's mayor. The occasion was a fund-raiser, but not for La Salle: Expedition II. The mayor was trying to find money to rebuild Fort Crevecoeur, a structure first erected by La Salle in 1680.

By now illness had begun to spread through the entire crew. Clearly, Ken had been sick and Sohn had the flu. Hess was now sick. Campbell, who had been sick but returned to the line of march, was feeling poorly again. He and Hess booked a room at the local YMCA. Cox felt tired, achy, and feverish, and he was far from alone. The crew remembered how many of them had come down with colds after visiting so many classrooms along Chicago's North Shore. Stillwagon hoped to find a day or two to take off so that the entire group could rest and recover. A doctor told him that the group had all been exposed to the flu, assuring him that Ken wasn't adding to the illness woes. Only seventeen crew members spent the night in the shelter, and Gross dropped out of the march the next day.

That afternoon Campbell had a run-in with Jan and Scavuzzo. He was helping Palmer and Baumgartner take down the sound equipment after the performance as the two older women smoked and drank coffee in the back of the room. Campbell, who had been in radio production with Baumgartner, blew up at them and said what many of the voyageurs had said to each other, that Palmer and Baumgartner did the work while Jan and Scavuzzo sat back and took it easy. After their sharp exchange, Jan apparently told Palmer that she would send Campbell home. That intention got back to Road Kill, who recorded it in his journal. The sword did not fall, but it hung over him for the next couple of days.

By now it was clear that no amount of bathing could remove the stink from the voyageurs for a substantial length of time. The clean bodies still put on underwear that went days, sometimes weeks, without washing, slid into sleeping bags that went months without cleaning, and covered themselves in woolen outerwear that was rarely washed.

If the men could not save their scent, however, they continued to offer ways that people could save the environment. At the forum that night, Dr. Richard Sparks of the Illinois Natural History Survey recalled that the Illinois Valley once produced thirty thousand pounds of commercial fish and was one of the best fur-producing areas of the Northwest.

"The Illinois River, in spite of all the horrible conditions that exist in the upper part, is still a beautiful river, and I hope this is a sunrise and not a sunset," said Sparks.

When asked what citizens could do to preserve the region, one of the voyageurs said that people tend to work more effectively in a group, and he suggested that citizens get involved in groups like the Izaak Walton League, the National Audubon Society, and the Sierra Club.

At Peoria the crew helped to dedicate a pavilion in the park meant to house a reconstruction of La Salle's Fort Crevecoeur, the place where the explorer intended to build a ship to take to the Gulf of Mexico. The woman who was the driving force behind the Fort Crevecoeur construction project, Mrs. Miller, gave the men breakfast the next morning. The day's events ended with a photo op at the marker site of the fort, sometimes called "the Plymouth Rock of the Midwest."

The reconstruction of the fort there was based on the long-held belief that the site was where La Salle had built his base in the Illinois wilderness, though the fort had been destroyed in the seventeenth century and no archeological evidence existed to verify it. The Daughters of the American Revolution had conducted a five-year study that decided on the site in 1902. In spite of the DAR's conclusion, several competing theories about the site continued to vie for acceptance. The Illinois State Historical Society undertook the task itself, naming a committee to study the location of the fort La Salle had anointed with the single word Crevecoeur—literally, broken heart. In 1921 the panel found that it was impossible to designate the exact spot on which the fort stood, and it agreed to adopt the DAR site. That same year the DAR erected a stone monument on the spot, with the inscription: "In 1680 upon this spot stood Fort Creve Coeur.... Here was centered the hope of Louis XIV for a broader empire of the French on American soil."

The crew's schedule would have been chock-full of appearances, except that Bill Dwyer, a veteran of the 1973 canoe trip, cut the crew some slack. He had moved to central Illinois, and convinced local officials to cancel several engagements. While the La Salle contingent was there, he exchanged some mutual admiration with one of the paddlers.

"There is no way in hell I'd make a trip like this," Dwyer told the voyageur.

"And there is no way in hell I'd paddle six hundred miles back up the Mississippi" like you, the voyageur replied.

Though the river was open between Peoria and Pekin, their next destination, the men hiked eight miles along railroad tracks to their next campsite. DiFulvio, Fredenburg, and Stillwagon were battling flu or diarrhea now, and none was among the marchers. Again, the crew found the liaison team had been no-shows in Pekin until two hours before the men arrived. Criticism of the advance work was less important to Campbell, however, than consequences of the criticism he had hurled at Jan earlier.

"This afternoon Reid found the chance to carry out Jan's work & send me home," Campbell recorded in his journal. He and Bardwell were trying to light a fire at the campsite when Reid called them over by their French names. He told them to let the fire wait. Campbell asked him to wait a second, Road Kill recorded. The seemingly innocent exchange apparently escalated into angry words. Reid alluded to a talk the two would have that night, Campbell said. By 11:15 p.m., Reid had not approached Campbell to have that talk and Campbell decided to go to bed, but not before writing in his journal, "If he wants to get rid of me he is going to have to kick me off, because I would not give him the satisfaction of me volunteering to quit for him." Nothing ever came of the flare-up. Both men had more important things to consider before the night was out.

The last voyageurs went to bed, their nightly home of paddles and canvas little more than a Little Pig's home of sticks and straw. Winter huffed and puffed outside, blowing so strongly that the men couldn't close the shelter entrance. Snow gathered on the canvas roof above their heads. It blew through the opening and over their bags. Finally, sleep overtook the weary travelers. Then whatever dreams had settled in with the snowflakes suddenly disappeared. The wind roared like a jet engine, drizzled away, throttled up and raged again. At 1:45 one mighty gust finally blew the shelter down. Trying to raise it again in that hurricane was impossible. Reid yelled for everyone to grab their gear and head for the Pekin Union Mission across the street. For only the third time since Aug. 3, the entire crew would sleep indoors.

At breakfast the next day the crew learned that the temperature overnight had been twenty degrees below zero. The wind had ripped through the camp at nearly sixty miles an hour, driving the wind-chill factor to seventy-five degrees below zero. The state pulled all snow removal equipment off the roads, and nine inches of snow lay on the highways around Pekin. Even back in Elgin the schools had been closed. Frese's secretary called with a message from him. He wanted them to know it was thirty-eight degrees in the Yukon, where dogsled races had been canceled and children complained because they could not ice skate.

FLOW, RIVER, FLOW

(Jan. 30–Feb. 14) Havana to Chester

The expedition left Havana, Illinois, on Jan. 30, heading for Anderson Lake. The temperature hovered near zero. Fredenburg returned to the line of march, but DiFulvio remained out. Even for Fredenburg, a veteran of the outdoors who had been ice fishing in temperatures of thirty degrees below zero, the cold was memorable. The crosswind along the levee road tore at the faces of the walkers. As the men crossed the lake where it was a mile wide, they turned directly into the wind. Across the surface there was bare ice where they slipped, and other places where they waded up to their knees in snow. At night the wind died out and stillness fell over Anderson Lake. The fire danced in the cold, almost brittle in its own light.

In the last several days, the group had taken the bus or vans from one place to another. They'd spent a lot of time indoors; and they'd begun to use paper plates. None of these modern conveniences authentically captured the voyageur lifestyle. None of the guys used the greeting *bonjour* anymore, either. Reid told them that they should stop spending personal time indoors, including activities such as reading, writing, sewing, or just sitting around.

While the bussing did not serve authenticity, it did serve the itinerary. Now it also saved the travelers' legs on Monday, Jan. 31, as the bus drove them halfway to their next destination. The men still had another ten-mile hike south from there to Beardstown, where weather had closed the high school the entire week before. Their path took them into a tough crosswind from the west. The river's broken ice reflected the bright sun so fiercely that the glare provoked headaches. DiFulvio's condition had not improved, and he went to the hospital. Doctors suspected he might have an ulcer, and he was advised to take things easy for a while.

Beardstown's students heard the crew perform the morning of Feb. 1. A thousand kids of all ages watched in the high school, but the presentation was marred at the end by a trio of knuckleheads who shot paperclips at the voyageurs. Hess, who'd gotten strafed, told a teacher. After the culprits were identified, the principal let Hess ream them out himself.

Near Grafton, Illinois, the tiny forms of voyageurs stand out against the broad white stripe of the Mississippi River, frozen over like all the others since the expedition left Chicago.

The men walked eight miles to the LaGrange lock while Hobart took a small plane south to St. Louis to look into river conditions. The pilot was a Beardstown insurance agent who moderated the forum the previous night. The Mississippi was frozen solid at least as far as Alton, Illinois, just north of St. Louis, and only partly open beyond there, though enormous ice floes able to crush a flotilla of canoes moved dangerously along the surface. In the awful cold, capotes stood up when placed by themselves on the frozen ground. Mittens hung over the campfire to dry would freeze overnight and require a second thawing. A beautiful sunset ended the day. At night a coyote howled for several minutes as a full moon crawled through the darkness. Back from his flight, Hobart called the Coast Guard and learned that the Mississippi was still closed all the way to Cairo and that ice jams were a problem as far south as Memphis, Tennessee.

On any given day, the expedition could be minus a crew member or two. During the long walk across Illinois, there were times when scarcely two-thirds of the crew slogged through the snow or slipped over the ice. Several men were absent from the march on Groundhog Day. Garcia and Marr and Wilson were still recovering from their injuries, of course. DiFulvio was resting on doctor's orders. Kulick had become ill and did not walk on. Now Foster was ill. Road Kill, who had hurt his knee wrestling with Buckwheat back in Mequon, found that his knee was so swollen that he could not walk. Father Loran, who could not paddle, certainly couldn't walk, either. The rest of the diligent band leaned into knee-deep snow on the river for miles until they found a narrow opening, and then they picked their way over a glacial landscape of ice sheets the barges had thrown aside. A few witnessed something rare: half a dozen bald eagles in flight.

After fourteen miles the men made an unscheduled stop Feb. 2 in Naples, a tiny hamlet where the liaison team had set up in a home being converted to a restaurant. A spot occupied more by dogs and trailers than people, it seemed, Naples is where two reporters from the *New York Times* caught up with the crew. Reid and Ken jumped at the opportunity to publicize La Salle II and, after the *Times* got a few quick photos, invited the newsmen indoors for a talk. Ken emerged briefly to tell the rest of the men that they could dry their clothing in certain rooms inside, but that they themselves were to keep their distance while he and Reid were being interviewed.

Tired and hungry, the other voyageurs ate their stew, many of them outside where additional pots were left for them. But when they started to bring their sleeping bags in to dry, they noticed Reid sitting at a table with Jan and Scavuzzo, who appeared to be eating chili and drinking Cokes. The image jarred some who had heard Reid preach just two days earlier against spending personal time indoors. The grumbling by some against Reid's leadership, which had been going on since Belmont Harbor, cranked up again. The next day, Watts overheard Reid confide in Fialko that he feared he had lost control of the group. Friday morning he addressed the men to try to regain their trust and rebuild the unity that had frayed so badly. Fialko recorded his own observations in his journal.

"So far we haven't come to blows, but I notice that there's a lot of back-shooting going on," Fialko wrote in his journal. "People usually wait for crew meetings to drop a bomb after they've talked it over with some friends first. Snide comments find their way into conversations within earshot of the 'offender' rather than on a direct approach to the person. . . . Babouef and Baron [Cox and Hobart] have quite a following amongst the crew. And I think that the seeds of doubt [about Reid's leadership] that were planted last spring by Joel Knecht have been nurtured well by some members of the crew."

Reid's leadership issues were little different from those that plagued La Salle himself. La Salle's hard-bitten men no doubt resented the morality imposed on them by the explorer, a former priest. They often went months, even years, before they were paid, and rumors of La Salle's death or financial ruin were enough to make the men walk off the job. Not unlike the subversion Reid faced, priests who feared civil control of their far missions stirred up both Native Americans and French voyageurs to abandon the projects that La Salle needed them to do. At least no one tried to kill Reid; La Salle was the object of several assassination attempts by his men, one of which finally succeeded.

Fialko noted that neither the crew nor the liaison team seemed to understand the problems of the other. Hiking through the bitter cold and snow instead of paddling down flowing rivers had taken a toll on the expedition's ability to interpret the voyageur life and the French pioneer history along the route, he suggested.

"I don't believe that the crew is hanging together like I think we can if the crew could bury some hard feelings that have developed over petty (I think) things," Fialko wrote. "I also think I know what Reid meant when he said that Ron [Hobart] wants this to be a 'college trip.' I think that we can travel from place to place, but the key is authenticity."

As the men hiked to Florence, they saw more bald eagles. The temperatures neared forty, which was an incredible heat wave for travelers used to extreme cold. Together the crew made a decision to walk the thirteen miles to Pearl before deciding whether to continue another four or five miles to Apple Creek. Again the group stretched out along the trail. Before everyone had arrived in Pearl, however, it appeared that Reid and Stillwagon had decided to press on to Apple Creek. To Cox, it shattered any notion from the morning's meeting that decisions would be made on a democratic basis. After another seventeen miles to Hardin, Fialko again recorded the discord.

"Morale low. Louie vs. René [Cox vs. Reid]. But Louie has more group support. René wants to push on. Louie is a restraint."

During those two days, voyageurs dropped like icicles on a warm day. Campbell, whose knee was killing him, had to stop. So did Braun, who in some ways was still rehabbing from the Hebron accident. Hess's foot was badly swollen. The next day Watts dropped out and Braun rejoined the march. Sohn soldiered on the whole way, though he was hurting. When the group straggled into Hardin more than eight hours after they began, only fourteen people were still on the march. The men who dropped out had set up camp for the others. The footsore men who shuffled into camp received a greeting that none of them could have foreseen.

"When we got off the river," Cox wrote, "we were met by a grade-A Cracker Moron. It was very dark, and I was walking right behind Reid. The Cracker was waiting for us at the shoreline with a lantern. His first words were, 'Welcome to Calhoun County, where the sun never sets on a nigger.' Perhaps Reid's face registered shock because the guy then said, 'You don't have any niggers in the group, do ya?' To top it off, he was a writer for the local newspaper. Now I know I can be a little intolerant, and possibly bigoted, but I've never greeted anyone in such a manner, and I doubt that I ever will."

The Jolliet reenactment dealt much more explicitly with conservation issues than La Salle II, but that didn't mean the Bicentennial voyage didn't care about the pollution it experienced on its way. The voyageurs had taken notice of the refuse dumped near Voyageur Channel in Georgian Bay and the soot and foul air of the steel mills in East Chicago. It was in Calhoun County, however, that Kulick and Sohn both remember people throwing garbage out of their houses directly onto the Illinois River. County residents they encountered chalked up such behavior to "city folk" who owned houses along the waterfront.

The group showered at the county high school and had a turkey dinner at the American Legion hall. The group performed for an audience of about forty. The newsman who had met the voyageurs at the river sat near Cox at dinner and said he wasn't very popular in Hardin because of his "liberal views." A forum on progress in Calhoun County seemed to corroborate his statement, as audience members agreed they would be best served by keeping industry, housing subdivisions, and racial minorities out of the area. The county was the only one in the state that did not have even one mile of railroad track. Bordered on three sides by the Illinois and Mississippi Rivers, the county was served by only two roads into it.

"We have walked 34 miles the last two days, & several of us are fairly footsore," Stillwagon wrote to his wife. "Tomorrow, of course, is a big day. We reach the Mississippi R. Morale is pretty low right now, mainly, I think, because everyone is tired of the cold weather & tired of walking!"

That same day in Hardin, Ken was interviewed by Chicago radio about the mood of the crew. "I'd have to describe the mood of the crew right now as sort of tight-lipped, grim determination to finish this expedition. It's been the most difficult month of the expedition, and for the crew it's been a very difficult time. We've been walking the entire length of the Illinois River Valley, and we've walked over four hundred miles so far. It's not quite the psychological lift for a crew as it is when they come sweeping into a town with their flags flying. It's a very determined line of half-frozen men walking on a windswept, frozen river."

Back in 1682, La Salle had arrived on the banks of the Mississippi River on Feb. 6. La Salle II had mimicked the explorer's itinerary exactly and planned to reach the big river on the same date. The schedule called for the modern voyageurs to hit Grafton, more than twenty miles away, just beyond the confluence of the Illinois with the Mississippi. The night before the long walk, however, Reid came up with a proposal that made financial sense but diverged from authenticity. The state of Illinois, he told the men Sunday morning, would give La Salle II a $2,000 bonus if the men camped in four state parks. Reid wanted the men to stop short of their goal and camp in Pere Marquette State Park, fourteen miles away. He also suggested that morale would go up if the men tried harder to be pleasant and reduced the bitching.

Hess, Campbell, Watts, and Kulick traveled with the liaison team while the other men hiked under gray skies in temperatures in the mid-teens. Apparently, the liaison team neglected to call ahead to the park, however, because Campbell reported that officials didn't know the men were coming. After camp was established, the voyageurs were driven further downstream, beyond Grafton, to Principia College in Elsah. One of the cultural forums was to take place there.

Perched above the Mississippi River, the eight-hundred-student campus was the world's only college of, by, and for Christian Scientists. Few of the students in the cafeteria knew who the strangely dressed men were. But a skit from their performance after dinner drew laughs and certainly lightened the mood. The students even formed a kick line for *"Chevaliers de la Table Ronde."* The forum focused on the preservation of Elsah, a town that appeared much as it did at least a century earlier. Elsah held fewer than 150 residents, but most of its buildings were built between 1855 and 1862, and thirty-five of them had been placed on the National Register of Historic Places. After the evening's program, students and voyageurs went off together to talk about outdoor education and Christian Science.

The men received a bus ride back to camp and, after a damp, subzero night in the park, walked back to Elsah, fighting winter glare all the way. The men walked south on the frozen river, stretching like a plain of ice between the banks. The Mississippi ice looked just like the Illinois River ice—solid as far as anyone could see. Viewed from above, the voyageurs looked like fleas against an enormous white cat. La Salle II finally made camp on the Mississippi shore that afternoon and performed for an appreciative audience at a crab dinner that night. Voyageurs were heartened by a rumor: Warm weather was around the bend.

On their way to Alton the next day, the men saw the Piasa bird, a painting on a large rock facing the river. The enormous mural depicts a fierce bird in red and green plumage, a warning from the Stone Age. The original had been described in Jolliet's seventeenth-century journal, and the Illinois tribes had claimed the painting was there when they first came to the area. A quarry company destroyed the original after World War II, however, so the voyageurs saw a reproduction, and it sat next to a Conoco gas station. The destruction of the original painting and the staging of the reproduction saddened Cox; as a social science teacher, he was particularly sensitive to the trivializing of historic places.

"I wonder if any other nation has so little regard for such things," he wrote. "History just doesn't seem to be very important to the majority of Americans.... Surely others destroy artifacts and other historic finds in the name of progress, but we seem to be especially cavalier about it."

While several students in Elsah had peppered the young men with questions about their journey, the men's short time in Elsah had also had a profound influence on several impressionable minds. Not only Christian Science, but religious faith in general had become a topic of conversation as the voyageurs plodded along. Months surrounded by nature and long hours of solitude had led some of the men to think naturally about God and their own places in the universe. The explicit nature of Elsah brought that thinking to a fine point.

"I've never seen—OK, noticed—the crew show so much curiosity about a religion," Fialko wrote, "maybe because it's so foreign to them." He listed the many religious experiences to which the boys had been exposed: Catholic masses, the Church of Saint Anne de Baupre in Quebec, the mission and shrine at Midland in Ontario, smoking the calumet with Hayne Sine and other Indian rituals, the Jewish school and temple at Belmont Harbor, the Baha'i Temple in Wilmette.

One lecture at Principia was by an older gentleman "who was about eighty," Bardwell said. The lecturer advised that the only reason for sex was procreation. After midnight, however, Bardwell and one of the female students went into a classroom, "where we indulged in fond embracing, the first time since the trip started. Boy, we did that until around 4 in the morning." In a side note to his own journal entry on Principia, Kulick said he learned later that Principia is called by some "the kissingest college in the west."

The constant challenges to his leadership had affected Reid, Fialko noted in his journal. "I'm noticing some change in Reid," he wrote. "One of his more common statements is 'The expedition is falling apart.' I know we're not as together on some of the things we do. Not like we used to be."

The mercury soared to fifty-three degrees on Feb. 9, so warm that many of the voyageurs walked with their shirts off. Some hiked in canvas pants instead of wool. The eight-mile stroll through an industrial area brought La Salle II to the Lewis and Clark Monument. The spot marks the confluence of the Mississippi and Missouri Rivers, but it also takes up the whole beach as a loading dock for barges. The guys were able to walk out onto the Mississippi's frozen surface for at least a hundred yards. From there they could see an icebreaker moving up and down the river.

"Icebreakers going north would back up then move forward, and you'd hear this ripping sound," Sohn remembered. The warmer weather also meant that melting ice and snow made for a muddy spot for campfires at night, though three bales of straw kept the sleeping bags dry.

Around 10:30 that evening, a man drove his car near the campfires and parked in the shadows about one hundred feet away. After five minutes passed without his getting out of the car, the man called out, offering sexual favors. Cox responded with a profanity-laced tirade. Undeterred, the man hollered that it would only cost $20 and that he could take on two at a time. After his latest bid was rejected in another salvo of finely parsed versions of four-letter root words, the man finally left.

The men went to bed after that, but soon another car drove up and several girls exited, making themselves at home around the fire. They had come with a proposition, too, but not the kind that had so lately been offered. The girls were from Principia, and they wanted to ask Hobart if they could canoe with the voyageurs for two or three days during their spring break. Hobart thought it sounded like a super idea.

The dawn brought a fabulous day for hiking. A glorious breeze brought warm air out of the south and heated the air to sixty degrees. The crew walked a dozen miles or more to the McKinley Bridge. Sun singed their noses. A big city crowded with cars and trucks lay ahead, and the survivors of Hebron took no chances. The liaison team met the men and drove them over the river and through urban St. Louis to Forest Park, where they made camp.

The voyageurs visited several schools in the area over the next two days, including one for mentally challenged children. Each school left an impression, but visiting the Principia Prep School so soon after Principia College made a special imprint on Kulick.

"I'm really amazed to see the maturing process that happens between high school and college," he wrote in his journal. "It just shows us all the more how much we've matured in the last year." He asked Lieberman if the crew were really like the high school kids they had just met. "He said he's sure we were, and we felt so mature then. I'm sure five years from now I'll look back and think how immature I am right now."

On Abraham Lincoln's birthday the rain came down hard, but the show went on for junior members of the historical society and for about forty Girl Scouts. After that, cars and vans took the men several miles south of St. Louis to Fort de Chartres, where another forum was held on the relevance of the fort to modern society. The vehicles stopped three miles short of the fort so the men could walk in. (The crew always liked to *show* authenticity, even when they were not actually *being* authentic.) DiFulvio rejoined his mates at the fort, no wiser about the mysterious virus that had forced him off the trail. For Reid, sleeping at Fort de Chartres was like visiting an old friend. It was where he and Frese had first bonded and where Reid had taken students to get a taste of French heritage in America's heartland.

However, Gorse and Hess were sent back to Utica to fetch the canoes and the rest of the crew's gear. Two United Parcel Service drivers went with them in a forty-five-foot truck to bring them to closer storage in Cape Girardeau, Missouri.

"We were never quite sure where we would need them," said Fialko. One of the UPS men was from Louisiana. Noting the long hair and beards of the voyageurs, he told them that after leaving Illinois they'd better go everywhere in groups—and carry their muskets. They'd soon be in super redneck country, and someone in a pickup truck had already flipped Hess the bird and called him a hippie. It was less than a decade after the film *Easy Rider*, in which a trucker guns down two long-haired bikers, and the shades of intolerance apparently still hung over parts of the South.

"It's depressing to think that we fought a war to keep these goobers in the Union," Cox wrote, hinting of a regional intolerance of his own.

Reid headed the crew to the Pierre Manard House, home of the first territorial governor of Illinois. His home was built in 1802 and contained many fine pieces of early American furniture. Three years earlier, Ken had seen the Mississippi spill over the top of the levee and the railroad tracks in front of the house. Now the river was much lower, perhaps as much as ten feet from that 1973 level. The next morning, however, it was moving three times faster than it had the day before. Reid called the Coast Guard for a status report on the river. The Guard reported that the Mississippi was still closed to all traffic.

The men spent the day visiting a school and two nursing homes, then they returned by walking a long gravel road through state property—the grounds of Manard State Prison, which housed notorious mass murderer Richard Speck. As they returned to the parking lot of the Chester Boat Club, the crew saw that unthinking vandals had trashed the Mississippi shoreline, leaving thousands of beer cans as well as other garbage tossed carelessly out the windows of passing cars and boats.

However, a Valentine's Day gift awaited the men. By six that evening, the Coast Guard had again opened the Mississippi River to all traffic. Reid dispatched Hess and Sohn with Fialko to pick up the canoes that had just been stored at Cape Girardeau, and Reid told the crew they'd be back on the water in the morning. The long portage had finally come to a close.

THE FATHER OF WATERS

(Feb. 15–March 14) Grand Tower, IL, to Rosedale, MS

The slow, plodding pace of the portage suddenly shifted into high gear as the canoes hit the water and a following current hurried the men along. Hikers once again became voyageurs. La Salle: Expedition II swept downriver on a flowing Mississippi, gobbling up the distance. The air was below freezing and snow blew in strongly from the north, but twenty-three miles after leaving Chester the clouds parted and the sun emerged as the crew reached Grand Tower.

Voyageurs make camp in the gathering darkness as a barge motors upriver, shining a light.

The town was named for three towering rocks that once stood on the Missouri side of the river. Now there was only one. The Army Corps of Engineers had blown up the other two. A community of twelve hundred people had lost half its population. One old man told the visitors that he wanted his children and grandchildren to make the town their home but that history alone couldn't help the people. They needed jobs, and employment was dying. The port authority hoped to build a barge terminal and create two thousand jobs, but the residents clearly feared industry coming to the area.

Dean Campbell, Reid's fellow traveler in 1973, headed the local committee. Campbell had been working on a steamboat from the 1830s, but he and others had already made a unique shelter for the voyageurs of 1977: an Iroquois long house. Smoke didn't vent very well, however. Sleepers found that it was better to lie down in the shelter than to sit or stand.

Some campers sat on a rocky hill and watched barge traffic and the dangers it posed. Sometimes tugboats shepherded islands of them, as large as four wide by four long. As two passed that night in the dusk, they roiled the river. Barges left a choppy mess in their wake and could force canoes to deal with five- or six-foot waves. They also rose like dark angels behind paddle craft and threatened to roll over them. Sunken barges, like icebergs, could punch holes in the fiberglass hulls of the canoes. At night a barge cast yellow eyes for a mile in three directions, one ahead and two to cover both shores. The engine hum growled as the spotlights swung side to side to seek out dangers. When the growling barges passed out of sight down the river, the world in their wake seemed to drift into deep silence. The tugboats and barges scared Foster more than anything else on the trip. Braun said that when the voyageurs paddled during a rainstorm, the rain drowned out the sound of the barges and tugs, making them potentially silent assassins.

Having walked more than five hundred miles across three states, the men's legs felt sore but strong. Now their arms and backs had to respond, to rely on muscle memory, to learn again to push down into the water and carry a cadence of fifty-eight to sixty strokes per minute. The current sped the canoes forward, and with lighter packs aboard, the voyageurs were quickly hurtling down the watery trace: twenty-eight miles on Feb. 16; then thirty miles to Cape Girardeau, Missouri; twenty-five to Cairo, Illinois; thirty more to Hickman, Kentucky; and thirty-two to New Madrid, Missouri. Here the cold began to moderate. Within a week, the temperature would rise from freezing into the seventies. Even in the forties, the air was warm to the voyageurs, and it made a special difference around camp.

"For so long we had been balled up around the fire," Bardwell said of the frigid days on the trail. "Now we scattered, wandering through the woods or strolling along the riverbank. People were just happy to get away. The constant search for warmth had worn on us."

As the expedition moved down the Mississippi, the circus tent no longer crowded the men together in a fetid bog of arms and legs and clothing, weary with perspiration. The modules returned with the canoes, providing three separate, more spacious accommodations. Braun's arm hurt on Feb. 16, so Campbell took over l'avant duties and said later he had no idea how much bending the bow men had to do.

The people of Cairo took the voyageurs on a tour of Horseshoe Bend Wildlife Refuge, home to more than 100,000 wintering geese. When their approach alerted the geese, an entire flock took off, and the thrum of wings and deafening honk of alarms filled the air.

"There were also a couple of herds of deer, which still fascinate me, even though I have seen so many," Bardwell commented. "They are beautiful. I don't see how anyone could kill them." The irony was lost on Bardwell. The expedition had supped on venison stew several times during the trip.

Wilson had returned to the expedition. He paddled briefly before the pain sidelined him again. With him came an additional element of conflict, noted by Fialko in his journal.

"He seems to align himself with anyone bucking Reid. Still leftover seeds sprouting from [last spring]," he wrote. He also took time to consider his own feelings about Reid, which he decided were not much different than they were at the outset of the trip. "Louie and a lot of the crew no longer trust [Reid]. They think he lies to them. They don't like to be driven. They like to be comfortable. And when he tries to push the expedition forward they bitch."

Garcia, who came down to Hickman with Mr. Lesieutre on Saturday, Feb. 19, said he hoped to get his cast off in three days. He had gotten his hair cut. Wilson had visited the campus of the University of Kansas. Neither voyageur was ready to take up a regular seat in a canoe. Wilson told his friends that the girls in Elgin could scarcely contain themselves waiting for the boys to return. He said the voyageurs were "big stuff" back home—"kind of like the Monkees." As always with Wilson, it was hard to know how much of his report was mere hyperbole. With injuries and illnesses decimating the expedition, only one of the canoes—Reid's—contained the full four-man crew, and then only because Dean had joined the crew.

The crew paddled to New Madrid in a gale on Feb. 20, the winds clocking in at thirty-three miles an hour. After breakfast of oatmeal and leftover beans, Wilson did get into a canoe en route to Picktonville, Tennessee. He said his back went out after twelve miles or so. The canoes approached their scheduled destination at a ferry landing just beyond a set of grain elevators, but Hobart the navigator just kept going, apparently without saying a word to anyone. There was a high-water landing downstream, as it turned out, but members of the crew saw Hobart's gambit as a study in power politics.

"This war that they are having—Hobart and Reid—is the type of thing that eats me up inside, not knowing what's going on and the two of them using what they have against one another," Bardwell wrote. "Hobart can get us lost, but Reid can keep us from getting fed or clothed or clean."

Old Man River played a prank on the travelers on Feb. 22. The air greeted the men warmly. The mercury rose to seventy-five, but the wind blew strongly out of the south, frothing the Mississippi into waves up to three feet high. In the contrary wind, Stillwagon's canoe twice spun 180 degrees in the current. At a bend in the river three miles south of New Madrid, five canoes maneuvered to the west bank. However, Stillwagon's ran into a wing dam that jutted out a quarter mile into the river.

"We were undermanned and didn't have the power to maneuver in the wind," Stillwagon said. "Since the truck accident some of the canoes are down to three men. When you're taking on water and one man has to bail and another man is steering, that only leaves one person to paddle and, in this wind, you just can't hold your own."

After waiting half an hour, Reid's canoe ferried upstream over to the Tennessee shore. But the current turned them, and they stopped their progress only after the river had carried them a quarter mile beyond Stillwagon's group. Then they stroked back upstream and landed on the eastern bank. The expedition remained separated overnight and stuck in place the next day as the wind gusted up to sixty-five miles an hour.

The expedition had scheduled a week in the Memphis area in order to stay true to La Salle's historic journey. In the original trip, Pierre Prudhomme, the explorer's armorer, had lost his way while out hunting and ended up wandering around for days before showing up again, nearly naked, drifting downstream on a log. La Salle put up a crude stockade while out looking for his prodigal paddler, calling it Fort Prudhomme.

The delay outside New Madrid left the crew wondering if they would fall behind schedule and whether some accommodation would have to be made in Memphis to make sure small towns beyond the city were not disappointed. Jan refused to cancel any of the Memphis appearances, but she canceled the Wednesday appearance in Osceola, Arkansas, because she knew it conflicted with local prayer meetings.

With no destination that night, Kulick lay in his sleeping bag and wondered why more Americans didn't camp out under the stars. Except for the wind, it had been a pretty warm day, a true breath of spring. The winter seemed brief to him and long ago. Kulick considered how strange it was to think so. He thought to himself that this must be how a new mother suppresses her memory of the pain of childbirth, swathed in the joy of holding her child. He also noticed that many people whom the voyageurs had met on this journey expressed the desire to do something different with their lives or to help their community. However, so many of them were too lazy or too mired in their own ways and afraid of change. Could he learn from their examples? Would he avoid the pitfalls and make his life count for others, or would he "become an old man telling his war stories until everyone's sick of them and him"?

The voyageurs rose at 4:30 and pushed off by 6:15 to tackle a sixty-mile leg despite the wind and the wing dams on Feb. 24, Cox's thirtieth birthday. The crossing of the two canoes to rejoin those on the western side of the river took up the first hour. Braun rejoined the crew. Then the little flotilla took off again. The day was warm, a bit of false spring. Temperatures rose into the mid-seventies. But the wind blew strongly, and the canoe teams protected themselves by paddling up the lee shore.

A couple of hours later, a tug came along pushing thirty barges in a huge block, five by six. Caught in a narrow bend in the river, four of the canoes pulled over to let the dangerous barges go past. But the wake threw Ken's and Reid's canoes halfway up a slanted rock wall along the shore. The impact cracked the fiberglass and punched six holes in the hulls. The waves drenched everyone. The expedition landed and unloaded. Fialko did his best to patch the damage with duct tape. Then they again braved the river, pushing into the wind and the barge-created waves.

An hour later the expedition ran into another first—a sandstorm on the Mississippi. The phenomenon occurred as the apparent result of dry conditions and a west wind, which had blown across Arkansas. The canoes had followed the coil of the river and turned directly into the wind, which had picked up dust, bank sand, and debris and hurled it upstream into the voyageurs' faces. The crew stopped at that point for lunch and waited for the wind to die down. Eventually, the canoes returned to the water and made it to Caruthersville, where the men had performed the night before.

That night Fialko spoke to Reid about the fact that no provision had been made for the voyageurs to celebrate with their families in New Orleans. It was the last real town where the families could have modern accommodations, and Reid had supported "family participation at the beginning and end."

"Our planned fiasco in New Orleans is really depressing for me," Fialko admitted in his journal. "It's one of our now-typical screw ups that at this point can be changed, but I think we all know that it will come out the way it looks now. It's almost like somebody doesn't want our people to join in for anything. Not just our family either but all those people who we've asked to come to New Orleans to our 'grand celebration' at the end of the voyage.

"Reid said they're 'trying to work something out' with the people in New Orleans. At this stage of the expedition, one would expect that the final celebration would be pretty well worked out. But I would expect a monumental screw up. I think we're even getting better at that."

Before turning in that night, the crew met to discuss their options for Memphis. The choices were (1) bussing to Memphis and return to Caruthersville the following week to continue by canoe; (2) paddling to Memphis and arriving a few days late; or (3) bussing close to Memphis and canoeing in while maintaining the schedule. Reid favored the third alternative, and the men readily agreed.

That night the men performed for a full auditorium at a high school. The audience sat hushed in their seats as four men walked both sides of the room with walkie-talkies. Later a girl told Stillwagon that the school's strict conditions were aimed at avoiding racial strife that plagued other area schools. She told him that the students didn't mind the climate, and that it helped make that school one of the best in the city.

Afterward, the crew set up at a campground and boat landing owned by Joe Thornton. Joe fed stomachs six days a week, but he fed souls on the Sabbath. A snack shop called Joe's Place anchored one end of the lot. A podium stood on a raised platform at the other end. A sign above it proclaimed: "Old Gospel Church, God-called preacher Evangelist Joe Thornton." A Bible verse urged the congregation to hear the word of the Lord. The La Salle II crew came in on a Friday and left on Saturday, so they never did hear Joe preach. But it was easy to imagine him standing in the Mississippi shallows like a latter-day John the Baptist, bringing the penitents to Jesus.

Dean, who was an early riser, took the liaison van down the river Saturday morning to get photographs of the men paddling into town. He stopped at a spot on the waterfront where he thought he might get some good shots. The neighborhood had once been a stylish section of Memphis, but in 1977, it was distinguished by its large number of boarded-up buildings. He left his camera in the van. He was only scouting possible photo opportunities for a later time.

"I hear something behind me," he recalled, "and I turn around and there's a guy with a knife."

"Gimme all your money," the robber demanded.

"Boy, did you pick the wrong person," Dean mumbled. He reached carefully for his wallet, opened it up wide, "and moths came out."

"Turn out your pockets," the robber insisted, refusing to be deterred. A single penny was all Dean could produce from those sources.

"You're much worse off than I am! Get out of here," the robber laughed.

Dean quickly complied.

At Tom Lee Park downtown, two hundred or more people came out to welcome the visitors. Among them were 4-H organizations, including several all-black inner-city groups. The groups brought food, including two live chickens. One group had grown its own corn and made corn meal from it. The local groups also made stew and homemade bread.

A handful of the men left camp to do something they knew would be seen as a compromise with authenticity. They went to an outdoor mall to look for reading material. Since leaving Toronto, the crew had leaned heavily on reading to ease the solitude of camp life. Books had become almost essential to some of the men, and fresh material was needed. Then they went into a truly forbidden place—a nearby Taco Bell, where they fed themselves with fast food. Thus fortified, they hit two more bookstores. At one, a woman captivated by their appearance thrust into their hands books she insisted would have been destroyed otherwise.

Despite cold and windy conditions on Sunday, Father Loran conducted mass. Then an Arkansas PBS crew came by to film the voyageurs as part of a documentary on Arkansas history. Reid rousted the men out of their sleeping bags when the film crew showed up. Later, the men were bussed across the river to West Memphis, Arkansas, where they were recognized as "official Arkansas Travelers," or goodwill ambassadors for the state. Audiences for the scheduled shows that day were puny, though. Only forty-six came to watch at an auditorium that held a thousand people. Only twenty-seven showed up for another, and that included the liaison team, Reid's parents, the devoted Dr. Brown, and the PBS crew.

The bus to bring the group back to West Memphis the next morning broke down. The temperatures on the last day of February had plunged back below freezing, and the shuttle in the back of a pick-up left most of the men chilled.

Four more performances brought in the month of March. The first two were for high school audiences. The third was for the Memphis Rotary Club, the largest in the South at 475 members. Kulick and Wilson sat at the table there with one Rotarian who said that if Wilson needed anything, he would call "one of those shines," by which he clearly meant a member of the African-American serving staff. Displayed on a wall in the room was the Rotary International Four-Way Test, a series of questions that called on Rotarians to check their ethical stance: Is it the truth? Is it fair to all concerned? Will it build goodwill and better friendships? Will it be beneficial to all concerned? Kulick wondered whether the Rotarian thought he was being fair or beneficial to "those shines." But Kulick and Wilson did make a connection at the Rotary dinner with Bill Sledges, vice president and part owner of the local Coca-Cola bottling plant. He invited them and their pals Gorse and Lieberman over to his house later that evening.

Sledges's home was in a lovely neighborhood. His wife was asleep in another part of the house, but his daughter, Phillipa, a recent graduate of Duke University, helped her father entertain the Yankee visitors. She seemed to have the world on a string. She was personable, beautiful, rich, and, with that Duke degree, obviously intelligent. Sledges served the young men Jack Daniels and Coke, and allowed Wilson to crank up the music to decibel levels more in keeping with the voyageur's taste. It did not allow for conversation other than shouting, however.

The rest of the Elgin crew relaxed with Lt. Hudgens and his wife at their home. Mrs. Hudgens was an English professor at Memphis State. The lieutenant had been a student in her classes three times before he married her. Hudgens, fifty-three, had been assigned to the voyageurs since Friday, and he had taken a real liking to his charges. He had laid in a supply of wine, beer, and chips.

Back at camp, there were more police to provide twenty-four-hour protection. Cox sat around the campfire, listening to their cop stories. One young officer said drunks and lowlifes prowled the riverbank, and rough barge crews frequented the bars nearby, where police refused to go without backup.

The last day in the area, the men traveled to Germantown High School, where teens in a work-study program provided lunch. The program gave the kids responsibility for ordering foods, cooking, and serving meals. In its own way, it offered the experiential learning that had been a hallmark of La Salle: Expedition II, and the men appreciated the parallel. Later the voyageurs performed at Memphis State University for the historical society. Marr flew in that night to join the liaison team, but more controversy seemed to be brewing. The crew now realized that no plans had been made for the crew's families and friends to join them in New Orleans.

Father Loren returned to the canoes for the first time since Blind River. The enterprise had scheduled three days to make the seventy miles to Helena, Arkansas. The warm days of late February did not follow the men as they shoved off. Wind-blown pellets hit them hard, and breakers hurled the river over the gunnels and forced the canoes off the water.

"I thought I was going to shiver myself to death," wrote Cox. "I now know what hypothermia is all about. I was shaking so badly I couldn't eat. At one point everyone was given a candy bar, but my hands were trembling so bad I couldn't unwrap it. Someone got it open for me, and then I couldn't eat it as my teeth were chattering so badly. Within a matter of minutes my neck and back were sore from the uncontrollable shaking. What really got me was the fact that a couple of other people were in just as bad a shape as I was."

The expedition continued after a pause to warm up, but the rain kept falling in sheets, reducing vision to about a hundred feet. With bends in the river, the wind alternately struck the men in the face and from behind. Ponchos stopped being any kind of rain gear. Canoes filled with water and the milieu bailed for several minutes at a time. "Father Loran was shaking even worse than I was at lunch," Cox observed. The men turned to shore and made camp, surprised to learn that they had traveled nearly thirty miles in those horrible conditions.

Many voyageurs began the following day in damp gear, but temperatures rising into the upper fifties helped the men wear their clothes into dryness. A water shortage aboard made for rock-hard peas in the soup, and there was not enough fruit to augment it. Of course, there was no water to drink, either. But there was a bottle of vodka. Late that night it made for a friendly campfire among the adults and some not-so-friendly talk about New Orleans and the problems shaping up.

In the word "March" the guys could see the end of the tunnel, the culmination of all their endeavors. Just the shift in the calendar month was enough to herald the end of the journey for travel-weary paddlers. The excitement of the trip had long since worn off for many of the voyageurs. Someone bought a Frisbee and a football in Helena, and several of the guys played football in a lot one night. The behavior, so natural for teenage boys, drew criticism from Reid, who saw the toys as a slap at voyageur authenticity. But authenticity had gone out the window almost from the beginning.

"I think you're either authentic or you ain't," John Fialko said, "and we picked a halfway point there somehow. We could justify everything we did, but sometimes you reach a point of making excuses for what you did. Maybe at the time it seems like the right thing to do, but then when you look back on it, you kind of second-guess."

"We are just flaming out," Cox recorded a few days later. "Guys are simply tired—physically and emotionally. This has been a lot to ask of a bunch of teens, no matter how mature they are. I guess we're like a punched out boxer who's just trying to hang on for a couple more rounds, and doesn't give a damn about how artistic he looks over the last few rounds."

At sunrise on Saturday, March 5, the travelers awoke to a barge horn. As the pilot navigated upstream he called out to the sleepy campers, "History in the making." Then he paused, as if thinking about the beached canoes. "You'll never get anywhere staying in bed so late."

Perhaps 150 people received them in Helena, including Miss Lily Peter, who had given Reid $10,000 for the voyage sometime earlier. Her ownership and management of two plantations had made her wealthy, and she had channeled her money into scholarships and environmental causes. In 1971 Arkansas Gov. Dale Bumpers had named her the state's poet laureate, a title she would keep till her death twenty years later at the age of one hundred. The local deference to Miss Lily, a gracious lady, was clear. The men would perform later that night at Helena's Miss Lily Peter Auditorium. A high school fraternity and sorority served hamburgers for lunch. Afterward, the DeSoto High School Rocket Club put on a presentation after lunch. An exchange with a trio of girls from the private school indicated that racism had not died out just because Congress had passed the Civil Rights Act.

"Hess, Stillwagon, and I were driven to the ceremony by three of the dumbest chicks any of us will ever encounter," Cox reported.

"One of them announced that they were from the private school [DeSoto], because 'the niggers here are soooo stuuuupid.' One of them asked us what kind of music we listened to. I said classical and was met by three very blank stares. They then asked what kind of dances we did. I told them I liked waltzes and minuets. One of them then said, 'Y'all get everything before we do. We're so slow here we're still doing the bump.'"

When the guys visited DeSoto High two days later, they got another earful, this time from an economics teacher, who gave the students a list of words to define. For open housing, the teacher immediately said, "Contrary to whatever the NAACP says, it can't be enforced." When he came to the word slum, he said, "You know what a slum is. That's Walnut Street."

"It was hard to determine if he was just a worthless cracker, or he thought he was being funny for the Yankees," Cox wrote. "Either way, it was nothing short of embarrassing. The sad thing is the students were laughing their asses off."

A Ford dealer who flew Stillwagon, Hobart, and Watts along the Mississippi and whose wife was running for school board said DeSoto had really helped Central, making integration so much easier by eliminating most of the troublemakers. One of the wealthiest men in town, he sent his own children to the public school, Central. He couldn't say enough good things about it.

Black men who drove the crew around town in a couple of vans also offered the visitors a perspective on the racial divide. One of the voyageurs told their driver that they were going to visit a private school. In the stereotypical drawl made famous by Stepin Fetchit,[3] the black star of the 1920s and '30s, the driver asked, "You means I gets to go to da private school?" When the van arrived, Kulick asked the driver if he was coming in. "They won't even let a dog in the front door, let alone me," he answered.

Back at camp, a festering boil popped as Gross blew up at Reid

---

3   Lincoln Theodore Monroe Andrew Perry (1902–85) became a millionaire from a vaudeville and film career based on playing this character, "the laziest man in the world."

over the lack of accommodations for loved ones in New Orleans. Gross was speaking on his own behalf, but he gave voice to the feelings of most of the crew. He had called his family and told them not to come, and he blasted Reid for a policy in which none of the men had a say. Reid defended his decision to keep family out of La Salle II's official celebrations and dinners. He used the "we decided" phrase, as he had so many times throughout the trip to cast the crew as participants in policymaking.

Then Reid spoke about the reputation of Paul Henderson, the official at Bank National de Paris (BNP), who had extended him credit and sponsored the banquet that was canceled while the men struggled to Belmont Harbor that awful day in December. Henderson was sponsoring a new celebration for the crew in New Orleans that, evidently, required their attendance but did not include the voyageurs' families. For this argument, too, Gross had no sympathy.

Dean had already made up his mind to leave the expedition in New Orleans. The decision had nothing to do with money, he said. If that had been the case, he might have left months earlier. In fact, though, money was part of the issue. Dean decided he'd had enough when he discovered that the La Salle II corporation had made a financial arrangement that cut him out of income he thought was to be his.

Another person who had fallen out with the leadership was Baumgartner, who had received a brochure on the Miss Elgin contest, a local event leading up through a state competition to the Miss America Pageant. Baumgartner thought she might have a go when she returned from the seventeenth century, but she was encountering a negative vibe from people she thought were in her corner.

"I am so excited about the Miss Elgin deal," she wrote her mother March 10. "It's my next goal (besides a hasty month till April 15!)." She deplored the cutting remarks she said Jan and Scavuzzo had made about Palmer behind her back. "I'm most sure they look down amusedly at my exercising and applying for Miss Elgin. Any more, they talk to me as if I were a three-year-old—quite annoying & frustrating. In addition, the other evening I came downstairs to hear Marlena [Scavuzzo] saying, 'Sharon is still young. I thought the Expedition would help her grow up, but it hasn't.'"

During the stay in Helena, DiFulvio walked off into the woods to do what they say bears do there. After more than six months in the natural world, he did the natural thing and wiped himself with a little nearby foliage. It turned out to be poison ivy, and the consequences both devastated him and entertained his comrades. Despite their amusement, they also felt pity for their comrade, whose privates not only itched but swelled. DiFulvio recuperated in the hospital for several days, and Stillwagon went to visit him there. When Stillwagon returned to camp and tried to explain what was happening, he began with a clinical approach but broke down laughing. With tears in his eyes, he said he couldn't adequately describe the affected parts. Not surprisingly, DiFulvio did not take a seat in a canoe the next day when the expedition moved on.

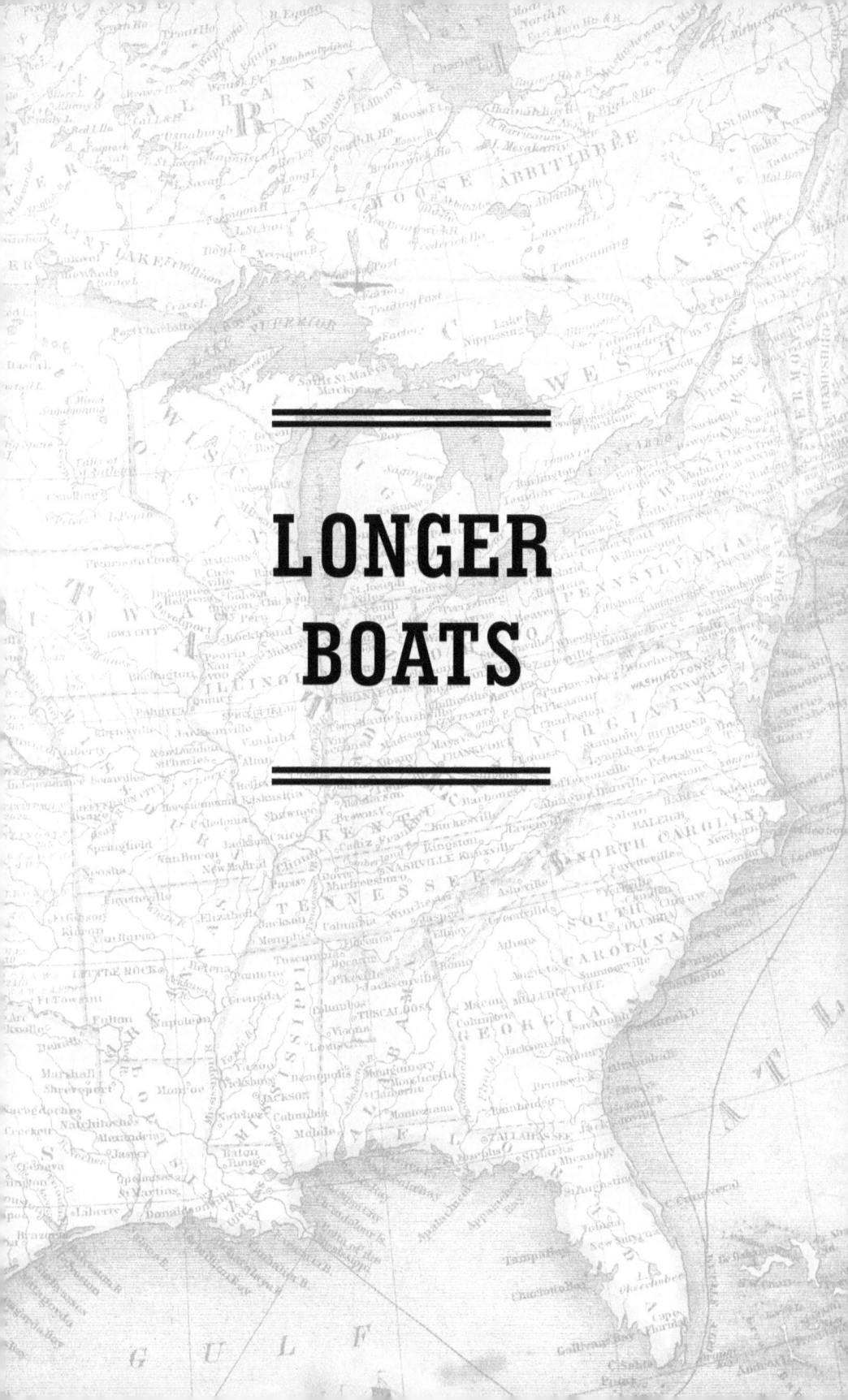

LONGER BOATS

I'LL GET DOWN TO THE SEA SOMEHOW

(March 8–April 9) Rosedale, MS, to the Gulf of Mexico

From Helena it's a six-hour drive to New Orleans, but it's nearly six hundred miles by the river, which coils tightly most of the way. One person at the National River Academy, a school for Mississippi River barge pilots, warned that the worst stretch might be below Baton Rouge, where the river narrows and freighter traffic picks up. Below New Orleans it was all freighters.

On March 8 the crew paddled nearly forty miles down calm water. Along the way the men saw a paddle wheeler. Temperatures once again wallowed in the warm sixties. With the river up several feet, water covered most of the wing dams. The men could paddle over them, but they had to slow down as they approached because the clearance was never sure. L'avants probed with their paddles, looking for small eddies that might announce the presence of a dam. A heavy concentration of trees on the banks complicated the progress, as some trees grew close to the water and some, dislodged by the river's flow, moved along with the current.

Veteran strokes made another thirty-six miles pass easily on March 9, and the crew shortened the journey by going through "the shoots," where the river had cut across an arm of land to create an island. On either side of the river, fifty- to seventy-foot banks rose over the six canoes.

A night or two later, Hess was eating dinner when he suddenly screamed and pointed into the sky. A meteor gleaming green and orange threw a long trail across the sky. It brightened, then it flared out. The astral passage was one of the more exciting events in Rosedale. Another was the women's basketball game that Friday, March 11.

Even in 1977, major colleges and universities offered little to women in the way of sports programs. Congress had passed Title IX in 1972 to prohibit gender discrimination in educational programs and activities. However, its application to women's athletics still fought for its existence in Congress and the courts, where the National Collegiate Athletic Association had sued to set aside the landmark law that provided equality in interscholastic sports for women. Until the issue was resolved and big schools started issuing sports scholarships to women, small colleges had an equal claim on the best female athletes in America, and some of the best basketball in the country was being played in tiny Cleveland, Mississippi, just a few miles down the road from Rosedale.

In a town of 2,500 people, the 4,200-seat gym was jammed with people. The Lady Statesmen of Cleveland's Delta State, winners of the last three national titles, faced off that night against the Crimson Tide of the University of Alabama. Delta State's star was 6-foot-3 Lucy Harris, who had played center on the US Olympic team. They had won the silver medal the previous summer when women's basketball was introduced as an Olympic sport. On this night, Harris scored a lot in the first half. In the second half, one of her teammates hit eight of ten from beyond fifteen feet, and another player, a 4-foot-11 guard, put on a dribbling clinic. The team also played outstanding defense, and Delta State won 87–57. The Lady Statesmen were to face the winner of Game 2 the following evening.

The second game featured Valdosta State and Mississippi College, whose players wowed the crowd with behind-the-back and between-the-legs passes during warm-ups. The game itself was a run-and-gun affair, with Valdosta State mounting a furious comeback before falling short, 104–100. The voyageurs were told that

Mississippi College had never beaten Delta State because they could not deal with the Lady Statesmen's slower pace.

Crewmen stow La Salle II gear in the shadow of a paddle wheeler in Natchez, Mississippi.

Reid announced on the bus ride back to camp that La Salle: Expedition II had received $600 from Kulick's father's company, $1,000 from Wilson's father's company, and $2,000 from the Illinois Parks Department for staying in four of the state's parks. The Illinois Legislature had also invited the crew to perform for elected officials in Springfield. Saturday night the crew crowded around a radio and listened to the women's national title game. Delta State hit more than 90 percent of its shots in the first half and built a large lead before cruising to a 101–84 victory.

Sunday dawned brightly with a light breeze and a high of seventy-five degrees. The city of Rosedale sponsored a lunch for the voyageurs at Great River Road State Park, near the confluence of the Arkansas and Mississippi rivers. It was there that Jolliet had turned back upriver in 1673, fearing a confrontation with armed Spaniards further south. Sixteen Mississippi state representatives attended the lunch. The legislature had spent a lot of money to establish the park, and it faced calls for an additional park appropriation of $1 million. The voyageur lunch was an opportunity to see how that money would be spent. A throng of picnickers filled the park on the sunny day.

The crew traveled across the Mississippi on Monday to Arkansas Post, the place on the White River where La Salle's top lieutenant, Henri de Tonti, established a fort in 1686. In 1783 British soldiers clashed there with Spanish allies of the American colonies near the end of the Revolutionary War. By 1819, the post was a thriving river port and the largest city in the region and selected as the first capital of the Arkansas Territory. During the Civil War, Confederate troops built a massive earthen fortification known as Fort Hindman at the Post, but Union troops destroyed it in January 1863. The post was now a national monument.

The men gave a couple of performances, but fewer than two dozen people showed up for them, and the occasion prompted an argument between friends. Wilson expressed his opinion that the sparse crowd didn't matter, that very little mattered anymore. Lieberman criticized him for his blasé attitude and ventured to tell him that it mattered very much, in fact. He didn't have to look very far for support. The Arkansas PBS crew that had shot events in Memphis had shown their footage to their editors and had received approval to do more filming of La Salle II. They had returned to follow the travelers down the Mississippi. Clearly, there was continuing interest in the activities of the reenactors. The crew performed again in the afternoon at Gillette (Arkansas) High School.

A crew meeting was held afterward. Jan had reported that *Life* magazine had contacted the La Salle II enterprise. The photo magazine wanted to get pictures of the voyageurs in New Orleans for a special issue on the biggest stories of the year. However, enthusiasm for the expedition had cooled downstream even as the temperature had risen. Below New Orleans, Reid found that communities had no interest in welcoming the neo-explorers. This meant that the journey would end as planned and that there would be no lingering visits to delta towns, no performances to keep giving. Some crew members greeted the news with relief, some with joy, and others with genuine disappointment.

No crew meeting would have been complete, by this point, without controversy. Ken expressed concern that some crewmen could not control their drinking, specifically citing the beer blast at Lt. Hudgens's residence. Hess asked pointedly if that concern applied equally to Father Loran. Then Lieberman said he thought the liaison team had to correct its attitude. Reid replied that the liaison team had the same kind of morale problems that the canoeists had. Then Stillwagon suggested that the entire enterprise could mute the squabbling and backstabbing and simply feel pride that the group would complete the journey.

Vicksburg was the next major target, roughly 150 miles away. On a day the crew voted the most beautiful of 1977 so far, the men paddled fifty-two miles under a sun that warmed into the upper seventies. Outside Greenville, Mississippi, the first words the men heard came from a boy who shouted, "You guys need a haircut." Wilson's dad arrived the next day with Garcia, who stayed with the liaison team for the rest of the trip. Greenville, a city of fifty thousand souls, had retooled its downtown to compete with shopping centers growing up on the outskirts of town. Citizens had at first resisted the new look, which included a broad and winding main street where greenery marked every turn. But the beauty and economic benefits had won them over.

The expedition traveled over ninety miles in the next two days before seeing Vicksburg high on the bluffs. They made camp on an island where vines made it hard to walk around, but the lack of river debris surprised the crew. The Big Muddy had lived up to its name, but there was scarcely any litter on the water. Without power plants, the river seemed much cleaner than parts of the Kankakee or the Illinois. The warm weather had some of the guys pulling out loincloths they had carried in their packs. The flashing markers along the western bank vanished in the fog on a Sunday evening, and Cox began to feel that the seven and a half months of the journey didn't seem so long after all. The Gulf was three weeks away.

"It's funny how quickly one can forget the bad times," he mused. "It's probably the only thing that's saved us—that ability to forget the bad stuff. The trip seemed so long during the winter, especially when we had to start portaging. You could only survive by falling into a rather mindless routine and just live day-to-day or hour-to-hour."

Reid missed dinner March 19 to be interviewed by a reporter for *People* magazine, which also took photos of him. The reporter had conceived her story as a profile of the modern La Salle. However, the *People* reporter shifted her emphasis from a personal profile to a feature on the expedition as a whole. The next evening she asked questions of the crew. She asked Cox whether anyone resented Reid and his role, and she asked him about Father Loran. Cox's answers were predictably frank.

* * *

That Sunday also saw the voyageurs arrive at Vicksburg around three in the afternoon. During the Civil War, the city had surrendered to Union troops under Gen. Ulysses S. Grant on July 4, 1863, after a forty-seven-day siege. The surrender came the day after the Battle of Gettysburg had ended the South's last effort to invade the North, and the fall of Vicksburg choked off the Mississippi River to Confederate traffic.

Afterward, Gordon Cotton, curator of the Old Court House Museum, took the crew on a personal tour of the Vicksburg battlefield, where loyal sons of the Old South continued to rue the War of Northern Aggression. Wearing a CSA belt buckle, Cotton referred to the Confederate side as "we" and made remarks such as, "We would have won if . . ." Cotton's bias had come naturally. In his 1998 book *Confederates in the Attic*, Tony Horwitz wrote of him: "Mr. Cotton lived in the same 1840s farmhouse where he, his father, grandfather, and great-great-grandfather had all been born. One of Cotton's cousins still slept in a bed riddled by bullets when Yankees killed her great-great-grandmother during a plantation raid." [4]

---

4 Tony Horwitz, *Confederates in the Attic: Dispatches from the Unfinished Civil War* (New York: Pantheon Books, 1998), 201.

Visits to Vicksburg High School and All Saints Episcopal School took place on Monday, March 21. A class from Meridian had traveled three hours to All Saints to see the voyageurs. All Saints, a coed boarding school for grades seven through twelve, had a canoe club, the Paddle Pushers, which had raised some funds for La Salle II. Thirteen club canoes escorted the expedition a mile to the river. Another SRO crowd warmly received the crew's performance at the Old Court House Museum, where the men gave out the scroll from the Quebec government. Ken became violently ill that night, the suspected victim of food poisoning.

People magazine concluded its crew interviews Tuesday morning before the canoes went back into the water. Ken, who had spent the night retching, continued to feel the effects of his stomach bug. But Reid delayed departure in hopes that Ken would fully recover. Every hand was needed for the journey's longest stretch to date, a sixty-mile paddle to an island downriver. A cold snap put some starch into the air, dropping temperatures down through the 50s and 40s during the day to near freezing overnight.

The twelve-mile trip to Natchez landed the crew next to the *Mississippi Queen*, a $45 million paddle wheeler complete with carpeting and modern appointments, including a pool. Without a place along the river to camp, a flatbed truck was needed to haul the canoes to the Grand Village of the Natchez, a replica Indian village that had recently opened. The tribe itself was destroyed by the French in the 1730s. The city was in the midst of the month-long Natchez Pilgrimage Pageant, first held in 1932. That night people paid $4 ahead to witness the Confederate Pageant, a series of tableaux celebrating the grace and gentility of the antebellum South and ending with the Confederate Ball.

"We, as a new generation in a changing South, recognize that our system had its evils," the prologue declared, "yet we take pride in preserving that which seems best in our glorious heritage." The program concluded, "We lived and died for Dixie—for a way of life and a state of mind that return to us in the soft, delicate fragrance of magnolias, and in the languid whisper of warm spring breezes drifting through the moss-covered oaks of our stately mansions."

In Vicksburg, Dr. Cotton had urged the voyageurs to ask the people of Natchez why they had so many beautiful antebellum buildings (mansions included) and Vicksburg had none. Wilson remembered, and asked a girl at the information center about it. "Oh, you've been talking to Dr. Cotton," she laughed. She explained that Northern industrialists owned most of the homes and that the city had voted against secession in 1861. The city greeted Union troops as liberators when they arrived.

Voyageur performances at Natchez South and Natchez North high schools drew little reaction. But one teacher at North, an all-black school, told the crew that it was the first assembly in seven years that the students didn't talk through. A show at the private Adams County Christian School followed, without a black face in sight.

The crew expressed discontent when it was discovered that an evening performance at the Indian Village would be a private show for an Air Stream convention. The show was an arrangement by the city for the Air Stream folks, who always spent a lot of money at the municipal pageant. Several voyageurs bristled at the idea of being used as a perk for businessmen, but it was too late to do much about the scheduled event. A chamber of commerce representative made the crewmen honorary colonels on the governor's staff.

* * *

Afterward there was a tour of houses on the Pilgrimage Trail, the oldest of which was The Wigwam, dating to 1793. A reporter for the *New Orleans States-Item* watched the voyageurs troop through the old house and couldn't help noticing the dichotomy. Hostesses in hoop skirts and men in gray Civil War uniforms who were used to guests of a later century now greeted barefooted, rough-hewn voyageurs from two centuries earlier.

"In one elegant, glimmering room of mahogany, crystal, and fine china," the reporter wrote, "a hostess was explaining to men who had done most of their eating outdoors lately that 'this is the informal dining room.'"

That night Reid imposed a two-drink limit on the men, first at a bar where a chamber rep took the men and later at the Natchez Village where the staff anticipated a party with the visiting voyageurs. Within half an hour the coolers were packed up and the village staff headed for the parking lot. During the evening, a black girl working at the Natchez Village said that she had never gone on the Pilgrimage or to the Civic Center, because she was afraid to. She had even worried about seeing the voyageurs that night.

Around midnight Kulick found himself on the gravel walk behind the Grand Village park. He thought about Elton John's "Goodbye Yellow Brick Road," and he turned the lyrics over and over in his head. The expedition had been his Yellow Brick Road, Kulick thought, and now it was coming to an end. His future lay beyond the last stroke of his paddle, one journey following another. He looked forward to closing the book on this chapter of his life. While he had reveled in what he thought was freedom on the trail, Kulick saw that the expedition had been, in a sense, a secure and protective world. Every day had been laid out, the rules "agreed upon," and the direction certain. Kulick felt a growing apprehension, and he knew it had much to do with the fact that he did not grasp what his future was to be. Perhaps, he thought, this is how we define real freedom.

The paddlers passed their first oil rig and a nuclear power plant under construction during another sixty-mile leg on March 25. The canoes made another forty miles as they paddled into Louisiana. Nights brought a special kind of torture. A man could choose to sleep uncovered and risk getting bitten to death by the mosquito swarms or seek cover in a sleeping bag that made him sizzle in his own sweat by morning.

Just as the cold and ice changed the travelers on their caravan through the Midwest, the passage through the South began to transform the crew. Stillwagon and Reid grew dark from the sun. Cox and others sunburned regularly as they shed layers down to their bare backs and legs. Months of travel without a visit to the barber shop left several of the teens with long hair, some of it shoulder length. The bronze skin and long hair turned the men into Hollywood images of Native Americans.

Exhausted paddlers found it easy to fall asleep in the heat, and the stroking motion had become so monotonously mechanical over time that even their mates in the canoe could not always tell when they had drifted off. One day Stillwagon noticed that his canoe was moving more and more slowly on the river. He saw that Braun, his l'avant, had slowed his stroke considerably. Gradually, it dawned on Stillwagon that Braun wasn't simply fading in the heat. In fact, he was asleep, though he had continued to stroke, however slowly, from his bow seat. He barked at Braun to wake up and admonished him to stay alert. Only a few minutes later, Stillwagon realized that he was falling asleep in the stern himself.

At Southern, the largest traditionally black university in America, welcome was made by the school president, the mayor of Baton Rouge, a representative of the French consul, and the chiefs of three Indian tribes. "Momma Jaguar" fed the crew in one of the halls. Passing students noticed the faces of the crew and asked why there were no African Americans among them.

The crew, many of whom had taken exception to racism in the South, did see the irony. Most of the suburbs north and west of Chicago were overwhelmingly white in the mid-1970s. Besides a lack of economic parity there, African Americans had for years faced redlining, which was an unadvertised tactic by banks to control access to home mortgages. Legal challenges to public housing also denied blacks opportunities to live in the suburbs, where excellent schools might have provided the chance for a better life.

The crew performed at a Baton Rouge junior high and Louisiana State University, visiting sororities and fraternities in the afternoon. Later at Bel Aire High School, the crew were scarcely halfway through *"A la Claire Fontaine"* when the final bell rang and students just got up and left for the busses without a second thought for the performers. After dinner the men strolled through a large mall, singing their songs, but no one knew who they were or seemed to care. One man asked if they were Jesus freaks and whether their songs were in the Bible.

Fialko mused that night about the end. Back in August, how had he imagined the preparations of two years and the journey of eight months would conclude? He possessed some vague vision of Reid erecting a cross of some kind on a swampy piece of Louisiana real estate and brandishing his sword in the air. With the Gulf so close now, Fialko thought of New Orleans as the psychological fulfillment of their mission. Everything scheduled after that, he thought, would be anticlimactic. He was not alone in thinking so.

* * *

Embarking took time on the morning of March 30. A thick fog blanketed the shoreline. Visibility was less than half a mile. In a stroke of good luck, the freighters on the river moved more slowly than the barges farther up, so the wake was a gentle roll instead of a troublesome chop. It helped that the channel in this area could reach two hundred feet in depth. The river drifted calmly south, the canoes gliding quietly in the current, scarcely disturbed by the paddles stroking through the surface. The canoes finally pulled into shore after dark, sixty miles beyond Baton Rouge in the town of Donaldsville. This was Cajun country, and the Northerners could only muddle through the local "coonass" dialect—English with a Louisiana flair—and merely sense their way to meaning of some kind.

A little rain accompanied the setting up of camp, but so did a throng of well-wishers crowded along the river's edge. It was impossible to unload without running into a host of children. The city welcomed their guests by making them honorary citizens, and a couple of French officials *parlez-voused* with Reid in their native language. Also on hand were French teachers from Quebec who had spent the school year teaching French to French teachers in Louisiana.

March did not go out like a lamb. The rain blew hard all day. Near Burnside, the men boarded the *Delta Queen,* a genuine wooden replica of the paddle wheelers that once plied the Mississippi and helped propel a young riverboat pilot named Samuel Clemens to fame. The vessel was much closer to the genuine article than the *Mississippi Queen*. The captain had dreamed all his life of piloting such a vessel. The boat was fifty-one years old and a national landmark. Its Mark Twain Saloon had pegged floors made of Siamese ironwood. After a tour, the captain stood drinks in the Texas Lounge. The voyageurs had to leave the ship, but as it churned the water and pulled away from the dock, the captain bade them farewell, blowing the whistle and playing a calliope on the back deck.[5]

The river played an April Fool's joke on Saturday. First, fog delayed launch. After the canoes got on the water, the skies opened up and it rained all morning. In the afternoon, the sun came out, bringing heat and humidity. Because the voyageurs didn't change seat positions all day, each man did all his paddling to one side of the canoe, so they were all sore on one side or the other after forty-six miles of stroking. Mosquitoes ruled the campsite near Kenner.

On April 2, Frese, Hobart's family, and many of the parents greeted the crew. So did the Leslies, who had been the crew's companions throughout the Toronto portage. They had said they would come, and they did. So did Howard Platt, who had been with the travelers during the crisis on Washington Island. At the city museum, a mock ceremony claimed the Mississippi Valley for the king of France. A celebration with family and friends had come together after all. The Lions Club hosted dinner, and more than a hundred people came from Illinois, including Elgin Mayor Richard L. Verbic and members of the Elgin Chamber of Commerce. Kenner and Louisiana state officials were on hand. The voyageurs were still in the suburbs of New Orleans, not even at the Gulf. But for all its hoopla, the celebration exposed a truth about La Salle: Expedition II. At its heart, the expedition was over. Reunited with their family and friends, the climax had come a week early. The rest would be a

---

5 The *Delta Queen* was declared a National Historic Landmark in 1989. It operated as a boutique hotel in Chattanooga (2009–2013) before going to Houma, Louisiana, for repairs in 2014.

denouement, a way to wrap up a story that had already been told. The realization saddened Kulick, who gave voice to his feelings in the official journal.

"I really feel like things are starting to fall apart and I fear they're going to get worse," he wrote. "A lot of people seem to think that because we're near New Orleans the trip is over. No one seems to care about anything at all."

Well, that wasn't exactly true. Palmer cared desperately. But the fact that her family had come down to visit her in New Orleans made for a wonderful reunion and an awful situation. The Palmers had only so much time and money. They were unlikely to take their younger sons, one of them still a toddler, all the way to California to see Disneyland, but the Magic Kingdom of Walt Disney World had opened just six years earlier in Orlando. Palmer's parents had planned this vacation to see their daughter, but they also planned to take advantage of this rare trip south to give their young sons the chance of a lifetime to enjoy a Disney theme park.

The problem was that the Palmers were also their daughter's way home, and they expected her to join them for their one-day stay in Orlando. This meant that she would have to leave the expedition just as it was poised to fulfill its mission. The decision denied her the closure that she had anticipated for so many months. It created friction between her and her family. As a teenager who saw things from her own point of view, Palmer could not appreciate fully the sacrifices that had been made by her working-class father to finagle the vacation time and drag his family along on her adventure over hundreds of miles. And she was unable to understand the sacrifice that would have been made by her family, especially her brothers, if they ignored this opportunity. She was angry, and she would stay angry for a long time. Eventually, she said, she grew up and gained maturity and grasped the situation for what it was. Years later she apologized to her parents. To their credit, they had wiped away any memory of Palmer's youthful petulance and protested that they didn't know what she was talking about.

* * *

On Sunday, April 3, the expedition reached a crowded Jackson Square in the heart of the French Quarter of New Orleans, near St. Louis Cathedral. Everyone was in good spirits as the Coast Guard escorted the canoes into the city. A fireboat shot streams of water over the river, and a thousand people watched from the levee. The crew were made honorary citizens and given keys to the city. Jackson Square offered barely enough room for three shelters. The Canadian consul and the state historical society hosted a cocktail buffet on the thirtieth floor overlooking Canal Street, and the lieutenant governor read a proclamation naming April as La Salle II Expedition Month. Dave Upton, their supporter from Michigan, called from Jamaica to congratulate the crew and said he would try to make it to town by Tuesday.

Dean took leave of his comrades around two that afternoon. The crew bestowed an expedition paddle on the journalist who so often stroked along with them and shared their campsites. Dean flew out as soon as he could after arriving in New Orleans. He was still broke and anxious to return home to California and begin seeking work in Hollywood. In some ways, it was long overdue. In 2008, Cox contacted Dean and others while reviewing his journal of the expedition and trying to augment his own memories. He asked Dean why he stuck with the voyageurs so long, since he was essentially unpaid and given little to work with.

"As to why I stayed, I didn't want to desert the crew and leave all your hard work undocumented," Dean replied. "I genuinely liked—or at least could tolerate—almost everyone on the expedition except for Reid . . . Even so, I respected what he was trying to do, even if I suspected his motivation for doing it . . . After [Chicago] I simply decided not to look at it as a job anymore; jobs pay. Instead I looked at it as an adventure, one I probably would have signed onto for free."

* * *

High school visits and a reception at the French Consulate took up Monday. Visits to a pair of girls' Catholic schools followed on Tuesday, ending with a reception by the city historical society next to St. Louis Cathedral. The crowd for the crew's performance was generally receptive, except for one heckler. Wilson's father told the man to stop. The man turned away, then jumped Mr. Wilson from behind. A local photographer had seen the guy coming and knocked him down, ending the confrontation. Later that day the photographer brought several of the boys up to his apartment above his studio for drinks, and after the expedition had disbanded he let Kulick, Gorse, and Lieberman crash in his studio for three days.

On April 6, the voyageurs paddled to Chalmette National Park, where Andrew Jackson had defeated the British in the Battle of New Orleans in 1815. Twenty-three young women in antebellum costumes met the travelers, who performed for a substantial crowd. The indefatigable Emily Brown, the stamp lady who had been among the expedition's best boosters, had come down to be with the voyageurs at their hour of triumph, and they presented her with an autographed paddle.

Later that afternoon, the crew paddled to Belle Chasse, south of New Orleans, the final scheduled stop in the expedition. A member of the liaison team had planted a flag there the day before to mark the landing spot, but the flag had disappeared by the time the canoes came by. Instead, the men unloaded at an old ferry landing and camped along a levee. A sixty-mile trip the next day took the voyageurs deep into the Mississippi delta. There they camped at Fort Jackson, built in 1820, and had dinner a short way beyond, in Venice. Many people think that this was where La Salle laid claim to the entire river basin and that no land existed further than this spot three hundred years ago.

Day broke well on April 8, as the men got a treat that had been absent for a long time—pancakes for breakfast. They stroked past Venice, where they had eaten the night before. They passed the end of the levee south of town. They passed the trailers, which half the town called home since the hurricanes of 1969 and 1973. They passed the new high school, standing out of the delta on concrete pillars. Soon they came to Pilot Town, a station for delta pilots and freighter captains on a spit of land where the Mississippi splits into multiple channels running to the Gulf of Mexico. Two dormitories house the pilots. One is for those bringing the freighters in from the Gulf. The other is for those taking the freighters north to New Orleans.

None of the pilots believed that the voyageurs would be able to navigate the fifteen miles of the narrow, swift South Pass and return. They promised to send out rescue boats when the canoeists discovered that the current was too strong for them. On that last night the pilots took bets against the voyageurs' return at the local bar. Parents and wives of the voyageurs showed more confidence, chartering a boat to follow the canoes all the way to the end of the journey.

* * *

The trip to the Gulf passed swiftly. The men awoke at 5:00 a.m. on April 9 and left at 6:10. They reached the Gulf by 8:30. Marr's dad wanted his son in a canoe heading into New Orleans. But Reid said no, he was "not interested in taking that risk for one shot at glory." Unable to keep a game voyageur down, the refusal only spurred Marr to hitch a ride on a Coast Guard boat and wield a paddle from the deck, well above the river but over its waters, a pioneer to the end. When La Salle: Expedition II finally reached the Gulf of Mexico, the men could simply have stepped out of their canoes onto the littoral as the broad expanse of water came into view. But that didn't occur.

"When it finally happened," Lieberman recalled, "it was exactly as we had imagined. All of a sudden the shore of the Mississippi dropped away and there—after 3,300 miles—was the ocean."

"There was something romantic about the horizon opening up before us, with no land in sight," Ken said. "To really say we're *in* the Gulf, we felt we should make it to the bell buoy at the end of the channel."

The canoes began racing, paddles churning the saltwater to froth as they sliced the half-mile between the shore and the channel marker. Then as the first canoe neared the buoy, the stroking slowed. Paddles came out of the water. The gouvernail adjusted his stern paddle so that the boat turned in a slow arc. Each successive canoe eased up as it approached, until all six canoes circled within a couple of feet of the floating bell. Then all at once the men slapped their paddles and tolled the true end of their long endeavor. In each canoe there was a bottle of La Salle champagne, and the celebratory wine was consumed out there on the water, the first expression of a job well done, a long journey finally completed.

Charter boats had tied up to a dock near the beach. Family, friends, and well-wishers mingled as the crews beached their canoes. Some of the voyageurs, their legs in casts, leaned on loved ones or hobbled on crutches. But before the long-delayed embrace with loved ones, the crew turned again to the water and ran toward it, diving flat into the shallows. Coming up yelling and screaming, they splashed each other to celebrate an achievement that they owned now.

The celebration presented an invitation to Father Loran that he could not resist. Because it was out of character with the man they knew, the voyageurs remember it vividly.

"He gave a war whoop and came running down the beach at full speed till the water was up to his waist," recalled Ken. "Then he dived into the water directly into a sand bar and just stopped, his black robe billowing around him like a beached whale."

The men then threw a series of people into the drink—Reid and Jan, Howard Platt, Pam Cox, Baumgartner, Scavuzzo, and Frese. Marr lumbered out on his crutches and dipped his cast into the water. The men played like boys for an hour, laughing and grinning and enjoying the moment. Then it was time for ceremony. They erected a wooden cross, as La Salle did, and buried a plaque with their names on it. Father Loran offered a prayer, and Reid, as La Salle, claimed the land for France.

Paddling back to Pilot Town, the men discovered that the pilots had an exaggerated idea of what constituted a daunting current. The river's flow was much tamer than they had encountered on the St. Lawrence, and the voyageurs came upstream at speeds up to five miles per hour. The man in the observation tower was stunned when a ship called in to say the canoes would be in soon after 3:00 p.m. About that time Frese's little navy came in sight.

* * *

The end of the journey, for most of the crew, came the next day, a Sunday, when they pulled their paddles one more time through the waters of the Mississippi River, moving up to Venice, where paved roads allowed motorized vehicles to come down to the river and load the canoes. Here, families were fully reunited with their sons, and the men pursued their separate paths back to the twentieth century.

"I knew [then] that I could put on my civvies . . . and stop calling myself a voyageur," said Gorse. "I'd gotten tired of people looking at me and having to talk to people. It was easier in the South and in New Orleans and around there, but I'd gotten to the point where I avoided people more and more. And all I'd wanted to do is be a normal person again and be able to walk into a store and not worry about . . . my image or anything like that."

AN ESTUARY OF LOOSE ENDS

The crew disbanded on April 10. The return to civilization was rapid. Couples grew together and split apart. Ron Hobart's girlfriend, Debbie, dumped him as soon as the men got back home. Judy and Ken Lewis eventually parted ways, as well. John Fialko married Linda within a couple of months. Dick Stillwagon reunited with Rowena and their children. Reid and Jan Lewis, now indebted for $30,000 in personal loans in addition to salaries they owed the directors, spent two weeks camping in Colorado, decompressing.

Five days after leaving Venice, Terry and Pam Cox found themselves back in Elgin painting their house, paneling the den, and tending their yard and garden back to health. Cox began doing some substitute teaching at Larkin High as the school year wound down. But a fight in the cafeteria and student chatter about "beating up some spear-chuckers" dismayed him. The bigotry echoed what he had seen in the Deep South and deeply disappointed him.

Clif Wilson's father left him a car in Louisiana, and Wilson began the drive home. The trip took him three weeks. His comrades had suspicions. Inquiries were met with a wink or a shrug. There were several young ladies he had met on his way south. The guess was that he may have renewed his acquaintance with a few of them on his way back north. Several others did so, too.

Keith Gorse, whose beardless face, tanned skin, and long hair made him look like an Indian brave, took a long while to trim his locks. In the 1970s there were many adults who viewed long hair in a negative light.

"When I got home I was very conscious of my long, long hair because people kept giving me strange looks," he said. They "gave me the cold shoulder all the time and they didn't treat me as fairly because I was a person with long hair. I wore my headband to church at my sister's confirmation, and quite a few people didn't like that, and I heard them say so myself. But yet I didn't think it was any of their business and it didn't matter to me."

Bob Kulick's family had moved to Connecticut while he was gone, and he would reunite with them there after completing a few expedition tasks. Almost as soon as he went east, he began to seek opportunities to share his experience with others. In this way, he also helped earn money for college. In fact, most of the young men who had put their lives on hold for nearly three years found jobs and began preparing mentally and financially for college.

But the crew was far from finished with La Salle: Expedition II. It hung over their lives like Spanish moss on Louisiana's live oaks. Reid had announced long before the trip ended that he expected everyone to be working on projects and other trip-related business for months after the expedition ended at the Gulf. He would not demand that the men attend evening sessions as they had while preparing for the trip. Such a move at the time might have courted disaster. But several loose ends needed to be tied up.

La Salle: Expedition II clothing and equipment had to find a home. Books on history collected during the training and expedition would go to the Gail Borden Public Library in Elgin and be shared with sister libraries in the U-46 communities of Streamwood, Bartlett, and Hanover Park. Reid sent a letter out to the voyageurs, reminding them that the articles of incorporation called for the expedition "to operate exclusively for educational purposes."

Dr. William Beecher, he said, was advising the expedition on developing displays similar to one he had designed at the Chicago Academy of Sciences. A number of organizations had already expressed interest in maintaining such displays, which included implements used on the journey, displayed with the names of the voyageur craftsmen who had created them. Among these organizations were the Elgin Historical Society; the Customs House in Cairo, Illinois; the Living Lakes Museum in Algoma, Wisconsin; the Louisiana Historical Society in New Orleans; and the cities of LaSalle, Illinois; Montreal, Canada; and Paris, France. Elgin would receive voyageur clothes, one of the canoes, and a large trove of mementoes collected from cities and organizations along the route. Another canoe and Tonty's (Marc Lieberman's) clothing were donated to Helena, Arkansas, "thanks to Miss Lily Peter, a long-time supporter of the expedition."

Keith Gorse, Bob Kulick, and Clif Wilson hustle Sharon Baumgartner into the waters of the Gulf of Mexico as the crew and liaison team of La Salle: Expedition II celebrate the successful completion of their journey through the heart of North America.

The items the men had to surrender included muskets, flints, powder horns, knives, fire-starting kits, paddles, canvas bags, tomahawks, and all clothing except for one complete outfit. Reid's letter specified the items in that outfit and allowed each man to keep his sleeping bag, his life jacket, and a paddle. The letter also carried instructions for the men about how to turn things in. The men were to clean their clothes and pack them in a large box or bag marked with their names. They were also to turn in an inventory list of the items they were holding. To catalog and distribute items to educational institutions, everything was to be sent to Reid at an Elgin address by Aug. 31.

Many miles away, several voyageur items turned up that summer in an unexpected place. Patricia Heinz and her husband had traveled from Laurel, Maryland, to do research work in Door County, Wisconsin. While spending time at the beach, they found voyageur equipment in the water. The couple contacted a local newspaper, whose staff told them about La Salle II and how one of its canoes had capsized there the previous autumn. The recovered items were added to those being collected for display.

The expedition received congratulations from President Carter, who wrote, "Ventures such as yours sustain my belief that increased knowledge of our past leads to a better future for our nation." Jacques Kosciusko-Morizet, the French ambassador to the United States, offered his best wishes, observing, "Each generation has its own frontier to explore, and it is very gratifying that these young men chose to reenact La Salle's wilderness journey. . . . Your determination and enthusiasm will serve as an inspiration."

One important post-trip exercise was to gauge the effect of the long journey on the voyageur's psychological makeup. Just as NASA checked out astronauts after long space missions, the enterprise hoped to learn how well the voyageurs could emerge mentally from their extended period at close quarters. On May Day, a woman from Governors State University administered psychological tests. Dale Guilsdorf was supposed to be on hand, but he was unavailable that Sunday, and after that day the test results seemed to disappear. The findings, if any, apparently were never published.

On May 2, Ron Hobart brought two new songs to a choral practice session for the crew to learn. The songs were intended to help fill in the second side of a long-playing record. The LP would be produced in a studio and include some of their skit scripts and much of their performance music from the journey. Directors hoped that the album would sell well and defray the costs of the expedition.

* * *

That Wednesday was "Welcome Back Day" in Elgin. The men dressed in voyageur clothing and met for rolls and coffee in the morning before dividing into two groups and visiting eight schools between them. The men didn't have to provide their audiences with much background. Teachers had prepared their students well, and every group had questions for the travelers. When the visits ended in the early afternoon, there was little to do but wait in the rain before a short paddle to scheduled events at Hemmens Auditorium.

* * *

Hundreds of well-wishers had gathered there to greet them, and Chicago's ABC and CBS stations had assigned film crews. The local library presented a plaque. Reid planted a Canadian maple. The voyageurs received one-year memberships in the local chapter of the Izaak Walton League. The ice cream social that followed charged $2.50 for adult admission, with the proceeds going to the expedition coffers. A class of schoolchildren had dressed as voyageurs, including one as La Salle and another as Father Zenobe Membre, the Franciscan played by Father Loran. Dinner came courtesy of the Elgin Teachers Association. The crew performed for their hometown, and Platt introduced a song he had written, inspired by their story. Then a parade of speakers took the microphone to praise the modern explorers for their vision fulfilled. Finally, the evening ended. The audience walked out of the auditorium and, with them, the spirits of 1682 drifted away to become the ghosts of 1977.

David M. Stamps, managing editor of the *Elgin Courier-News*, wrote a tribute to the local contingent after the Hemmens celebration. In echoes of Shakespeare's *Henry V*, Stamps said that the voyageurs would always be able to draw on the memory of what they achieved "while others sat and gauged the distance." Stamps said that, "like the fallen at Gettysburg, their deeds have gone beyond our power to add or detract. No, forevermore, they can tell themselves that of all the people that could have gone, they were the ones who undertook a three-thousand-mile journey using primitive equipment and suffering the century's bitterest winter, modern dangers, and plain hard work."

Unfortunately, the warmth of the Elgin send-off gave way within a week to a cold dose of financial reality. The adults met May 10 with Sumner Rahr and Company and members of the Special Gifts Committee at 209 S. LaSalle Street in Chicago. Until then, only the executive committee of the corporation—the Lewises and Mike Afelt—really understood the depth of La Salle: Expedition II's financial hole. The corporation's deficit amounted to roughly $300,000—half the total budget. Rahr felt the amount could be raised quickly, despite his firm's own failure to do so during the previous nine months when the expedition was a going enterprise. Rahr suggested continuing to meet on a monthly basis, taking in $300 each month to supervise those meetings. Paul Henderson of the National Bank of Paris did not share the fund-raiser's optimism. He expressed the belief that few people would be willing to contribute to an expedition that had already concluded. Even sources that had been expected to produce substantial amounts while the expedition was ongoing had proven to be chimerical. Reid had expected the New Orleans Committee, for example, to raise $40,000. Instead, it produced only $600.

The massive debt weighed heavily on Reid's mind, but some of the activities left on the crew's plate involved potential income-producing devices. Len Olson made good on his promise of a case of *Decidons Demain* for each voyageur, and each also received a bottle of the wine when they gathered for the May 2 song practice. Olson had planned to produce a thousand cases of the vintage and charge $200 per case. Now he considered a greater run, as many as 1,900 cases. Adding a wine rack and information about the La Salle reenactment, he planned to charge $240 per case and market the wine to wholesalers and retailers along the expedition's route. Each case would return $180 to $210 to the nonprofit corporation. Not only would that make a lot of money for La Salle II, he imagined, but it would produce some great publicity for Tabor Hill. Reid, too, thought the sales would harvest a substantial amount of money. Doing the mental calculations, he said that even at $150 for 1,700 cases (still a lot of money to pay for wine), the enterprise could realize $250,000. In the end, however, Olson's wine raised only $5,000 for the expedition.

The final live performance of La Salle: Expedition II took place at the Palmer House hotel in downtown Chicago before the Illinois Junior Women's League's state convention. Afterward, the ladies gave the enterprise a check for $4,400. Several hours later, the men gathered in a recording studio at the Chicago Board of Education and put their songs on a master tape for the record. Ken and Judy Lewis and Howard Platt provided narration between songs. The vinyl would include an insert with photos of the trip and information written by Ken about the expedition. Proceeds would also benefit the nonprofit corporation. Some people bought the voyageur album, *The Voices of La Salle: Expedition II*, but sales of the album never provided substantial profit.

Cox and Hobart were convinced that there had been financial misconduct by the La Salle II nonprofit corporation. Though Illinois law enforcement officials were consulted, however, no evidence of wrongdoing was ever found. In the end, Reid managed to pay off every financial obligation, including the salaries, though it took fifteen years before adult directors received the last payment.

Randy Foster had always faced pressure from his family to earn money, and the workaday world beckoned to him and one or two others. For most voyageurs, college had always been an important consideration. After all, they had been selected specifically for their academic ability and leadership, qualities of young men whose ambitions would demand higher education. College had already been postponed for a year, and the academic year fast approached. The need to make money for tuition, board, room, books, and other expenses weighed heavily on the priorities the young men now set for themselves.

There was some attempt to provide personal journals. Bob Kulick, who was part of the journal project headed by Ken, kept what was designated the official journal of the expedition. Among the adults, Fialko, Cox, and Stillwagon all kept journals. Fialko wrote extensively but skipped long periods of time. Cox kept a detailed, daily account of the expedition, and it reflected every raw emotion before, during, and after the trip.

Among the student voyageurs, Campbell, Braun, and Bardwell wrote in journals. Bardwell diligently wrote into two leather-bound books all the way to the Gulf. Braun compiled a detailed account, but it lurched to a halt soon after his frightening birthday experience in East Chicago. No comparative study of the 1976–77 journals with those of original voyageurs was ever done, and the full collection and processing of the journals from all those who kept them may not have been possible. Clearly, Kulick's family focus pulled him toward the East Coast and college there, though he did make a start to interview expedition members about their experiences, and completed half a dozen.

Reid, who had taken leave from his public school teaching duties to pursue his La Salle dream, never returned to the faculty in U-46 schools. The district had given him a leave of absence when the expedition was first approved, and it extended his leave several times over a number of years until U-46 and Reid mutually closed the curtain on his classroom teaching days. His absence from the faculty may have distanced him from the teachers who had been recruited to coordinate the projects. However, he continued to give interviews and make presentations about the expedition. Any speaker fees he generated from such appearances were applied to expedition debts. He also stayed in touch with groups and individuals that he viewed as supporters of the expedition. Since 1975 he had supplied them with updates on La Salle II's progress, and he continued to do so long after the canoes had come out of the water.

* * *

A year after the voyageurs disbanded, Reid wrote "Dear Friend of La Salle: Expedition II" to update his benefactors. "As we beached our canoes on the ocean shore . . . I thought of all of you, who, in your own ways, supported and encouraged our crew and thereby made the Expedition a success. . . . Although the voyage is completed, the Expedition is far from over. Work is continuing on many fronts to place the experiences of the Expedition into a permanent form so that its lessons and inspiration may endure for future generations."

He explained that the crew members were so scattered that Carlson and his staff of twelve teachers were trying to coordinate their work with them by phone and by mail. Reid expressed his appreciation to the U-46 school board for his unpaid leave of absence for 1978–79 and noted that it would be his fifth year working full time on La Salle II. Reid had to touch on the financial situation, of course. He said that the expedition "must still raise $190,000 to assure the completion of our work."

"Interest in the Expedition continues to run high around the world," Reid insisted, claiming to have received articles from Thailand, Germany, England, and the South Pacific. The specific publications mentioned included foreign issues of *Reader's Digest* and a few US magazines—*Americana*, *Boatmaster*, and *Mariah*. His brother, Ken, had written the articles for *Mariah* and *Boatmaster*. *People* magazine's article had appeared in April 1976, as soon as the crew completed their journey to the Gulf of Mexico.

In July 1978 Reid communicated on La Salle II letterhead with the crew, the liaison team, and parents. Again, he said, "Interest in the Expedition seems to be growing rather than diminishing." Calling attention to the need for money, he pleaded for help in selling the album. Kulick had been selling records and passing out donation cards in Connecticut, he said, and Gross had sold eleven records at a voyageur gathering in Elgin. However, only five hundred of the records had been sold. Another 3,500 albums remained in inventory.

There was even talk of producing a feature film, though that never came about.

* * *

In November 1980 Reid gave an interview to Mercedes Meyers of the *Elgin Courier-News* to publicize a fund-raiser to help pay for the expedition that had ended three and a half years before. Reid, by then forty years old, said that a $140,000 debt remained. The sum included tuition for a group of teachers at the National College of Education in Evanston, where the teachers worked on the research projects that were to be the expedition's legacy, the article said. Lewis told Meyers that 50,000 pages had already been written for materials designed for students from kindergarten through adult education. The most tangible result of La Salle II's educational projects, however, was a lengthy article full of color photographs in a low-literacy reader published in the late 1970s by academic publisher Scott, Foresman.

Reid started a business, a French language immersion program, which grew to include a number of schools, especially on Chicago's North Shore. But he never completed work on the educational materials that he long insisted would be the true legacy of La Salle II. In 2013, after an accumulation of inherited odds and ends had swelled his house with various boxes, Reid mused that La Salle II's educational materials might well be among the boxes somewhere in his house. But he did not seem eager to search for them. Their time had long passed, and other adventures awaited.

ALL EXPERIENCE
IS AN ARCH

So many of those who contributed to the La Salle II experience have gone, as the great English poet Alfred Lord Tennyson put it, "beyond the sunset, and the baths of all the western stars."

David Lane, whose journalistic efforts for the Tri-centennial expedition gave Bart Dean a blueprint to follow; Perry Lewis, who contributed time and money to his son's expedition and held down the fort at home; Sumner Rahr, who devoted his working life to financing worthy nonprofit ventures; Father Loran, who stayed the course despite his age and balky back; Bob Olson, whose Jolliet and Marquette video of 1973 captured the voyageur life in ways that two-minute snippets of local coverage did not; and Joel Monture Knecht, whose talents, despite a sudden snag midstream, helped frame the picture of authenticity which was a hallmark of La Salle II.

"The Fox" died Oct. 3, 2001, at Countryside Care Center in Aurora, Illinois, of complications from diabetes. Jim Phillips was seventy. On a day in late November, nearly two months after his death, Frese arranged a memorial service along the banks of the Fox River. Among the five dozen or so in attendance were voyageurs with whom he had shared a paddling adventure nearly three decades earlier. Four of them paddled against the brisk breeze to the middle of the river. Chuck McEnery, no longer a priest, carried a box fashioned of oak from the Phillips homestead. He broke a canoe paddle over his right knee to signify the end of Phillips's journey. Then he opened the box and poured his ashes into the current. As they settled slowly into the river bed, a flock of wild geese flew over the Fox.

Ralph Frese died in December 2012 at the age of eighty-six, honored in his time by the American Canoe Association and the Cook County Forest Preserve District, among others. His canoes were used in NBC's 1978–79 miniseries *Centennial*, based on James Michener's novel about the taming of the American West. Steinmetz High School celebrated its seventy-fifth anniversary in 2009 with space devoted in its program to two of its most celebrated alumni, both from the Class of 1944. Hugh Hefner, who launched the Playboy empire, was given half a page. Frese got a full one.

Voyageurs swap stories around a fire while considering the adventure of tomorrow.

A year after providing food and briquettes for the aging voyageurs at a campsite once more, Sharon Baumgartner was murdered in 2014, stabbed to death by a mentally troubled sister. True to her nature, Baumgartner had been trying to help her. The voyageurs attended her memorial service and mourned her death. Then they gathered at Sohn's home to remember the young woman who had served them so faithfully so long ago.

The current has carried La Salle II forty years downstream. Those who had a hand in the odyssey have individually explored a considerable future for which, Reid once quipped, they relived the past. Did the journey of 1976–77 inspire their progress or inform their discoveries? Did it fill in the "Unknown" regions of the maps of their lives? Long before the voyageurs sighted the Gulf, every one of them knew he had been changed. Shortly after the expedition ended, Ken was interviewed on Chicago's WBBM radio and asked whether he would do it again, knowing what he knew now.

"The hardships and difficulties seemed insurmountable at times, and there were some very bleak days in the dead of winter where we were having all our problems," Ken answered. "It's been very challenging, and anytime a group of twenty-three men can hang together under that type of conditions and not lose a single dropout, I think there's some kind of chemistry, some kind of magic going on there that I certainly would want to repeat if I ever had the opportunity. . . . I'm sure no one will be the same exactly after having undergone an experience such as this. There are about to be radical changes in everyone's personality. I think they're changes for the better, especially the sixteen students who set out on this trip. I've watched them gain in maturity during the last eight months. At this point, they're probably more mature than most adults I know."

In some cases, their very maturity made it difficult for voyageurs to acclimate when they went off to college. Academics were not the issue. The young men had steeped themselves in modern studies and arcane instruments for two years. On the trail in Year Three they had read and they had written. They had tested theories, recorded data, examined reactions, and drawn conclusions. They had made useful items with their hands and turned over great questions in their minds. Inured to hardship, there was little privation far from home to which they could not adapt. But immaturity is almost standard with freshmen, and the kind of socialization that usually takes place in college was already well behind the modern voyageurs. It was neither high school nor college that was the crucible of their education. It was La Salle: Expedition II. What had they learned, and how did they apply those lessons?

EDUCATION

The expedition had revolved primarily around education. The voyageurs taught people of the Midwest and the South about their French heritage, demonstrated the importance of conservation, and inspired people to learn more about the land upon which they lived and worked. Many became hooked on the idea of teaching as their life's work. Even some who found themselves pursuing business careers, like Kulick and Bardwell, began their college years considering education as a path.

The adult teachers, of course, found ready application of their experience. Marlena Scavuzzo returned to teaching with a new appreciation of positive reinforcement. The expedition had empowered the boys, giving them the sense that they could do anything, because it focused on what they were able to accomplish instead of their weaknesses, she said. Scavuzzo understood that students who could achieve real mastery in real tasks would build confidence in their own abilities. She applied that lesson to her instruction in English in Orion, and Jan Lewis returned to the teaching of English with a new sense of how to reach her students at Streamwood High School, one of five now in U-46, the second largest school district in Illinois.

Terry Cox returned to Downers Grove North to teach American history, and the unit on exploration was not only a particularly powerful one for his students but a special treat for him before he retired in 2002. In 1979 Pam gave birth to their daughter, Stephanie. "She gave us the best of both worlds," Cox said. "We traveled with a kid that couldn't get enough of it. And she forced me to grow up—at least a little bit." In 2012 he and Pam returned to Toronto and walked the portage route together.

John Fialko spent only a few more years in Elgin after the expedition before moving to Fort Collins, Colorado, where he taught at Rocky Mountain High School. John made occasional classroom presentations on La Salle II for history and French classes. In his first year at Rocky Mountain, another teacher organized a rendezvous like those the mountain men took part in during the early nineteenth century. John agreed to demonstrate beaver trapping, and he continued to be a part of the reenactment for twenty years, until it moved to a city park and many aspects of the rendezvous, like open fires, were discontinued. Standard-based academics by that time had forced social studies classes to focus on testing and left little time for authentic reenactments. Now retired from teaching, John stays active with youth as facilities director for Buckhorn United Methodist Camp and takes martial arts classes.

Several of the student members of La Salle II also went into education. After college at Southern Illinois University, Rich Gross got his teaching certificate and returned to the Chicago area. His close encounters with rivers and lakes gave him unique insights into the teaching of biology and chemistry at Conant High School in Hoffman Estates. His school district lies just east of Unified School District 46.

Chuck Campbell earned a bachelor's degree in recreation and a master's in experiential education and has devoted most of his working life to education, recreation, and youth development. Employed by the city of Duluth, Minnesota, "Road Kill" has worked with several environmental education programs, the National Park Service, the YMCA, the National Youth Leadership Council, and the United Methodist Church. Handing his training down through the generations, he had his grandson sleeping in a snow shelter at age two and a half, and paddling the Boundary Waters Canoe Area Wilderness at age six.

Cathy Palmer had always wanted to do something out of doors and saw herself as an outdoors person. She went to Elgin Community College for two years, intending to transfer to the University of Wisconsin at Stevens Point. At a college night at ECC, however, a rep from Northland College gave a slide presentation about the small private school on Lake Superior in northern Wisconsin.

During one segment of that presentation, she saw a group of students dressed in voyageur garb and heard the strains of "*En Roulant*," and she was hooked.

The cost of a private school was a burden for a blue-collar family in Elgin, but once again her parents backed her choice. They even packed up their sons and headed up to Northland College to see what had drawn their daughter like a lodestone to the Great North. Northland was an environmentally conscious liberal arts college of 650 students at the time. Classes were small, and students called their teachers by their first names.

After college, Palmer first became a young mother. Later she served as a camp director for twenty-five years for the YWCA, the Girl Scouts, and the YMCA. Listening to National Public Radio, she heard about Conserve School, which was established not far from Northland. Palmer had been impressed with the Boyd Conservation Center, the residential learning center in Toronto, when she passed through the city on the 1976 portage. She had been won over by the allure of experiential learning, the sense of learning by living instead of simply being told about something. "I thought I had a knack for it," she said. She interviewed and got the job, and now she serves as a school administrator and director of outdoor programs and student life.

"I am what I am today, I do what I do today, because of what I did when I was eighteen," Palmer declared recently.

Reid continued to give his vision to educational endeavors. He founded the Council for Study Abroad, La Compagnie des Amis de Fort de Chartres, and Aventure Française, Inc., a total-immersion language school with weekend and summer programs for middle school, high school, and adult students. Reid has portrayed La Salle in many presentations and mini-reenactments since 1977, notably in Jacques Cousteau's television special on the Mississippi River, when the famed underwater explorer took his vessel *Calypso* down the river from Lake Itasca, Minnesota, to the Gulf of Mexico.

Reid continues to talk about La Salle II and gives motivational speeches. One step. One paddle stroke. You take one. Then you take another. *Voilà!* The journey of 3,300 miles is done. Anyone can do it. The beauty of La Salle: Expedition II, he said, is that neither he nor anyone else who went through the arduous trip was an icon or a celebrity or a famous explorer. He was a "no name" who simply dared to make his left foot follow his right.

His commitment, step by step, to French language studies and the advancement of French heritage in the Americas has won him recognition from the French government, which named him a Chevalier in the order of the Palmes Academique in 2002. In 2011 Renaissance Française–USA presented Reid with its Gold Medal, given to those who have devoted themselves to public service or social works intended to improve quality of life. Perhaps his greatest tribute comes from letters he has received over the years from ordinary people who, having heard from him of La Salle II, dared to take that next step in their lives.

A Washington state principal told French language students that a field trip was impossible because funds had already been spent. Inspired by the story of La Salle II, however, the students raised the money in a whirlwind of car washes and bake sales. A Colorado high school student facing daunting personal problems found "that I could hang on, I could survive, and I have taught myself to live again." A teacher in Massachusetts said of the voyage that "its lessons and impact make it truly a dynamic tale of how to thrive, not just survive, in one's lifetime." There are hundreds of such stories from schools across the country. The lessons of the latter-day voyageurs moved the director of the foreign language laboratory at Yale University to write that their tale was "an inexhaustible source of inspiration for all those who are concerned with the education of teenagers. It should be of the greatest interest to all teachers and administrators in secondary schools throughout the country."

For all those voyageurs who taught, the expedition drove home the value of authentic experiences in learning. To an older generation, it might be called the "school of hard knocks" or "learning by doing." A search engine can provide facts. A teacher can explain the hows and whys. But there is nothing like actually performing tasks or seeing things for oneself to make a lesson real.

HISTORY

Clearly, the expedition of 1976–77 was also about history and France's role in developing the heartland of the United States. The expedition has enhanced Sid Bardwell's love of history and especially burnished his need for context, what life was like for the people he reads about. Living history himself, he said, he understands better than most how important those details are: what people ate, how hard their lives were, whether they felt exhilaration, fear, or loneliness.

Ron Hobart, who had gathered the songs for La Salle II, couldn't stay away from that part of history. He joined the Wisconsin-based *Les Fils du Voyageur* (Sons of the Voyageur), a French-language singing group that dresses as seventeenth-century adventurers and sings professionally. Does that sound familiar? The group, created in 1976, performs for organizations from Lafayette, Indiana, to Winnipeg, Manitoba. After a years-long hiatus, they re-formed in 1996 for the album *Bien Travailier*. Their latest CD is called *Canot d'Ecorce*.

Gross never lost his interest in La Salle, and his historical research over the past thirty-five years has been a key to understanding the explorer's mission in America. Gross has served as historical consultant for Great Lakes Exploration Group, an underwater salvage company whose president, Steve Libert, has been seeking the wreck of La Salle's *Le Griffon*, the first ship to sail above Niagara Falls. Gross enlisted Reid's help when Libert needed the help of France's Ministry of Marine.

ENGINEERING AND THE ENVIRONMENT

La Salle II, like the Jolliet Tri-centennial, concerned itself with conservation of natural resources and preservation of the environment. At the time of the expedition, the United States was not only beginning to protect its natural resources through the EPA, but it was also entering a new stage in its ventures into space. Both absorbed the attention of the voyageurs.

Doug Sohn and Gary Braun both went into businesses that deal with water-quality engineering, Buckwheat in Illinois and Braun in Washington state. As a wetlands biologist, Braun was engaged in dredging and scrubbing Wisconsin's Fox River where the 1973 Jolliet reenacters encountered significant pollution.

John DiFulvio earned a bachelor's degree in environmental studies and a master's degree in public administration before spending twenty-six years as a forest ranger. The lesson he learned from another ranger's mindless obedience to rules at Sand Banks was not lost on him. He is currently operations director for a property security company near Madison, Wisconsin. DiFulvio married his childhood sweetheart, Tami, who came to see him every weekend during the expedition between Manitowoc and Peoria. Together they raised a son and a daughter, both of whom learned French and worked as counselors in Reid's language immersion program.

After portraying Jacques de La Metairie, La Salle's notary, in La Salle II, George Lesieutre attended Massachusetts Institute of Technology, earning his bachelor's degree from MIT in aerospace engineering in 1981. He also received a PhD in aerospace engineering from UCLA in 1989. He is currently head of the department of aerospace engineering at Penn State University.

COMMUNICATION

Every voyageur learned to communicate effectively with a wide variety of people. The men lost any stage fright they had in order to perform. They developed patience to answer questions from both children and adults, often the same questions they had heard hundreds of times before. They acquired empathy for others as they saw themselves as spokesmen for a heritage that bound them to the people they met.

Randy Foster, who became an electrician in Chicago's western suburbs, said that these communication skills prepared him to talk with customers and build his business. Sid Bardwell's English teacher told him he could be a writer despite his creative spelling, but it was his dogged determination to keep a journal throughout the trip that turned him into a writer.

"Learning to deal with people and the public has changed my life," said Steve Marr, who has spent nearly a quarter of a century, all told, with Honeywell, using his education as a watchmaker in the Mississippi River town of Quincy, Illinois.

SELF-AWARENESS

The voyageurs had plenty of time to look inward during their days and nights away from the public. You look at the scenery and think about what it means to you. Then you think about what anything means to you. You stare into the campfire at night and watch the sparks pop into the blackness and it is only you and your thoughts about what you value.

Years of late-night discussions with fellow directors and months of thinking while staring at campfires helped Dick Stillwagon take stock of himself and his path in the world. Stillwagon made it through a couple more school years before he hit the wall in the spring of 1979. In what he described as "a classic case of burnout," he walked away from teaching. Then in his forties, he was no longer a young man. He had no job prospects lined up. But he fully knew now who he was, and school did not have the same meaning for him that it once did. Walking through snowdrifts, paddling down foreign rivers, his commitment had always been to his family. Now he determined to protect his integrity and provide for them in a different role. He found his calling in the private sector, but La Salle II still affects the aspirations of his children and grandchildren, who take pride in his work for the expedition.

Keith Gorse, who has spent his working life in the computer industry, observed a significant difference between the calm world of the seventeenth century and the helter-skelter world of the twentieth, a difference he could see in his own behavior.

"When I was home in the beginning, I constantly had things planned for the future, either that day or the next day, or college or whatever. It's always on my mind and I'm always in a hurry, and I always have to be doing something," Gorse said soon after the journey. "I can't just sit . . . unless I listen to music. It relaxes me. . . . But if I'm sitting, I have to be playing with something in my hand or I have to be reading a book, chewing my nails. But on the trip, that all stopped . . . I felt very comfortable with myself. I had a lot of time by myself during the day, while we were paddling or while we were walking, to think. I got to think about a lot of things, and that kept my mind occupied, and I wasn't nervous about anything. Nothing bothered me."

Terry Cox, who could scarcely believe the trip was finished when the canoes returned upriver to Venice, had written hundreds of pages in his journal. The daily habit of putting his thoughts on paper continued for weeks, eventually spending itself like the dying embers of a campfire. But he did have some observations to make when rereading his journal for the first time many years later.

"I must say that I was more than a little surprised when I went back and reread these journals as to how withdrawn I was by the end of the trip," he said in 2008. "I guess I felt that the only way to endure was to withdraw and keep everyone—crew members and visitors—at arm's length. . . . I obviously just wanted to finish things up and get home ASAP. Even now it's hard to objectively assess the expedition. We really did accomplish something rather significant . . ."

For Clif Wilson, the expedition helped him grow up. The self-confessed party animal may have been spoiled by his circumstances. But years of working with boys of different backgrounds, the politics in his own canoe, and the response of comrades to his crises off Washington Island and Route 2 seasoned him. He came back home in a more serious frame of mind. The journey certainly brought him more clarity about what to do with the immediate future.

"I knew I wanted to go to school the following year" after the trip, he told Kulick soon after the expedition ended. "But at the time I really didn't know what I was going to do. I didn't even have a good idea. The expedition kind of made it clear as to what I wanted to go into. I'm going to go to school at the University of Kansas and take mass media communications and political science as a double major or possibly a major-minor . . . I'd like to go into political journalism, television . . ." Wilson did enter the world of media and became vice president and director of sales for a radio group operating several Chicago area stations.

CONFIDENCE

Each voyageur acquired a quiet confidence, not from hearing a lesson taught but from achieving mastery. When the expedition reached the Gulf, it had been the journey itself, not the destination, which had built the men's character. Any one of them could call a counsel. Every man's opinion mattered. Every man was responsible for himself, but he was also responsible to his companions. And when crises struck the travelers, each man held himself accountable to protect the safety of all.

"I grew up a lot on this trip," Marr said recently. "We had no one but ourselves to depend on. I was only seventeen when the expedition began, but I had to do my part. Learning to deal with people and the public in all kinds of situations changed my life."

"I've changed. I know that. I'll never be the same again," Marr said in the January/February 1978 issue of *Boatmaster* magazine. Marr, who admitted to being in poor physical condition when he signed on as a voyageur, lost forty-five pounds along the way but gained a new perspective. The challenge of training, he said, "sort of scared me. I didn't think I could do it all. Sometimes, if someone [had given] me two cents, I would have dropped out. But I stuck with it. The harder I worked, the easier it got. I began to see that almost nothing is impossible if you set your mind to it."

Reid's limitless optimism, his absolute conviction in what he was doing, filtered through the ranks and filled the entire expedition with faith that the voyageurs would achieve their goal. For all the calumny they heaped on him, even Reid's most vocal detractors agree that La Salle II would never have succeeded without him and his beacon of confidence.

COURAGE

The twentieth-century voyageurs and their families accepted the physical risks of their trip up front. It was a requirement, part of the buy-in to adventure. Eventually, the risks became real. Illnesses and injuries mounted. The honest prospect of death lurked in sudden gales, ten-foot swells, island-sized barges, and highway traffic. Every day became a test of bravery. Then trucks hit Braun and Marr and Garcia and Wilson. And each voyageur not only knew but felt the price of his courage. Years later when a banker threatened to pull the plug on a loan Wilson had taken out to finance a real estate project, the voyageur had no sense of fear. What could the banker do but call the loan? Wilson had faced far worse in the cruel waters off Wicked Point and Death's Door and on the bleak landscape south of Hebron.

Clearly, their sense of courage went beyond the physical. The voyageurs had met challenges of many kinds. They had overcome stage fright, general timidity, and self-doubt. They had overcome social divisions, learning differences, internal trust issues, and general indifference that audiences showed toward their cultural, historical, and environmental messages. Each person knew he could handle anything life threw at him. Stillwagon saw the expedition as a test of fire that might have altered the pattern he would follow. The trials of the trip had empowered him to step off into the unknown.

"I can safely say that it was a major event in my life," Stillwagon said. "I believe that it had a great effect on my whole family; even a couple of grandkids have seen things about LaSalle that relate to me. I changed careers. Was it directly related to my experiences on the expedition? I can't say. I do know that I felt that I had the courage to try new things and that, probably, was a result of the expedition."

The boys who started the voyage became men while enduring its hardships. They knew that the experience of the journey had prepared them for the future in ways that the classroom never could have. The expedition changed not only the crew but also, in some cases, those who were left behind. Though they did not face a test of strength or pain, their courage was no less real.

Pam became the bread winner while her husband was away. While Cox was still in Canada, Pam received notice that their property taxes and auto insurance were going up. At St. Ignace, she told Cox that she couldn't make it on one salary, not with the house payment. To help with expenses, she took in a boarder. The couple had sold their car and bought an old Honda to help pay expedition expenses, and eventually the repair bills caught up with her, too. She paid $100 for repairs in September. She drove up to Washington Island after the Hog Island incident. On the way home, the Honda broke down. She had to rent a car to get home. The unanticipated cost of that event alone included a $15 tow, $95 to repair a timing chain on the car, $56 to rent a car plus a $25 drop-off charge—nearly $200 in all at a time when such an expense truly hurt her budget. In March she negotiated the purchase of a new Honda Accord before the canoes hit New Orleans, but she lost her boarder at about the same time. Friends and expedition families often invited her to dinner, which did help with food costs.

* * *

Finances weren't the only thing that made life harrowing for Pam while she was home alone. As the expedition reached Georgian Bay more than a month into the trip, Pam received a threatening phone call from someone who knew her name and Cox's. The caller said, "I know who your husband is. He's gone, and he won't be back for a long, long time." Nothing came of the sinister call, but it made for some anxious moments. In the midst of this, Pam's grandfather became ill during the trek and passed away as the expedition neared the western end of Georgian Bay. The emotional toll that this took represented yet another test of Pam's courage. And throughout the journey, she taught a full load of classes at school and worked with other teachers to try to wrestle expedition documents into some kind of organized form for publication. Cox is the first to admit that he came home to a different woman than the one he had left at home, one who was proud and strong. She had passed through the fire herself and emerged a confident, capable individual who, like the men, could face whatever situation life presented.

FLEXIBILITY

The expedition taught the voyageur band that the world was not only full of dangers but also full of opportunities. The voyageurs balanced risk and reward every time they chose to shove off into the water. By New Orleans they understood that fear of the unknown only encased their feet in concrete. Progress could only be made by recognizing opportunity when it appeared, weighing the risks but not fearing to move forward.

Reid found himself reassessing situations all along the route. If the crew were wind-bound, it was an opportunity to repair gear or speak to students. If a reporter showed up at the campsite, it was a chance to spread the word of French heritage or water conservation. If tempers were boiling over, it was a chance for problems to be worked out and unity to be built. In other ways, the ability to see opportunity led some voyageurs into life paths that might never have occurred to them had they not developed such flexibility on the trail.

Kulick bussed tables at a restaurant while working on his bachelor's degree from Colorado State University. After graduation in 1982, his boss asked him to join him at JMC Restaurant Distribution Inc., a subsidiary of CiCi's Pizza. Kulick set aside his ambitions to teach, took the invitation and eventually acquired a stake in one of the largest pizza chains in the country. He served as director of purchasing and distribution, then as president of CiCi's from 1994 to 2012. He still owns a piece of the company and serves on its board of directors. With exploration still in his view,

Kulick signed up in 2010 with Virgin Galactic, holding ticket No. 195 to become one of the first space tourists when that opportunity presents itself.

Dean had put his post-college life on hold for the expedition. While he never expected to make money from the trip, the money woes that had fallen on Reid and Jan at the epicenter of La Salle II carried in ripples to Dean's shore. But he never left the expedition, despite his many intentions to do so. Dean also saw the trip as an opportunity that he could not waste.

* * *

"I admit that I nearly did leave the expedition in Belmont Harbor," he told Cox in 2008, "but by then I knew we were in for a long, rough portage that would provide the best pictures yet—pictures that I knew would get published all over the country and possibly the world. And they were. So, truth be told, I hung on through that middle phase of the trip for purely mercenary reasons."

In Los Angeles Dean sought work in television and wrote and produced episodes for *Taxi* during its three-year run of Emmy Awards (1979–81) as the top comedy show on TV. Dean also worked on *The Bob Newhart Show* and *The Larry Sanders Show*. Nevertheless, Dean saw the expedition as one of the touchstones of his life. Even the awful saga of the winter portages did not deflect his pride in accomplishment.

"We were companions in misery at the time. But no matter what happened, I'm glad I did it," he said. Dean's Emmy for producing *Taxi* is reportedly gathering dust in a closet. It is the expedition paddle from La Salle: Expedition II that has an honored place, mounted on the wall of his office.

Bardwell's journey through life has resulted from taking one opportunity after another. When social science classes he wanted were all filled at the University of Iowa, Bardwell decided to take a survey course in Asian studies. The only thing he "knew" about the Far East was the popular TV show *Kung Fu*, he said. Bardwell enjoyed the course, and then decided to take another. And another. One professor told him that Sony Corporation was offering money for a University of Iowa student to study abroad but that no one had signed up. Bardwell took the offer and studied a year in Japan. During his senior year, he took two semesters of Japanese on his way to a degree in Asian studies and a minor in business.

After graduation Bardwell applied for a job to teach in a rural prefecture in southern Japan. It was considered a tough assignment. The previous two people who had taught there left not enjoying their experience. Bardwell was still not the first choice for the post, but one line from his essay caught the attention of those reviewing applications. He had talked about La Salle: Expedition II, commenting that it had taught him "to keep a smile on my face even when my feet are cold." He had come to understand how interesting people can be wherever you are. He signed up for a two-year stint and stayed for four after falling in love, marrying, and having a baby.

When he returned to the States, he got an MBA from Cornell, where he also took language courses. The dean of the business school, a former executive for John Deere Co., told him that Deere was looking for someone with language abilities. Bardwell's working life has been in international marketing for Deere, most of it in Asia. He also spent six years opening up Deere's Russian office in Moscow.

"I feel particularly lucky. I never had a grand plan, but I've always been open to opportunities," he said.

RESILIENCE

For every voyageur, overcoming obstacles was a way of life during his journey. If there wasn't enough to eat, he still paddled. If the ice prevented river travel, he sucked it up and hiked over the frozen land. If no hall had been prepared, he stood on the levee with his companions and performed in the open air.

When the truck accident forced Marr to drop out of the line of march, the disappointment taught Marr a lesson about resilience. "I had to learn . . . when my plans were shattered to pick up the pieces. I had to learn not to live in the past or the future [but] to take things as they happened."

That ability to bounce back from disappointment gleamed brightly in the example of the Fialkos. John and Linda lost everything they owned in the High Park forest fire that raged around Fort Collins in the summer of 2012. Undaunted by either their loss or the task ahead, they began to rebuild in 2013 in Rist Canyon next to Rocky Mountain National Park. Thousands of dollars were raised by the former voyageurs to help them recover.

The resilience of the voyageurs seemed to have rubbed off on one of their ardent admirers, the owner of Tabor Hill Vineyards. Len Olson, the vintner who introduced twenty-seven different grape varieties to Michigan, hosted a five-year voyageur reunion at his vineyard, and much time was spent singing inside one of the vats. By then he'd added a small restaurant and an outdoor eating area that his wife ran, but he later lost the entire operation when they divorced. The vine had withered, but the root was strong. Len returned to winemaking in southern Michigan in 2009, launching Founders Wine Cellar that year in Baroda on the same date he had sold his first bottle of Tabor Hill wine: July 14—Bastille Day.

In 2012 the men and women of La Salle: Expedition II gathered with their families once again in New Orleans, thirty-five years after their youthful saga ended. They celebrated their achievement and marked the passage of time. In choruses that grew stronger with repetition, they sang the voyageur songs of old. Terry Cox gave a short speech. And in spite of the anger he had felt toward Reid and Ken so many years before, he acknowledged their roles in making the expedition such a success.

"Reid brought us together with his passion and vision. Ken helped us entertain thousands of people . . . Fortunately, we had the 24/7 love, support, and encouragement from some remarkable parents, some incredibly understanding wives and girlfriends, and wonderful friends—old ones and new ones we met along the way like Ralph Frese, Dave Upton, Thor Williamson, the Leslies, and so many others." And then he spoke of resilience.

"I know many of you have had some serious setbacks since the expedition—personal and professional," Cox said. "But from what I've seen and heard, you've reacted to those setbacks the same way you reacted to obstacles during the expedition. You have not allowed the setbacks to define you. The confidence and determination that the trip helped nurture has served you well over the years. That may be La Salle II's ultimate legacy."

SPIRIT

When he was no older than twenty-four, Tennyson wrote "Ulysses," a poem about the aging Greek hero who fought at ancient Troy and was punished by the gods, forced to wander the seas for years. Despite his advancing years, Ulysses says of himself and his fellow wanderers, "That which we are, we are: one equal temper of heroic hearts, made weak by time and fate, but strong in will . . ."

Now in their fifties, their leaders in their seventies, the twentieth-century voyageurs display the same kind of will. Like the aging hero, they still yearn for adventure. They still hope to tread untrammeled shores. They lean toward the unknown edges of their lives as Ulysses, bound to the mast of his ship, leaned toward the sirens' song. Like true explorers, they have shown themselves willing, as they were in their youth, to test boundaries.

George Lesieutre remains extremely active in outdoor activities. He has ridden his bicycle in road races: from Boston to Minneapolis and from Seattle to Portland, Oregon. An avid runner, he has participated in many races in distances from the mile to the marathon. The same guy whose time bested the rest of the voyageurs has run Boston several times, posting a 3:10:20 in 2010. He belongs to the Nittany Valley Running Club. And he is still married to Annie, his high school sweetheart.

Marc Lieberman, an active attorney who lives in Arizona with his wife, Cindy, is a national winner of the Moeller Prize for excellence in journalism. Testing his writing in a completely different way, Lieberman's first novel, *Sign of the Anasazi*, drew excellent reviews. A self-published version of the science fiction adventure made Lieberman a finalist for the Indie Awards and Best Books, USA Book News in 2007–08.

Every year Sam Hess plans a trip with Lieberman and Kulick. In 2007 their trip took them to Africa, where they summited Mount Kilimanjaro together. Wilson accompanied them on the trip and, even with his injuries from Hebron and a condition that strictly limited his altitude, he climbed with them far up the mountain's heights. Wilson has also paddled a kayak in an overnight vigil for a friend swimming the twenty-one-mile San Pedro Channel from Santa Catalina to the Palos Verdes Peninsula.

Rich Gross was one of two men Ralph Frese entrusted with the name of his business, Chicagoland Canoe Base, and the molds and tools used to make the custom canoes that brought home the latter-day voyageurs of both the 1973 Marquette-Jolliet Tri-centennial and the 1976–77 La Salle: Expedition II. With everything else he is doing, Gross still hopes to make kits available and engage young people in canoeing and river adventures, as Frese once did.

In the summer of 2013, while working with Great Lakes Exploration Group, Gross arranged for his fellow voyageurs to gather at a camping area in northern Michigan, near the dive site for *Le Griffon*. He and Reid wanted to show French officials and naval archeologists how their own fur traders once plied the waters of America. Gross sent out a mass invitation email, and he had reserved a campsite just a few miles from the shore. The media had already begun to gather, hoping for a scoop if divers could identify *Le Griffon*.

Some voyageurs were busy with work, and others lived too far away. Nevertheless, crewmen came like a flock of seagulls to a beach picnic. As French interpreter, Reid was already at the water's edge with Ken. Ever the historical interpreter, Dean Campbell of the Tri-centennial expedition was also there in full voyageur regalia along with a pair of reenactors from Indiana. But the true campsite lay up the road at a state park.

* * *

Once again, Sharon Baumgartner gathered firewood and food for the voyageurs she had supported long ago, and drove it to the destination. Cathy Palmer had duties at her outdoor school and would have been there if she could have, Baumgartner let everyone know. Hobart and Cox arrived in the glade. Gorse, Foster, Hess, and Wilson were there, some with their sons. Kulick had come up from Texas on a motorcycle outfitted for an extended stay on the road. Buckwheat and Road Kill came, and even Braun had come in from Seattle.

* * *

Once again the veteran canoe men set their craft in the water. Once again they donned their costumes of long ago. Arranging themselves on seats and bales, they shoved away haltingly from between piers. Then, stroking ever more strongly out into the lake, the voyageurs neared the place where the French officials had been promised a surprise. Reid, once again the La Salle of old, dressed in the broad hat and livery of a nobleman, raised the call and response of their paddling song.

"*Trois beaux canards s'en vont baignant,*" Reid sang.

"*En roulant, ma boule,*" the men responded, paddles pulling with the cadence.

"*Les fils du roi s'en va chassant,*" he sang again.

"*Roui-roulant, ma boule roulant,*" the men chanted. Now the voyageurs broke out in a full-throated chorus.

"*En roulant, ma boule roulant!*" Reid called.

"*En roulant, ma boule!*" the voyageurs sang in refrain.

Once again, it was 1681. And it was 1976.

That night the voyageur band gathered in the lengthening shadows, their hamburgers dripping fat into the crackling fire and their hands full of good cheer. Together they remembered the tribulations of a youthful quest in which their commitment to each other and to their goal helped them to endure. In the next few evenings, some would stay in campers, others in nearby motels, and others in authentic voyageur shelters on the edge of Lake Michigan. And each would consider in his or her own way the next step in a life lived with passion every day.

ACKNOWLEDGMENTS

Hard Rivers could not have been written without the input of virtually every man and every woman who participated in the memorable journey that wound its way through the heart of North America in 1976–77.

I have personally contacted every living person who was a crewman or liaison team member for La Salle: Expedition II. Almost everyone has been open and giving in various ways to help me tell their unique story. Even those few who declined interviews spoke volumes with their reticence, and I have tried to give them a voice through the contributions of their peers. I am indebted to each person whose words at the time and whose memories of those days have helped to express this adventure of their youth. Some people have been especially helpful.

Rich Gross provided me with contact information for his crewmates, Bob Olson's 1973 Jolliet/Marquette reenactment video, hundreds of photographs from 1976–77, radio interviews with crewmen, and an itinerary of the trip. He also invited me to a rendezvous of La Salle II veterans in Michigan, where I got to know many of the modern voyageurs, including the late Sharon Baumgartner, a delightful woman who shared fully in the men's hearty sense of adventure.

Terry Cox sent me his incredibly detailed journal on CD. When he digitized it in 2008, he augmented his entries with asides he solicited from Clif Wilson and Bart Dean, who provided rich stories from the trail. Matched with Rich's itinerary, Terry's journal provided a scaffold on which to erect everyone's memories.

He also gave me a copy of his remarks for the thirty-fifth crew reunion in New Orleans.

I am indebted also to Bob Kulick. He and his wife, Jacky, graciously welcomed me to their retreat in north-central Texas. Bob supplied copies of the official expedition journal he kept, training and evaluation documents from 1974–76, newspaper clippings, and expedition journals kept by John Fialko, Gary Braun, and Chuck Campbell. Bob's boxes of expedition material included copies of letters sent home by crewmen and liaison team members. Bob also provided his transcripts of post-trip interviews with Fialko, Wilson, Keith Gorse, leader Reid Lewis, and assistant liaison director Marlena Scavuzzo.

Marlena gave me a sense of the difficulties experienced by the liaison team, and she allowed me to take possession of her mother's enormous and well-kept scrapbook of newspaper clippings. These were especially helpful in fleshing out the "attack" in Gananoque, the indefatigable Dr. Brown, and the fascination of the Natchez heritage pageant, among other stories.

Sid Bardwell sent me the two-volume, leather-bound journal he kept on the trail in 1976–77. Along with input by Steve Marr and Bart Dean, his perspective on life with both the crew and the liaison team provided an important balancing view of the feud between members of those two camps.

Gary Braun sent me a slide presentation that he had made at his children's school. This not only helped me visualize the trip from a voyageur's point of view, but it also gave me a window on how I might present their story to other groups.

Reid helped by providing details that few others knew. He provided letters from the important individuals who endorsed the trip—Sir Edmund Hillary, Jacques-Yves and Philippe Cousteau, Marcel Marceau and Sigurd Olson—and dignitaries like US President Jimmy Carter and Canadian Prime Minister Pierre Trudeau who recognized the special contribution the expedition had made to understanding their common heritage. Reid presented evidence of the impact the story of La Salle II has had on the lives of those who have heard it. More than all of these, however, he provided encouragement to tell the tale. Reid believes that everyone has the ability to live a life of adventure. He rejoices in the fact that he and his crew were not famous or particularly gifted. If "no-names" like the folks of La Salle: Expedition II can succeed in such a difficult adventure, against all those odds, any person can accomplish great things. All that's needed is a little imagination and the willingness to put one foot in front of another. Step by step, even the journey itself becomes a victory.

A manuscript does not become a book without a lot of help from a lot of people, and there was a battalion of folks at Greenleaf Book Group and River Grove Books who helped bring *Hard Rivers* into the world. This team included Project Manager Emilie Lyons, Assistant Editor Lindsey Clark, Justin Branch, Sam Alexander, and Carrie Jones, and I know there were others. As an editor myself, I am especially grateful for the guiding hand of editor Elizabeth Brown. Liz took all the rocks and wing dams out of the manuscript and left *Hard Rivers* an easy stream for the reader. It's not an easy thing to conserve the beauty of a story while keeping the reading environment clean, but Liz did it with a keen eye, a deft touch, and a kind heart.

Acknowledgements wouldn't be complete without honoring my late parents, Jeanette and Jere Howard. Mom taught American literature, introduced me to the parts of speech, and encouraged me to write. Dad had the largest vocabulary of anyone I ever knew and led me to such romantic adventure stories as *Kidnapped, The Three Musketeers,* and *The Prisoner of Zenda.*

Finally and importantly, I want to thank my wife, Dorinda, and our daughter, Wendy. Wendy provided guidance by reading many of these chapters and giving such tough-love observations as, "Easy does it, Robert Frost" and "Must you start every chapter with your cheesy transcendentalism?" Dorinda suggested that I seek the answer to "Whatever happened to . . . " and gave me the freedom to fly to Green Bay to camp out with the guys. She set me up in my writer's "cave," where her sewing notions and gift wrap gave way to my books and papers and computer equipment. And her good nature sustained me when the project of a few weeks became that of a few years.

A tout le monde, je dis, "*Merci beaucoup.*"

ABOUT THE AUTHOR

CRAIG P. HOWARD grew up along Salt Creek, a tributary of the Des Plaines River, at what was then the edge of suburban Chicago. The weed-choked stream and the woods on its banks formed a playground for children with imagination. Craig played sixteen-inch softball on a diamond that neighborhood dads carved out of a ragweed swamp. He swam in Lake Michigan, canoed on the Des Plaines, and camped in Indiana and Michigan. Craig studied social sciences at the University of Illinois and came home to write for local newspapers, covering the appearance of the La Salle: Expedition II crew in Elgin in January 1977. He followed his fiancée to Houston, where he worked twenty years for the *Houston Chronicle* and taught for several years in area schools. Craig still lives in Houston with his wife, Dorinda. He enjoys jogging, gardening, and fantasy baseball.

www.ingramcontent.com/pod-product-compliance
Lightning Source LLC
Chambersburg PA
CBHW020352080526
44584CB00014B/991